Twitter™
FOR
DUMMIES®

Twitter™ FOR DUMMIES®

by Laura Fitton, Michael E. Gruen,
@pistachio   @gruen

and
Leslie Poston
@geechee_girl

Foreword by
Jack Dorsey
Inventor, Founder, & Chairman, Twitter

WILEY

Wiley Publishing, Inc.

Twitter™ For Dummies®

Published by
Wiley Publishing, Inc.
111 River Street
Hoboken, NJ 07030-5774

www.wiley.com

For general information on our other products and services, please contact our Customer Care Department within the U.S. at 877-762-2974, outside the U.S. at 317-572-3993, or fax 317-572-4002.

For technical support, please visit www.wiley.com/techsupport.

Wiley also publishes its books in a variety of electronic formats. Some content that appears in print may not be available in electronic books.

Library of Congress Control Number: 2009928743

ISBN: 978-0-470-47991-9

Manufactured in the United States of America

10 9 8 7 6 5 4 3

WILEY

About the Authors

Laura Fitton: Laura "@Pistachio" Fitton is leading the charge of sussing out intelligent and productive business uses of emergent technologies like Twitter, where she is read by thousands of community members. The first to publish a white paper on "Enterprise Microsharing" (popularly called "Internal Twitter"), she also writes for and runs the TouchBase blog and is an early beta tester of Seesmic and Qik. She relaunched Pistachio Consulting in September 2008 to connect businesses to new ideas and innovations using all the tools of microsharing. Pistachio comprises the TouchBase blog (covering business use of microsharing), the TouchBase Link Blog (stream of Twitter and microsharing articles for businesspeople, wherever they are published), and serves clients like Johnson & Johnson, Ford Motor Corporation, PeopleBrowsr, The Sister Project, Transplant-1, and CommuNteligence.

Laura is a magna cum laude graduate of Cornell University's eclectic College Scholar program. In "past lives," she studied science writing with Carl Sagan, rock climbed, sailed on a schooner, raised a niece, ran a hobby farm, traveled, and lived abroad.

Today she lives in Boston with two toddler daughters and a giant Leonberger. She practices Ashtanga yoga and plays ice hockey in her "spare" time and is a stroke survivor dedicated to raising awareness.

Michael E. Gruen: Michael E. Gruen has earned significant respect in the corporate sphere and within the startup community as a trusted advisor since 2003. In many cases, he has fulfilled the role of interim Chief Operations/Chief Technical Officer with several organizations in need of innovative leadership during crucial developmental periods. In 2006–2007, Michael briefly joined Morgan Stanley as an Analyst. Currently, Michael is CFO/COO at NOM, a Digital Services Agency, and the CEO of a new healthcare startup.

Michael graduated cum laude from Hamilton College as a Senior Fellow with a BA in Computer Science. He lives in New York City and, on the off-hours, races taxis on his road bike through the city streets.

Leslie Poston: Leslie Poston is passionate about helping people and businesses find their way to success via technology. As a writer, she has more than 200 ebooks and books in her repertoire and several more in development.

As a speaker and leading authority in social networking, new media, brand and business development, she is the Founder and CEO of Uptown Uncorked social media and business development consultancy. She is also the cofounder of Film Pop!, a digital and new media services development agency for independent film as well as a long-time consultant to the entertainment industry for new media development and marketing.

A firm believer in translating online relationships and successes into the offline world, she has also founded Social Media Breakfast New Hampshire, PodCamp NH/ME, and the nationwide Strong Women in Tech initiative. Her educational background is in English Literature and Clinical Psychology.

When she isn't watching or playing sports (especially hockey and UFC/MMA), playing piano, hiking, sailing, skiing, supporting local bands, playing with her Rottweiler, or working, Leslie can be found on Twitter, meeting new people and making connections with the world.

Dedication

To our Twitter friends, thank you for your support, help, and assistance in writing this book. To our families, just plain thank you.

Authors' Acknowledgments

Writing and publishing this book was a team effort. The three of us would like to thank the Twitter community who have shared their ideas on BrightIdea (`http://tfd.brightidea.com` — thanks also to Matthew Greeley and the BrightIdea team for use of their Webstorm software) and have helped us target important facts to include in this book. We're also grateful to every follower on the `@dummies` account and everyone who retweeted for and about *Twitter For Dummies*.

If it were not for our wonderful editors and production team, this book would not have come together as quickly as it did. Thanks to Kelly Ewing, Jodi Jensen, Andy Cummings, Mary Corder, Mary Bednarek, Laura Miller, Elizabeth Kuball, Steven Miller, Mark Burstiner, and Jennifer Webb.

Many thanks to our acquisitions editor, Steve Hayes, for allowing us to write this book in the first place, and to Chris Webb and Ellen Gerstein at Wiley for tirelessly explaining Twitter to their colleagues and introducing Laura to Steve.

Laura particularly wants to thank her co-authors, mentors, friends, Twitter readers and everyone who has written for, commented on or read Pistachio Consulting's TouchBase blog. Special thanks to Alexa Scordato (`@alexa`), Alex Howard (`@digiphile`), and `@mdy`.

And a very special thanks to Caroline McCarthy (`@caro`) for lending an extra hand when we needed it most.

Publisher's Acknowledgments

We're proud of this book; please send us your comments through our online registration form located at http://dummies.custhelp.com. For other comments, please contact our Customer Care Department within the U.S. at 877-762-2974, outside the U.S. at 317-572-3993, or fax 317-572-4002.

Some of the people who helped bring this book to market include the following:

Acquisitions and Editorial

Project Editor: Kelly Ewing

Acquisitions Editor: Steve Hayes

Copy Editor: Laura Miller

Technical Editor: Steven D. Miller, Mark Burstiner

Editorial Manager: Jodi Jensen

Sr. Editorial Assistant: Cherie Case

Cartoons: Rich Tennant
(www.the5thwave.com)

Composition Services

Project Coordinator: Patrick Redmond

Layout and Graphics: Melissa K. Jester, Ronald Terry, Christine Williams

Proofreaders: Melissa Cossell, Penny Stuart

Indexer: Julie Kawabata

Special Help

Elizabeth Kuball

Publishing and Editorial for Technology Dummies

Richard Swadley, Vice President and Executive Group Publisher

Andy Cummings, Vice President and Publisher

Mary Bednarek, Executive Acquisitions Director

Mary C. Corder, Editorial Director

Publishing for Consumer Dummies

Diane Graves Steele, Vice President and Publisher

Composition Services

Debbie Stailey, Director of Composition Services

Contents at a Glance

Table of Contents

Foreword

. . . .

*L*et's be honest: You're not a dummy.

Technologies are often designed to guard against the seemingly errant desires
and mistakes of the commons. What's remarkable about this technology you
intend to learn is its ability to immediately expose and evolve the true desires
of the commons.

Although it may seem so, simple technologies like this don't happen over
night. What looks like a story of 1 to 3 years actually has a shadow of over
15 years of work, dumb mistakes, false starts, late-night frenetic insight, and
patient distillation. Twitter is a life's work built around three tenets: minimize
thinking around communication, expose trends in local and global circles,
and spark interaction. What you're holding in your hands describes an
essence of communication upon which millions will build their own value.

While not everything can be conveyed in under 140 characters, the essence
of Twitter can: "Expect the unexpected. Whenever possible, be the unexpected." I expect you to build something unexpected. Start small, start here.

Jack Dorsey
Inventor, Founder, & Chairman, Twitter
San Francisco, California

Introduction

. . . .

*H*ave you heard? All the world's a-twitter!

Twitter is a tool that you can use to send and receive short, 140-character messages from your friends, from the organizations you care about, from the businesses you frequent, from the publications you read, or from complete strangers who share (or don't share) your interests.

As a user of Twitter, you choose whose updates you want to receive — which people you want to *follow.* In turn, other users can elect to follow *your* updates. You can send messages publicly for the entire Twitter community, semi-publicly to users whom you approve to receive your messages, or privately from one user to another. You can view these messages, called *updates* or *tweets,* either on the Internet or on your cellphone.

Twitter has changed and enhanced the way that people communicate with each other, with brands and companies, and with social movements and initiatives. Twitter has empowered users to raise money for people in need, coordinate rescue efforts in the wake of a natural disaster, and alert authorities to emergencies and illegal activities both domestic and abroad.

Skeptical of what you can say in 140 characters? The first paragraph of the Introduction weighs in at 41 characters. This paragraph? 137.

You may also find, over time, that you communicate more effectively and that your writing becomes shorter and more to the point. You can say a lot within very little space; and because it takes only a little time to read and update, you may be surprised about how much value you, your friends, and your family can extract from Twitter.

About This Book

We, the authors (Laura, Michael, and Leslie), aren't employees, representatives, or shareholders in Twitter. The opinions that we give in this book represent what's worked for us and our networks, but not necessarily the Twitter world at large. We've been on Twitter for quite a while, and we have a good sense about how people are using it. But Twitter is a living, breathing, and constantly changing dynamic community. Much of Twitter's value comes from the ecosystem of tools built by others to work together with Twitter.

Hundreds of these new tools launch every month. Twitter itself may change its feature set, its privacy features, or general direction overnight, which changes the way that people use it.

In fact, from the time we started writing this book to the time we're completing it, about a dozen things have changed on the interface, including one complete layout overhaul. Although the layout and the exact location of everything may change around a bit, the basics of Twitter likely will always be the same. After you understand how the service works, you can pretty easily find any feature that may have moved since the publication of this book. *Note:* While things change, keep in touch with `@dummies` or our personal accounts (`@pistachio`, `@gruen`, and `@geechee_girl`) for the latest on our thoughts about Twitter. You can also keep up with the Twitter for Dummies community at `www.TwitterForDummies.org`.

We wrote this book to help more people understand, try out, and benefit from the incredible results and opportunities that can happen on Twitter. There's been so much recent fuss over Twitter that you may think it's just a fad. The truth is Twitter's been changing lives for years now. Twitter can be fun, productive, supportive, and surprisingly powerful.

Just ask Laura. Before she "got" Twitter, she was practically homebound with two kids under two, trying to rebuild her personal and professional network in a whole new city. Twitter has been like a generous ocean. Treasured new friends, mentors, and incredible opportunities continually wash up on her beach. After 12 months of meeting incredible people and all her business leads, along with speaking at events all around the world, Laura finally took the hint and refocused her entire career on Twitter itself, to help others experience the benefits of mobile social networking. This year, her Christmas and birthday wish — to raise $25,000 for charity: water to build wells in developing nations — came true, you guessed it, because of Twitter.

Conventions Used in This Book

In this book, we stick to a few conventions to help with readability. Whenever you have to enter text, we show it in **bold**, so you can easily see it. `Monofont` text denotes an e-mail address or Web site URL. We capitalize the names of Twitter pages and features — such as Settings. Numbered lists guide you through tasks that you must complete in order, from top to bottom; you can read bulleted lists in any order you like (from top to bottom, bottom to top, or any other way).

Note: Screenshots in this book show you what the interface was like in spring 2009, and significant changes took place four times during the writing of this book. If you ever run into Michael and he looks kind of nervous when you talk about the Twitter interface, it's because he had to go back and change so many descriptions and screenshots over and over again. Give him a hug for us, please?

What You're Not to Read

We wrote this book for the first-time Twitter users. If you've already created an account that has some friends and followers, you can probably skip the chapters that talk about how to sign up and get moving — but you might find it useful to review the sections on how to dress up your profile. If you're a business and have already gotten rolling on Twitter, you can probably safely ignore many of the starting chapters and check out Parts III and IV. If you're a Twitter pro and could have probably written this book, feel free not to read anything, use this book as a doorstop, and recycle it when you're done. Okay, we're kidding — it'll make a great gift for the Twitter-skeptics in your life!

Foolish Assumptions

In this book, we make the following assumptions:

- ✔ You're at least 13 years of age. (You have to be at least 13 years old to have a Twitter account.)
- ✔ You have access to a computer and the Internet (and know how to use them!).
- ✔ You have a working e-mail address that you can access.
- ✔ You have a mobile phone and know how to send text messages (if you want to access Twitter by using your mobile phone).
- ✔ *Bonus:* You have a smartphone (if you want to use a mobile Twitter application).
- ✔ You can read.

How This Book Is Organized

Like other *For Dummies* books, each chapter in *Twitter For Dummies* is self-contained, and you can read them in any order you want. However, we've organized the book into four parts, and if you read them in order, you can get a strong understanding of the Twitter landscape, from signing up to tweeting like a pro.

Part 1: Twitter? Like Birds Do?

Part I introduces you to the very basics of Twitter, from understanding how the Twitter feeds work to getting up and running with an account. You can figure out how to find and invite your friends to Twitter and start communicating with them in public and in private. We also look at the different things that you can do with the Twitter.com interface, including some things that may not be immediately obvious.

Part 11: Joining Your Flock on Twitter

After you become familiar with the basics of Twitter, you probably want to know how to find the sorts of people you want to follow and how you can start communicating with them in a way that makes sense on the medium. We give you all that information in this part, and we provide a list of many resources that you may find useful in getting Twitter to work best for you.

Part 111: Twittering in High Gear

Part III goes in depth into all the ways that you can interact with the Twitter interface, from desktop clients to mobile phone tricks to short-hand commands that can drastically improve the efficiency and information that you can get from Twitter. We also go over third-party solutions, search tools, and other content discovery tools and metrics that you may want to try.

Part 1V: Knowing Why We Twitter

In Part IV, we ask you to ask the big questions about why you'd want to use Twitter and what sort of presence you might want to cultivate. We go through the different ways in which people, businesses, not-for-profits, and other organizations can use Twitter. We also provide case studies and examples for how brands and organizational presences have benefited other users on Twitter and themselves, and how they've successfully used Twitter to improve their brands' transparency and customer relations. Lastly, we show how Twitter has started to effect social change and how grassroots efforts by users have helped raise money, expose news, and even elect presidents.

Part V: The Part of Tens

The final section is typical of every *For Dummies* book. In these chapters, we provide you with highlights of our ten favorite Twitter tools, ten favorite ways to use Twitter, and even some other applications that have the same or similar functionality as Twitter that you can check out.

Icons Used in This Book

Icons in this book point out important tidbits for you to look at, remember, and absorb. In this section, we go over the icons that we use throughout the book to guide you on your Twitter journey.

The Tip icon points out helpful information that's likely to improve your Twitter experience.

The Remember icon marks interesting or useful facts that we cover in detail in earlier chapters or something that's so important that you need to remember it while you're using Twitter.

The Privacy icon denotes that you should be careful about the Twitter activities that we're discussing. You may find yourself with a security or privacy concern.

The Warning icon highlights potential danger. When we use this icon, we're letting you know that you should proceed with caution.

Whenever you see this icon, rest assured that we're letting our inner geeks run wild. Here we point out information that's interesting but not absolutely necessary to your understanding of the topic at hand. If you want all the details you can get, read these paragraphs. If you just want to know the basics, skip it.

Where to Go from Here

If you haven't used Twitter before, mosey on over to Chapter 1 and start reading — we can get you up to speed in no time. If you've been using Twitter for a while and understand where everything is, but you want a better idea of how to use the service, head over to Part III, where we shift Twitter into high gear. If Part III is old hat for you, Part IV (particularly Chapters 11, 12, and 13) goes over some interesting businesses, personal, and not-for-profit stories that can help you grow as a Twitter user.

With that, we'll see you online!

Part I
Twitter? Like Birds Do?

The 5th Wave   By Rich Tennant

"He saw your laptop and wants to know if he can check Twitter."

In This Part . . .

You may find getting started with Twitter a bit daunting because Twitter.com doesn't make obvious why you'd want to use Twitter in the first place.

In this part, we cover the basics of why you may want to use Twitter and how to set yourself up with a Twitter profile that you can call your own. Additionally, we show you where to find all the basic stuff you need so that you can get started in no time.

Chapter 1

Sharing Your Thoughts, 140 Characters at a Time

In This Chapter

▶ Understanding what Twitter's all about

▶ Seeing how individuals, organizations, and businesses use Twitter

▶ Discovering what you can do with Twitter

▶ Looking into third-party Twitter applications

---

*Y*ou may have heard of Twitter but have no idea what it actually is. Twitter is basically a powerful *mobile* social network that enables you to keep up with the people, businesses, and organizations you're interested in — whether you know them personally or not. It also lets you share what you're doing with the world — everyone from your family and friends to complete strangers. (You'll have to bear with us to find out why you would want to do that.) Harvard Professor Andrew McAfee (@amcafee) describes Twitter this way: "With Twitter, my friends are never far away."

And www.Twitter.com itself says that *The New York Times* calls Twitter "one of the fastest-growing phenomena on the Internet." *Time* magazine says, "Twitter is on its way to becoming the next killer app," and *Newsweek* noted that "Suddenly, it seems as though all the world's a-twitter." What will you think?

Every day, we see dozens of new ideas and ways to use Twitter. In this chapter, we do our best to introduce the basic ideas and explain how Twitter works and why it's so powerful.

Figuring Out This Twitter Thing

Twitter is a fast-evolving, surprisingly powerful new way to exchange ideas and information, and stay in touch with people, businesses, and organizations that you care about. It's a social network — a kind of map of who you know and who you're interested in (whether you know them personally or not) — that you can access from your computer or your cellphone.

Twitter has one central feature: It lets users instantly post entries of 140 characters or less, known as *tweets,* through the www.Twitter.com site or your cellphone, or by way of the numerous applications that are available for both. (We talk more about the different ways to tweet in Chapters 8 and 9.)

On the most basic level, Twitter is a mobile social network that combines elements of short messaging services (SMS or *texting*), instant-messaging communication tools, such as AOL Instant Messenger (AIM), and blog publishing software, such as Blogger or WordPress. Like blogging, your tweets are generally published to the world at large where anyone can read them on Twitter.com (unless you choose a private account, so that only those you choose can see your tweets). Unlike blogging, you're limited to just 140 characters. Like instant messaging, you can communicate directly with people (through direct messages), but unlike instant messaging, each message has its own unique resource locator (URL), so each message is actually a Web page. Instant messaging also lacks the social network "following" features of Twitter and basic ideas like "publish-subscribe" and one-to-many broadcasting of messages.

Think you can't say anything meaningful in 140 characters? Think again. Not only are twitterers innovating clever forms of one-liners, haiku, quotes, and humor, but they're including links — in 23 percent of all tweets by one measure — and links carry a lot more information and context. Writing 140-character messages seems trivial. But headlines and very short advertising copy are famously hard to do really well — and known to be powerful.

The idea of Twitter sounds simple — even a little too simple. But when you think that millions of people around the world are posting Twitter messages, following other people's Twitter streams, and responding to one another, you can start to see the significance behind Twitter's appeal. True, Twitter can look like it's full of noise. But once you find interesting people and accounts to follow, your Twitter stream shifts from a cascade of disjointed chatter to one of the most versatile, useful online communications tools yet seen — that is, if you take the time to learn to use that tool correctly.

In the beginning was the word: The origins of Twitter

Twitter connects a wildly diverse array of people from all over the world, erasing barriers and boundaries all the way. Some of the media hype has called Twitter nothing short of revolutionary. And because Twitter is so easily customizable and open-ended, it has continued to become more and more popular with people and companies.

But Twitter's beginnings, like so many other digital innovations, were humble. Twitter was built in 2006 by three technology entrepreneurs — Evan Williams, Biz Stone, and Jack Dorsey. All three were then employed by a San Francisco–based Web company called Odeo, which specialized in publishing software for *podcasting* (audio broadcasting over the Web). Dorsey was the one who came up with the original concept, and the three subsequently built it as an internal tool for Odeo employees. At first, they had no idea that it would catch on the way it did.

A management shakeup led to Twitter and Odeo's reincorporation under a new company, Obvious Corp., and shortly thereafter, Twitter was released to the public. Already a favorite among Silicon Valley's geek elite, Twitter had its real coming-out party at the South by Southwest Interactive Festival (SXSWi) — an annual confab of tech and media innovators in Austin, Texas — in March 2007 when it was about a year old. Not only did it win the conference's Web Award honor, but its rapid-fire messages became the de facto coordinating and communicating tool for thousands of SXSWi attendees and the company became the digital world's new darling.

Shortly after SXSWi 2007, Twitter was spun off once again, becoming its own company separate from Obvious Corp. — Twitter, Inc.

Now, millions of people use Twitter to keep in touch with family and friends, to launch and expand careers, to connect businesses and reach customers, to build a brand, to report the news, and a whole lot more. No two people or businesses use Twitter in exactly the same way, and that fact is part of the secret to Twitter's success. You might argue there isn't really a wrong way to use Twitter, (as long as you mind the terms of service and don't try to actively do harm) so you get to completely tool it to your own needs.

Twitter is a great way for you or your company to connect with large numbers of people quickly and personally, just like you were having a conversation. In tech-speak, Twitter is a microblogging or microsharing tool; however, you can more easily think of Twitter as a giant cocktail party with dozens of conversations you can join (or start) at any moment. Or, if you prefer a work metaphor, Twitter is like the office water cooler where any number of informal (or formal) conversations can take place.

If you're familiar with blogs, instant messaging, and Web-based journals, you can start to understand what makes Twitter so unique. The Web offers a lot of information. Twitter can turn those long articles, lengthy conversations, and far-reaching connections into easily digestible facts, thoughts, questions, ideas, concepts, and sound bites. In other words, when you have only 140 characters, you have to be succinct.

How Individuals Use Twitter

Tomorrow I begin the archeological dig that is my desk. I will Twitter each item as I process it.

— Author and comedian John Hodgman via Twitter, December 4, 2008
(http://twitter.com/hodgman/status/1039327071)

Looking at Twitter for the first time, you might be compelled to ask, "But *why* are all these people, many of whom seem like just random strangers, talking?" At first glance, Twitter seems flooded with disjointed conversations, interactions, and information. You can find news headlines, political debates, observations on the weather, and requests for advice. The idea of Twitter can be a bit confusing for new *twitterers* (people who use Twitter).

People have many reasons for using Twitter:

- ✔ **To connect:** Most people start using Twitter to forge connections and be a part of a community. Others just want to be heard. Twitter lets millions of people around the world hear what you have to say; then it lets you connect with the ones who want to hear from or talk to you about your passions, interests, and ideas.

   For more on the social side of Twitter, check out Chapter 12.

- ✔ **To record:** Some people tweet as a way to take notes on life. They use Twitter at conferences, events, or just walking around and may even jog their own memories later about something that happened or what they've discovered. For example, if you're walking down the street and you notice a new restaurant you want to check out when you have more time, you might tweet about that. Now everyone who follows you knows about this interesting-looking place, and you have a way of remembering to go back there yourself.

- ✔ **To share:** Some people use Twitter to share what they think, read, and know. They may tweet links to great articles or interesting items, or they may tweet original thoughts, ideas, hints, and tricks. Some tweet notes from speeches or classes, and others share choice bits of their inner monologue. Even when this information can get pretty obscure, with millions of listeners, someone's bound to find it informative or interesting.

- ✔ **To stay in touch:** Whole families and groups of long-term friends use Twitter to stay in touch. Twitter can send public or private notes to your friends, and it stores all sent messages, which means that you don't lose your thoughts when you close your browser (or your desktop application). Connecting to one another on Twitter is a great way to preserve an initial contact, such as at an event or conference, in a way that lets you gradually get to know them more over time.

Twitter is pretty easy to actually use, meaning everyone from your 8-year-old cousin to your 90-year-old great-grandma can figure out how to use Twitter and say hello. Because you can access Twitter by using either a computer or cellphone (or both!), it fits into mobile lifestyles and brings you closer to the everyday thoughts of those you're interested in.

How Organizations Use Twitter

Barack Obama's successful presidential campaign in 2008 was perhaps the best example of an organization using Twitter to solicit donations, raise awareness, and call people to action. During the campaign, tens of thousands of Twitter users followed Barack Obama at `http://twitter.com/barackobama`, where campaign staff used the service to provide the then-candidate's whereabouts on the trail and kick off new donation initiatives. (Even though election laws mean the account can no longer be updated, it has hundreds of thousands of followers at the time of this writing.)

The power of Twitter works for much smaller organizations, too. Groups such as churches and local charities can use Twitter to provide an additional way for members to connect, plan, and reach out beyond their immediate community. Preachers tweet about their planned sermons, youth group directors tweet about events, and local soup kitchens tweet when they need help. Whether it's extra hands for a project, far-reaching assistance with a fundraiser, or some other big idea, Twitter can enable organizations operating on a budget to think on their feet.

New organizations have also sprung up through Twitter. Some people have started their own donation campaigns on Twitter and encouraged other Twitter users to donate and then tweet about it. But Twitter isn't just for charities. Enthusiasts of just about any interest have banded together on Twitter. For example, you can find organizations for food and wine lovers, sharing recipes and swapping restaurant reviews on Twitter. (You can search for the subjects that interest you on `http://search.Twitter.com`.)

For example, musicians use Twitter to spread the word about concerts, song releases, charitable efforts, and their daily lives as celebrities. (Even Britney Spears has an official Twitter account: `@BritneySpears`.) John Mayer (`@JohnCMayer`) live-tweeted from the Grammies. Musicians working hard to make a name have used Twitter to engage thriving, and involved, fan bases.

Twitter has also been a big help for community efforts. Whether it's Amber Alerts, fundraisers, searching for kidney donors, or rescuing James Buck from an Egyptian jail (`http://twitter.com/jamesbuck/statuses/786571964`), Twitter has shone as a tool for social good. Plenty of people in the world want to lend a helping hand, and Twitter's platform makes it easy, in real time, with a global network of connections.

For more on using Twitter for your business, turn to Chapter 11.

Businesses That Use Twitter

If individuals, community groups, and nonprofit groups, can use Twitter (as we discuss in the preceding sections), businesses large and small can use it, too.

Discount airline JetBlue uses Twitter to advertise fare specials, put out weather alerts, and conduct customer service (`http://twitter.com/JetBlue`). Coffee retailer Starbucks uses Twitter to connect with customers and spread company culture (`http://twitter.com/Starbucks`), as does online shoe retailer Zappos.com (`http://twitter.com/zappos`). Early on, computer manufacturer Dell started a Twitter account (`http://twitter.com/DellOutlet`) to promote special deals on returned equipment and has said that, as of December 2008, its Twitter account has generated over a million dollars in revenue. You can bet, Dell now has many more accounts: `www.dell.com/twitter`.

So why would a business want to establish a presence on Twitter?

✔ To network with customers and see what they're saying.

✔ To answer questions.

✔ To finely tool a company image.

✔ To poll and pull in feedback.

✔ To take advantage of an innovative form of 140-character advertising. If you have a limited quantity of something to sell in a short amount of time, you can't find a better channel than Twitter to make it known.

✔ Even a business with *no* customers on Twitter can take advantage of five off-platform benefits that we talk about in Chapter 11.

But none of these reasons really scratch the surface of why so many people use Twitter. Whether you want to use it for mostly personal or mostly business reasons, or even a blend of the two, you'll find that your reasons for tweeting multiply over time while Twitter becomes more and more useful to you. Each chapter in this book clearly explains why Twitter has caught on like wildfire and how you can join in the fun (and enjoy the business benefits) of this microsharing service.

If you're not sure where to begin, you'll be glad to know that many professions are comparing notes about the best ways to use Twitter. For example, ExecTweets (`www.exectweets.com`) shines the spotlight on executives who use Twitter. You can find dozens of industry-specific blog posts and guides on how to use Twitter most effectively. Laura's company started one list of these guides here: `http://pistachioconsulting.com/featured-articles/industry-guides`.

For more on putting Twitter to use for your business, turn to Chapter 11.

Getting Your Tweet Wet

Having breakfast and getting ready to ride. 6 hours today...

— Cyclist Lance Armstrong via Twitter, December 20, 2008
(`http://twitter.com/lancearmstrong/status/1069006436`)

When you log into Twitter, a question appears in large print across the top of the screen: "What are you doing?" The most basic activity on Twitter is to answer that question, whenever and however you feel like it. The beauty of this simple question is that you can answer it in so many different ways, and your answer can spark so many conversations.

While you get more comfortable using Twitter, you may find that you ignore the question of "What are you doing?" altogether. That's okay. Twitter is inherently flexible and open-ended, so you don't need to stick to a rigid set of rules. In effect, Twitter is what you make it.

The "What are you doing?" prompt can get some new Twitter users stuck in a rut. Sometimes, twitterers freeze up out of self-consciousness, concern that they're not doing it right, or just plain old 140-character writer's block. You know these Twitter accounts when you see them: The twitterers end up twittering only about what they had for breakfast, that they're leaving the office to go home and watch *Heroes,* or various other mundane life updates that don't spark much conversation. Many of these Twitter users don't end up getting involved in the Twitter culture, and some then stop using Twitter altogether.

If you're brand-new to Twitter and you're ready to try it out, turn to Chapter 2 for information on how to sign up, customize your profile, and adjust your settings. Chapter 3 fills you in on the Twitter.com interface — it's sort of a road map of the site, so you know where everything is.

You can get much more value from Twitter — and have a lot more fun — if you just let yourself relax and talk about what's on your mind. Passionate about aardvarks? Send out a few tweets with aardvark facts and see who talks back to you. Have a burning desire to change careers from accounting to roadie for a rock band? Talk about it! You can probably get a response or two.

How Twitter differs from Facebook

"Facebook is closed, Twitter is open. Facebook is structured, Twitter is scattered. Facebook is people you've known, and many you might have wanted to forget; Twitter is people you never knew, but might have wanted to meet. And because of all of that, barring an acquisition or failure to execute . . . Twitter will overtake Facebook and become the backbone of the real-time web."

— *Brightidea.com CEO Matthew Greeley (@brightidea)*

If you're a regular Facebook user, you may be wondering how Twitter is any different from the status updates that are part of Facebook. The main way in which Twitter differs from Facebook is that with Facebook, you're broadcasting your status updates to people you've allowed to be your friend and view your profile on Facebook. On Twitter, you're by default sharing your updates with the world. You can protect your Twitter updates so that only people you allow can see them, but that's not very common. Instead, most people leave their tweets open to the public, which means anyone who's interested in what you're saying can follow you — and you can choose to follow them back or just ignore them. You don't have to know the people you follow, and your followers don't have to know you.

Replies work much differently on Facebook, and as a result, the system is much less dynamic. On Facebook when people reply to your status update, their replies appear with your update itself, which moves farther and farther down in the feed, until eventually it's not even seen anymore. On Twitter, the most recent replies are always at the top of the stream, which means the conversation continues to be relevant and visited for as long as people are talking.

On Twitter, people frequently repeat your tweets for their own followers. It's commonly called *retweeting*. If your band is playing at a club on Friday, you might tweet, "MyBand rocks out Blondie's, 123 Main St, LA, Fri 9/3 @ 9 pm www.myband.com for tickets" If any of your followers want to spread the word, they might tweet, "RT @yourname: MyBand rocks out Blondie's, 123 Main St, LA, Fri 9/3 @ 9 pm www.myband.com for tickets" That RT is shorthand for *retweet*, and by putting your name after RT, they're letting their followers know you're the one who originally posted it (and that you're the one whose band is playing at Blondie's). If you want to encourage people to retweet something, you can even put something like, "Please RT" in the tweet. What all this means is that your tweets can spread like wildfire, and you can get the word out (fast!) about the things you want to share.

It's really striking to see how much faster, more easily, and farther messages spread on Twitter. Sharing and passing along information is what makes Twitter a sensitive global news detector, a powerful tool for social change or marketing, and an interesting and dynamic flow of ideas and information.

Tweeting Like a Pro

We'd like to thank you in 140 characters or less. And we just did!

— Twitter co-founder Jack Dorsey, accepting Twitter's Web Award honor at the South by Southwest Interactive Festival in March 2007

Simply put, a *tweet* is what you call the 140-character message that you send out onto the Web by using Twitter.

Why call it a tweet? It's convenient, tying into the whole theme of birds chirping. Also, like much of the Twitter vocabulary, *tweet* is a term coined by the users, rather than the company — evidence of the playful loyalty that avid users have with the Twitter brand.

Twitter limits the length of tweets to 140 characters (letters, numbers, symbols, and spaces), a length that may seem short at first. And it is. How in the heck are you supposed to say anything in this tiny bit of space? How can you distill your company pitch into 140 characters, or review a book or movie by using so few words? With time, you get used to this length restriction. Perhaps one of the coolest things about Twitter is that the more you use it, the easier it is to write short, sharp, clear tweets. As you get more accustomed to tweeting, you find that squeezing thoughts into 140 characters often makes you refine the point in ways you wouldn't have thought of before.

Some Twitter users have reported becoming better salespeople offline, or better writers, because Twitter's mandated brevity forces you to focus your thoughts into concise, direct sound bites. Because Twitter's communication format encourages brief but engaging ideas, Twitter sparks conversations faster than almost any other Internet conversation format.

Where the name Twitter comes from

We want to get this out of the way: Yes, Twitter is a silly name. It calls to mind images of birds chirping, or the all-night gab-fests at junior high sleepovers. But to be fair, a whole lot of Web services have silly names — in an industry peppered with companies that have names such as Meebo and Veoh, a company called Twitter doesn't stand out as having a particularly odd moniker. And co-founder Jack Dorsey has argued from the start that Twitter is a fitting name for the service. In an early interview with Jack, Ev, and Biz, (when Twitter was still owned by Obvious, Inc.), the founders answered a question about where the name came from. Jack said, "If you look it up in the dictionary, it's actually just [a] short burst of activity, and it's something that birds do. It's just like chirping." In this case, the name Twitter reflects the short bursts of "noise" (or tweets) that Twitter users make when they conduct their digital banter. (If you haven't made the connection already, this definition explains why Twitter's logo is a cartoon bird. To watch a video of the interview in its entirety, go to `www.podtech.net/home/?s=obvious%2C+twitter`.)

Branching Out with Third-Party Applications

At the risk of sounding like a Twitter cheerleader, don't ask "What *can* you do with Twitter?" Instead, ask yourself, "What *can't* you do with Twitter?" From its inception, Twitter has had a very open *application programming interface* (API), which is the geek-speak term for code that lets external developers and programmers weave the Twitter service and functions into other applications and services on the Web. The open nature of the Twitter API has led some people to come up with very interesting uses for Twitter.

The most popular Twitter applications are downloadable client programs that let you manage and update your Twitter feed from your desktop; vying for most popular are TweetDeck (www.tweetdeck.com) and Twhirl (www.twhirl.org), but people access Twitter dozens of ways, including (about half of average use) Twitter.com.

More than a thousand already exist. Some are silly (such as HereBeforeOprah [http://herebeforeoprah.com]), some are annoying (such as Magpie [http://be-a-magpie.com]), and some are incredibly useful (such as TwitPic [http://twitpic.com] and HootSuite [http://www.hootsuite.com]). (We cover these tools in Chapter 9.) The beauty of Twitter means that even the silly ideas have a chance to succeed, if the Twitter community responds to them. Because Twitter can do so much, so simply, the array of third-party applications offers a nice balance of work and play.

If you want to stick with using Twitter just as a status update service, that's fine. In fact, many people do. But if you want to really maximize your use of Twitter, you may want to check out all the neat ways you can use it — for example, to track expenses, request restaurant reviews, follow gas prices, read the news, find out the weather in your area, give hurricane relief to people in need, fundraise, drive cancer awareness, and a whole lot more. This diversity of use makes Twitter a vibrant community that you can tap into both for fun and for business.

Chapter 2

Hello, Twitter World!

Twitter is a deceptively simple, yet powerful conversation tool that enables users to broadcast short messages to the world and to connect more closely with people they care about. Intrigued about why this "stupid"-looking tool is so well-loved and popular? Then this chapter is the place to get your feet wet. It usually takes a while of using Twitter to get what about it could be really interesting and valuable to your life. Luckily, Twitter is not only easy to use, but it's also quick to set up and a piece of cake to get going.

In this chapter, we go over the very basics of Twitter: getting a username, beautifying your profile, finding people to communicate with, and getting yourself situated and ready to start tweeting like a pro in no time.

Signing Up

For many Web services, signing up is the easiest part of an otherwise complicated process. With Twitter, using the site is just as easy as signing up.

To sign up for a Twitter account, follow these steps:

1. **Use your Web browser to navigate to the Twitter Web site at `www.twitter.com`.**

   The Twitter splash page appears, as shown in Figure 2-1.

2. **Click the large green Get Started — Join! button.**

   The signup page appears, as shown in Figure 2-2.

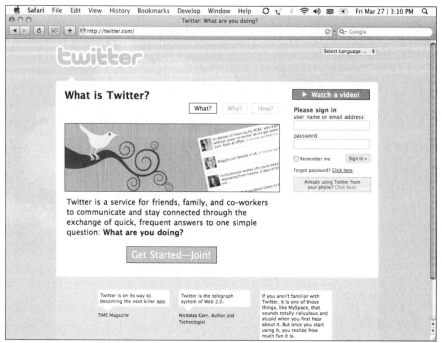

Figure 2-1:
The Twitter splash page.

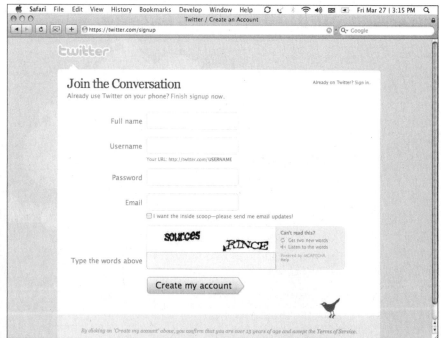

Figure 2-2:
The very short and simple Twitter signup page.

3. **Enter your desired username and basic information in the appropriate text boxes.**

   The only information Twitter requires from you is a username, a password of your choice, and a unique e-mail address where Twitter can contact you for notifications. (You'll probably take longer to decide on a username than to actually sign up. We cover how to choose a good Twitter name in the following section.)

4. **Type the CAPTCHA code in the Type the Words Above text box.**

   This step is a standard Web tactic to prove that you're a human and not a spam program. (For more information on this code, see the sidebar "What's up with the CAPTCHA?")

5. **Click the Create My Account button.**

   By clicking the Create My Account button, you're agreeing to Twitter's Terms of Service. You see a link at the bottom of the page where you can read those Terms of Service if you like, or you can go to `http://twitter.com/tos` to read them.

   You're taken to your newly created Twitter account (see Figure 2-3).

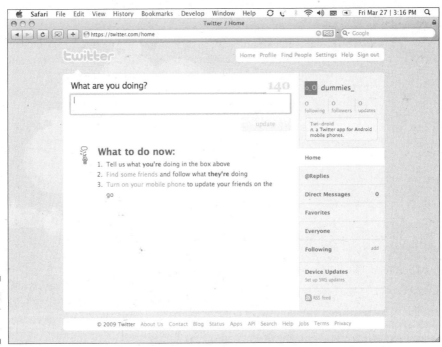

Figure 2-3:
A Twitter
blank slate.

What's up with the CAPTCHA?

A CAPTCHA is a quick check to make sure that an actual person, rather than a computer program, is using the Web site. Web applications use CAPTCHA (which stands for Completely Automated Public Turing test to tell Computers and Humans Apart) as a standard defense against spam and automatically generated user accounts.

You may find the CAPTCHA a bit tricky to read, but that's largely the point. Computers have a hard time reading text that's distorted in any way, but humans can adjust rather quickly.

Sometimes, you may run into a hard-to-read or ambiguous CAPTCHA. If you're having trouble reading the CAPTCHA, Twitter uses the popular reCAPTCHA tool, which can easily generate another CAPTCHA for you: Just click the Get Two New Words link to get another CAPTCHA. There is an audio version of the CAPTCHA on Twitter, but it really doesn't seem to work well.

If you can't read a CAPTCHA after a few tries, you may be a computer. If you think that you may, in fact, be non-human, please consult your doctor or trusted medical professional.

Did you know you can register for Twitter entirely by text from any cellphone? Get a friend started while you're away from a computer — you can create a new Twitter account from any cellphone at any time. Just send an SMS text message with the word "join" to 40404 and follow the directions that are texted back to you to choose a username. Later, go to Twitter.com and look for the button labeled Already Using Twitter from Your Phone? Click Here. (To find out more about using Twitter on your cellphone, check out section "Adjusting Your Text-Messaging Settings," later in this chapter.)

If you already have a Twitter account, **do not** text "join" to 40404 or you will lock your phone into a separate new account. You will not be able to add your phone to your original account until you delete the new one. See instructions on how to set up your phone to work with your existing Twitter account below.

Picking a Name

On Twitter, your username is your identity. Laura's Twitter name, or *handle,* is @Pistachio, and it has become the way that many people know her. She's met thousands of people in real life after initially connecting with them through Twitter, and it's not unusual for her to hear, "Hey, Pistachio!" from across the street or across the room at a party. @Pistachio has, in effect, become her nickname. If you want a quick glimpse at the search engine "optimization" (SEO) value of Twitter, just run a Google search for the word pistachio and you'll find her Twitter account is one of the very first search results. Crazy.

Why @Pistachio?

Many people have asked where the username @Pistachio came from. Simply, Laura's first office was painted an unfortunate green color — that precise, indescribably ugly shade of Grandma's favorite ice cream on summer nights at Friendly's by the rotary in Gloucester, Massachusetts. Laura first adopted the color as a company name in 1997, and over the years it has become part of her identity. Thus, she now is @Pistachio.

When we refer to Twitter usernames in this book, we follow the convention of putting an at sign (@) before the name, because that's how you refer to other users on Twitter. (For example, if you want to say that you're reading Laura's book, you might say, "Reading @Pistachio's book." That way, people who follow you on Twitter can easily click over to Laura's Twitter profile, in case they want to follow her, too!) But when you're actually choosing a username, the @ isn't part of it. The only characters you can use are uppercase and lowercase letters, and the underscore character (_).

That story emphasizes that you should think about how you want to be perceived both on and off Twitter and how your username fits into that perception. Twitter is a far-reaching service, and if you get really involved in the culture of Twitter, like the rest of the social Web, it undoubtedly spills over into real life. The days of choosing anonymous handles such as sexybabe44, like you may have when you used instant-message programs or chat rooms in years past, are long gone.

If you can sign up for Twitter by using your name or a variation of it as your username (assuming somebody else isn't already using it), we recommend doing so. It makes your experience with Twitter much easier when the line between online and offline blurs.

For example, if your name is John Ira, you may want to pick a Twitter username such as @johnira or @john. If users have already claimed those monikers, try adding an adjective or descriptor, such as @handsomejohn or @johntheterrible. If you prefer for people not to know who you are, you can choose a name that's a bit more generic. You can also use a handle that you've established on other Web sites. You may also want your username to match your e-mail address — for example, if your e-mail address is doglover1980@whatever.com, you may decide to use @doglover1980 as your Twitter name.

Be forewarned! If you choose to use your last name only, like Michael (@gruen), you may find yourself without a first name in the eyes of other twitterers.

Using Twitter for your business? You can use your company or business name as your username, and you can fill in that business name in the Name text box on the Settings page for your account. But if you do, be sure to include the names of anyone who handles the company Twitter account in the 160 character "Bio" text box on the Settings page for your Twitter profile. (We cover how to customize your profile in the "Customizing Your Profile" section, later in this chapter.)

If you're looking to be a bit more removed and really would prefer to use a nickname rather than your name, or your company or product name, be sure to choose a username that's friendly and accessible. On Twitter, you want people to respond to you, not be put off by a risqué or otherwise questionable handle. And if you run into your Twitter pals at networking events or other real-life social situations, you want to make sure that you don't mind having your username written on your nametag or shouted out in greeting.

Lean toward using a short Twitter username. ***Remember:*** Tweets are only 140 characters, so when people are replying to you, if you have a longer name, you leave them less room for message content. Twitter limits your username to just 15 characters for this very reason. (For more on how to reply to another person on Twitter, turn to Chapter 5.)

Your Twitter name has power and influence on *search engine optimization* (SEO), or how close to the top of a search results list you appear in a search engine such as Yahoo! or Google. Businesses should consider using valuable keywords as their Twitter names.

Finding Contacts

When you first sign up for Twitter, you're prompted to see if your friends are on Twitter (see Figure 2-4). Finding contacts on Twitter can be a lot of fun! The easiest way to find your friends is to import your friends and contacts from other services that you already use (such as Gmail, Yahoo! Mail, AOL, and Hotmail). You may be pleasantly surprised at how many people you know who are already busy tweeting away.

To import contacts and make them part of your Twitter world during the registration process, follow these steps:

1. **Select the e-mail account type from which you want to import on the left-hand side of the screen.**

2. **Type your e-mail credentials (username and password) in the Your Email and Email Password text boxes.**

Figure 2-4:
See
whether
your friends
are on
Twitter by
importing
your e-mail
address
book.

Having Twitter automatically find your contacts involves entering your e-mail account password. Although Twitter has established itself as a trustworthy service, in general, be very cautious about sites that ask you for your e-mail address and password.

3. Click the green Continue arrow.

Twitter looks at your contact list from your e-mail account and gives you a list of all the people from your address book who are already on Twitter.

4. Select the check boxes for the people you want to follow.

If you click the Select All check box, everyone is selected. If you uncheck the Select All check box, everyone is unselected, and you can go through your list of contacts, picking and choosing who to follow.

When you follow people on Twitter, you see their updates on your Twitter Home screen.

5. When you finish selecting people, click the green Continue button.

If you didn't select all the people in your address book, you're asked whether you want to invite any of the people you didn't select to join Twitter. (For more on inviting people to join Twitter, see "Inviting Contacts," later in this chapter.)

If you're not careful about where you click, you can accidentally send an e-mail to everyone in your address book. However, if you want to invite all your contacts to join you on Twitter, go ahead and share the Twitter love!

6. Repeat these steps for all your other networks, if you have them.

If you skip this step during the registration process, you can always search for people by first name, last name, or e-mail address by clicking the Find People link at the top of any Twitter page.

Using useful people-finding tools

Jumping into random conversations is a great way to find like-minded Twitter users, but it's not the only way. You can use a few tools to discover people on Twitter who share your interests or live near you.

One of the more interesting tools out there, TwitterLocal (www.twitter local.net), helps you find Twitter users by geographic location. It's a great way for people interested in real-life meet-ups, as well as those in localized industries (such as real estate and car sales) who use Twitter to drum up business, to contact each other.

Twellow (www.twellow.com) is another handy tool for widening the scope of your Twitter universe (which, yes, some call a *twitterverse*). Twellow sorts Twitter users by categories based on keywords found in the Bio sections of their profiles. Users can also claim Twellow profiles for any Twitter user-names that belong to them, by proving who they are. Claiming lets you edit the entry to add more categories or remove incorrect categories. Twellow is searchable by name, location, or category, similar to an online yellow pages for Twitter (hence the name Twellow).

Part III explores more of these third-party tools.

Searching by using Twitter Search

Twitter also has its own search engine, known as Twitter Search, which you can access by clicking Search at the bottom of any Twitter page or by going to http://search.twitter.com. You can enter any keyword of your choice into the Twitter Search text box and click the Search button, and Twitter not only brings you results in chronological order (with the most recent at the top), but also lets you know when people have made new tweets that match your search criteria and gives you the option to refresh the search results page.

Everything in moderation: Making sure you don't follow too many people

Be cautious when following new people. You can easily get excited and start following a ton of random people, but this approach has some potentially negative consequences. It takes time and genuine interaction to build relationships on Twitter, so many of the initial people you follow (who don't personally know you) may not opt to follow you back immediately. As a result, you may at first find that you're following many more people than are following you, and your follower/following ratio is skewed heavily to the following side.

To some Twitter users, an account that's following 500 people with only 1 or 2 people following it back is a warning sign that it may be a spam account — and you don't want people to think that you're a spammer. Take a relaxed approach, following a few people at a time, talking to them, and giving them time to follow you back before increasing your follower circle. Over time, your numbers swell on their own just because you're building a network and interacting with it.

Twitter users are often interested in meeting and talking with new people and want to hear fresh voices. If you talk about your passions, interact with people in and out of your network, and are genuine, you'll have no trouble finding people to follow and getting them to follow you back.

If you have a blog or Web site, create a friendly "Hello, Twitter people!" Twitter landing page that introduces yourself to people you follow or who may want to follow you, and link to that page on your Twitter profile so that it directly welcomes curious new people. Companies that tweet should definitely mention it on their own website so that it is clear whether or not their account is authentic. Todd Defren of SHIFT Communications (@tdefren) has pointed out that it's a particularly good idea for businesses to use a Twitter landing page to explain how they are using Twitter and offer ways to opt-out of any connections or communications.

You can use Twitter Search to find new people on Twitter by typing keywords connected to your interests or profession in the text box. Bonus: Because Twitter Search sorts results based on how recent they are, the people you discover through this search are likely very active Twitter users.

Twitter Search was originally built by another Web startup called Summize, which had earned special privilege and access to Twitter's application program interface (API) to create a search engine for the microsharing service. Although Twitter officially acquired Summize and has since renamed it Twitter Search, Summize is still known to many (and affectionately referred to) by its original name. (Michael somehow never got over the name change, and Laura's been caught referring to Summize in her speeches frequently.)

Inviting Contacts

During the registration process, after you import your contacts from your e-mail address book, you have the option to invite any of your contacts who aren't yet using Twitter.

The process is really simple:

1. **On the Why Not Invite Some Friends? screen (see Figure 2-5), select which of your contacts you'd like to invite to join Twitter.**

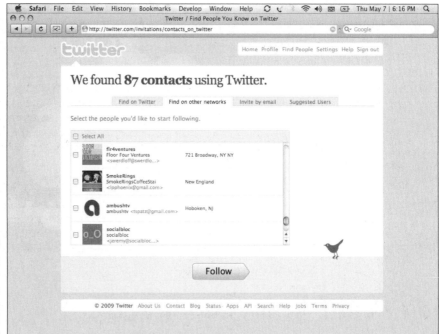

Figure 2-5: Ask your friends to join the party!

2. **Click the green Invite arrow.**

   An invitation to join Twitter will be sent to the people you selected, letting them know that you're on Twitter and they can follow your updates by signing up for Twitter themselves.

If you've used the Find on Other Networks tool, you've already been prompted to invite friends from your address book who aren't on Twitter. If you want to invite your friends by hand, without having Twitter go through your address book, take the following steps:

1. **On the top navigation bar of any Twitter page, click the Find People link.**

   The tabbed navigation loads below the navigation bar.

2. **Click Invite by Email.**

   A text box appears.

3. **Enter the e-mail addresses of the people to whom you want to send an invite.**

   Separate each e-mail address with a comma and a space.

4. **After you enter all the addresses you want, click Invite.**

   You're done!

If you choose not to do this now, you can always go back and do it later. Simply click Find People in the toolbar at the top of your Twitter profile to make the input screen for e-mail invitations appear.

If you don't opt to invite people during the registration process, or you want to invite people down the road, you can always e-mail people you know whom you think would most enjoy or benefit from Twitter, sending them a link to your Twitter profile and writing a note explaining what Twitter is. Many people choose this approach when they first join Twitter so that they can keep the invitation process personal.

Many Twitter users, co-author @geechee_girl included, have put Twitter handles on business cards and in e-mail signature lines. These actions are indirect invitations for the people who meet us in real life or interact with us in business to connect with us on Twitter, as well. The more people who join you on Twitter, the more effective your network becomes.

Say Hello! Your First Tweets

The entire premise of Twitter is to answer the question "What are you doing?" in 140 characters or less. So, go ahead! Tell Twitter what you're doing right now. Type a message in the What Are You Doing? text box, keeping under the 140-character limit. When you're done, click Update. Congratulations! You've just made your first tweet.

If you're thinking, "Wait, that's it?" you're right: That's it. Tweeting is that simple, but that simplicity makes it powerful. Your first tweet was probably something mundane, such as, "Trying out this Twitter thing" or "Hello there, Twitter. I'm reading *Twitter For Dummies!*"

But while you start to add more and more updates, people begin to see what's going on in your life and what you're thinking about. Twitterers following you or searching for keywords in Twitter, in all likelihood, start talking to you about what you're doing. The conversation starts with those simple exchanges: Talk about your favorite band's new album, your mechanic and how she fixed your car's catalytic converter, or really anything at all. If you've already found your contacts on Twitter, they probably respond to you pretty quickly. If you don't have any followers yet, don't worry; they'll come.

We discuss suggested Twitter etiquette, culture, language, and all that stuff in Chapter 7. This chapter simply tells you how to get your Twitter profile up and running so that it reflects who you are and what you want to get out of Twitter.

Your tweets, right now, are publicly visible and searchable, even if you delete them immediately after hitting Update. This situation isn't life or death, but be careful. If your updates are unprotected, what you tweet ends up in Twitter Search and on Google, even if you delete it quickly. (Chapter 9 discusses search tools in depth.)

Customizing Your Profile

Your public page on Twitter, also known as your profile, is other Twitter users' first impression of you, and it can make a big difference in whether they decide to follow you. Take a few minutes to dress it up a little! Making sure that it reflects you or your business makes all the difference when it comes to whether people stick around to see what you have to say.

After you sign up for Twitter, one of the first things you should do is personalize your profile. Make sure that you have

- ✔ An *avatar* (a picture that shows up to the left of your tweets, representing you or your company)
- ✔ A background image or background color for your home page
- ✔ A bio that's 160 characters or less
- ✔ A link to anything else you want to share

Some of the best profile pages on Twitter are the ones that give you a look into that user's personality. Someone who loves to ski might upload an image of his favorite mountain range as the profile background and pair it with an avatar that depicts him in ski goggles. You don't have to bare your soul, but people on Twitter want to know something about you, and the public page is where they can first discover it.

After you log into Twitter, you can customize your profile at any time by clicking Settings in the top-right navigation bar.

Changing your avatar

Your avatar is displayed to the left of all your tweets, so it's your official face on Twitter. Some Twitter users change their avatars almost daily to different photos of themselves, some users leave their avatars the same all the time, and still others change their avatars according to a specific occasion — holiday-themed photos for Christmas or Halloween, for example. Your avatar is your face, some other picture, or the default oogily eyes emoticon: o_O. It's your choice.

People don't like following back if your avatar is just the default. Show your smiling face and set others at ease!

To change your avatar, follow these steps:

1. **Sign in to Twitter and click Settings in the top-right menu bar.**

   The Settings page opens.

2. **Click the Picture tab (see Figure 2-6).**

Figure 2-6: Smile for your Twitter avatar photo, instead of using the default oogily eyes.

3. **Click the Browse button and navigate to the picture that you want to upload.**

   Currently, Twitter supports the .jpg, .gif, and .png file formats.

4. **Click the Save button.**

   Your picture is uploaded to Twitter.

The size of your profile image is restricted to 700 kilobytes (which is a rather large image), and Twitter crops it automatically into a square for your public profile. Choose an image that's square or close to square, or make sure that the part of the image you want featured in your avatar's thumbnail version is in the center of the image.

Try to find a picture that's at least 73 x 73 pixels. Otherwise, Twitter stretches the picture out, causing some distortion.

If you upload a photo and it doesn't look quite right, don't panic! Just find a new picture (or adjust the original file) and try uploading it again. You can upload a new picture at any time.

Changing your background

In addition to changing your avatar, you can change the background of your profile page from the default blue to another color. You can even upload an image of your choice (or do both!). You can *tile* an image (make it repeat, like tiles on a floor), make an image large enough to cover the entire background, or choose a smaller image that doesn't cover the entire background (and leaves a solid color behind it).

To change your background by using Twitter's tools, follow these steps:

1. **Sign in to Twitter and click Settings in the top-right menu bar.**

   The Settings page opens.

2. **Select the Design tab.**

3. **Select a pre-made background or use your own image or pattern.**

   The pre-made Twitter backgrounds appear in square thumbnail images inside the Design tab.

   If you don't want a standard Twitter look, but instead want to use a background image or pattern from your computer, click the Change Background Image link below the pattern images. Then, upload a file by clicking the Browse button and finding your image on your computer.

4. **(Optional) If you want your image to tile, click the Tile Background option.**

5. **If you want only to change your image, click Save.**

6. **(Optional) To customize your text and links, click the Change Design Colors link.**

You may want to make your Twitter page match the color scheme of your blog or Web site. If you can access the hexadecimal codes on your blog's color scheme, you can enter those same hexadecimal codes in the appropriate boxes. After you finish, click Save Changes to update your colors. If you mess up before you save your changes, you can always hit Cancel or navigate away to retain your current color settings.

Hexadecimal codes are the six-digit codes used in Web site design to assign colors; each combination of numbers and letters corresponds to a different shade. For example, 000000 is black, and FFFFFF is white. Plenty of places on the Web offer easy-to-understand guides to hexadecimal color codes. Check out Adobe's Kuler (`http://kuler.adobe.com`) if you're looking for a nice color palette.

7. **Click each of the color swatch squares that you want to change.**

A note above each square tells you what part of the text or design is affected.

8. **When you're happy with your color scheme, click Save.**

If you're using Twitter for business purposes, use your background to reflect your company's identity — tiling your logo as the background, for example. Figure 2-7 shows an example of JetBlue's Twitter background.

Figure 2-7: A customized corporate background.

Editing photos for your Twitter avatar

Many of the photos that you want to use for your Twitter avatar may include other people. Or the picture composition may not allow you to get a good head shot. Thankfully, both Macs and PCs have tools available so that you can quickly put together an avatar without needing third-party photo-editing software. As an added bonus, these tricks show you how to take *screenshots* (pictures of what appears on your screen).

Start by finding a picture on your hard drive, the Web, or your digital camera and open the picture.

If you use Mac OS X, follow these steps:

1. **With the picture file open and visible on the screen, press ⌘+Shift+4.**

   Your cursor changes into a crosshair.

2. **Click and drag your cursor over the area that you want to include in your profile picture, and then let go.**

   On your desktop, a new file (usually titled something such as Picture 1) appears, ready for uploading.

On a Windows computer, follow these steps:

1. **With the picture file open and visible on the screen, press the Print Screen button on your keyboard.**

   This button may read PRNTSCR or a similar abbreviation.

2. **Press Windows+R.**

   The Run dialog box appears.

3. **Type** mspaint **at the prompt and click OK.**

   MSPaint opens.

4. **Press Ctrl+V.**

   A screenshot is pasted into MSPaint. By default, the Move tool in Paint is selected.

5. **Drag the screen shot up and to the left to mark the upper-left corner of the picture you want as your avatar.**

6. **Click outside the selection rectangle to deselect the screenshot.**

7. **Scroll to the bottom-right corner of the image.**

   A small, dark blue box appears directly outside the bottom-right of the image.

8. **Click and drag that tiny blue box toward the upper-left.**

   Stop where you want to mark the bottom-right corner of the image.

9. **Choose File⇨Save As.**

   The Save As dialog box appears.

10. **Save the file as a** .jpg, .gif, **or** .png, **give it an appropriate name (such as twit-teravatar), and save it in a place where you can find it later.**

    You're ready to go!

If the default themes or images don't appeal to you, or if you're looking for something simpler or more casual, you can find free background images at sites such as TwitterPatterns (www.twitterpatterns.com). TwitterPatterns offers a variety of pattern graphics to choose from, all of which are sized specifically to fit Twitter profiles. If you're feeling adventurous, you can hunt online for interesting background images on your own and upload them yourself. Just make sure that they're the right shape and size.

Your background image is almost always overlaid with your Twitter stream, so people usually won't be able to see the middle of the image. Their screen width dictates how much of your background they'll actually see.

Using your background image to expand your profile

Because Twitter's user profiles are so limited, some avid Twitter users take advantage of the background image to add more information or personal links than Twitter allows for in its short Bio section. In many cases, a Twitter user includes a short professional biography, accompanied by more links and ways to connect with that user (see Figure 2-8). This idea is a great way to let people know where else they can find you.

To customize your background image, you need to use a custom template application or create your own template from scratch by using a program such as Photoshop or a free image editor such as Gimp or Seashore. You can also use Microsoft's PowerPoint.

Figure 2-8: @Pistachio's extended profile information contained in a background image.

TIP

If customizing your own background image from scratch isn't your speed, don't worry! Several sites generate free Twitter templates that are designed just for Twitter neophytes in your situation. One of these sites is TwitBacks (www.twitbacks.com), which offers you a fill-in-the-blanks form to create your own Twitter background. Alternatively, you can grab a template from BoinBlog (http://boinblog.com/2008/07/02/twitter-profile-customization-photoshop-template). You need Photoshop on your computer to open the file, but it's a fast and easy way to create a template for yourself or your company if you're pressed for time.

Adjusting Your Text-Messaging Settings

By using Twitter cellphone notifications, you can keep tabs on your friends, your spouse, or someone who randomly says the funniest things. Some users, though, are more inventive: They use this feature to keep tabs on their current client roster to try to gauge those clients' happiness levels before calling them for project updates.

You can interact with Twitter on your cellphone via Short Message Service (SMS) text messages, on a mobile Web site, or by using a client application on your smartphone. You can opt for tweet notification from your network in several ways, as well.

Before you can do anything with your new Twitter account on your cellphone, though, you have to associate your mobile device with Twitter. Like most things about Twitter, it's pretty easy to do.

To associate your cellphone with Twitter, follow these steps:

1. **Sign in to Twitter and click the Settings link in the top-right menu bar of your Twitter home page.**

   The Settings page opens.

2. **Select the Devices tab.**

3. **Enter your cellphone number in the text box and select the check box below it to confirm that you allow Twitter to send messages to your phone; click Save.**

   A screen appears giving you a code that you need to text to 40404 (brief instructions are provided).

4. **Send the code to 40404 from your cellphone.**

5. **On the right side of your Twitter home page, under Device Updates, click the Phone radio button.**

   If you find the notifications overwhelming or need to stop them for a while, just turn them off, which we talk about in the following section.

You can turn on cellphone notifications even more easily if you sign up for Twitter by texting a message to 40404. But if you've already signed up at the Web site, use the Web site to add your phone. If you sign up both on the Web site and by using your phone, you end up with two accounts that aren't connected to each other.

Controlling the text-message flow

If your account has text-messaging device updates set to On, you receive a text message each time someone in your network sends a tweet. (To find out how to turn on cellphone notifications, see the preceding section.)

At first, receiving text-message updates from all your new Twitter friends is fun. But when your network grows, you may find all those tweets a bit noisy, to say the least — not to mention the fact that your cellphone plan may charge you for each text message you receive. To change this, look at Settings and then the tab called Devices. We give you more detail on what you can adjust, and how to do it, in Chapter 4 and Chapter 7.

Plenty of avid users of Twitter never even receive SMS updates; others swear by them. Part of the beauty of Twitter is the many different ways that you can access it. You always have a choice.

You can also set quiet time, which (in our opinion) is a very underrated feature. Basically, quiet time can ensure that your phone doesn't wake you up in the middle of the night when tweets come in from the other side of the world.

To set up quiet time, follow these steps:

1. **Click the Settings link on the top navigation bar.**

   The Settings page opens.

2. **Select the Devices tab.**

3. **Select the check box labeled Turn Off Updates During These Hours.**

4. **In the drop-down menus directly below the check box, select the times between which you don't want text messages to come into your phone.**

5. **Click Save.**

Selecting your text notifications, person by person

If you start following hundreds of people, you probably don't want to receive text-message tweets from all of them. Thankfully, Twitter lets you receive texts only from users of your choice so that your phone isn't vibrating and beeping all day.

To turn off device notifications for some of the people you're following, follow these steps:

1. **Go to your following page (`www.twitter.com/friends`).**

2. **Next to each person that you follow, you have the option to turn their individual device updates On or Off by clicking one of the radio buttons.**

3. **If you can't see the device updates On and Off options after each name on your following list, you don't have device updates turned on for your account. Turn it on and you will be able to adjust each individual's settings.**

Chapter 3

Stroll Around the Grounds: A Tour of the Twitter Interface

*F*or the power it wields, Twitter is one of the simplest and, we think, most elegant Web sites for mass communication. The interface makes interacting with other people — some you already know and others you'll meet — incredibly easy, and it cleanly organizes a lot of information.

As you use Twitter more and more, you may want to know where to locate things quickly and manage your communication flow more intelligently. In this chapter, we dive down into each Twitter page view, showing how it relates to the conversations going on around you and the conversations you're having directly.

Starting Out on the Home Screen

When you first log into Twitter, the Home screen is your first stop. After you set up your account, you go to this screen to touch base with your followers and the people you're following. On the Home screen, you can also see who's talking to you directly through *@replies,* which are public tweets in response to individual users, and *direct messages* (DMs), which are private, one-to-one tweets. (For more on using @replies and DMs, see the sections "Tweeting to One Specific Person: @Replies" and "Shhh! Sending Private Notes via Direct Messages," later in this chapter.)

Additionally, the controls along the top of the Home screen let you change your settings, update your profile background, upload your avatar, toggle your SMS notifications, and more. (Chapter 2 covers most of these setup features.)

The Home screen, shown in Figure 3-1, has a standard layout. The header has a Twitter logo on the left and a list of links on the right, which appears on all Twitter pages. Those links' names describe where they take you:

- ✔ **Home:** Your Home screen. Clicking on the Twitter logo at left also takes you to your Home screen.

- ✔ **Profile:** Your Profile page.

- ✔ **Find People:** The people search tool.

- ✔ **Settings:** Where you can configure your Twitter account (see Chapter 2).

- ✔ **Help:** FAQs and support.

- ✔ **Sign Out:** Exactly what you think it is — signing out of your Twitter account.

Figure 3-1:
The Twitter
Home
screen,
where you'll
spend a lot
of time.

Twitter is a living Web application. Its interface changes from time to time, so if you can't find something immediately, it's likely taken on a different name or moved to a different location on the interface. For up-to-date information about what's going on with Twitter, visit the company's blog (`http://blog.twitter.com`).

The sidebar

The area on the right side of most Twitter.com screens (Home, Profile, Replies) is called the sidebar. It's both a reference for what you're looking at in the main content area and a controller for the Web site, and it's configured a little differently in each view. Here's a breakdown of what's on the sidebar. Except where noted, this description applies to the sidebar on your Home screen:

✔ **Your information:** Your avatar picture and username. When you're logged in to Twitter and on your Home screen, you'll see only your avatar and username. Your Name, Location, Web, or Bio appear only on your Profile page. Click your avatar, the Profile link, or any @username link for your name to see your Profile page.

✔ **Your stats:** Your following and follower counts and the number of updates you've posted, followed by a box that displays definitions of various Twitter related words, tools, and services.

✔ **Your communications:** @username is a link to your *mentions* (all the tweets posted by other people that either mention you or are replies to you), and underneath it you will find your Direct Messages, and Favorites.

For more on using favorites, see the section "Playing (Twitter) Favorites," later in this chapter.

✔ **Your searches:** Next is the Search text box, followed by several sections that you can expand to a bigger view or shrink down to a single line by clicking a down or side arrow in a small circle to the right of each heading. As soon as you save a search to refer to it later, Saved Searches becomes the first of these sections.

✔ **Trending Topics:** Trending Topics shows you the most commonly tweeted words and hashtags at any given time. The Trending Topics view is a surprisingly powerful peek at what is going on in the world (at least, the world according to twitterers) at any given moment.

✔ **Your community:** Following is the last section on the sidebar, and it shows a grid of the avatar photos of those you follow (or a random sampling of them if you follow more than it can display).

✔ **Your community:** A grid that shows a number of avatars from the roster of other Twitter users you follow.

The "What are you doing?" box

Directly atop the wide left column, you find a box in which you can post your latest update. If you continually use Twitter's Web interface to post updates, you'll become very well acquainted with that box. (We go over how to update without using Twitter's update box in Chapter 8.)

You've probably noticed a light-gray 140 sitting on top of the upper-right portion of the update box. While you type in your message, that number decreases, letting you know how many more characters you can type before you go over the limit. When you get to 19 characters remaining, the number turns burgundy, and when you get to 9 characters remaining, the number turns red; if you go over 140 characters, the number starts counting into the negatives. If you can't click the Update button, you've likely gone over the limit, so be succinct!

As soon as you type a new tweet and click the Update button, your tweet appears in the area directly below the "What are you doing?" box and in the Twitter feed below that.

If your last tweet was on the long side, you might notice that it was shortened and an ellipsis (. . .) at the end of your tweet. If it was abbreviated, you can click that ellipsis to see your full tweet. If you replied to anyone or included a link in your tweet, you can now click that link. Additionally, the timestamp saying how long ago you posted that update in fact contains that update's *permalink*. Click that link and a page dedicated to that tweet — and that tweet alone — opens. Cool, huh?

This seemingly subtle fact is a big part of what makes conversations on Twitter different. Unlike IM or a chat room, every single tweet can be uniquely bookmarked, linked to, replied to, and archived. Right now, you can go online and view famous tweets you may have heard about, such as @JamesBuck's "Arrested" at http://twitter.com/jamesbuck/statuses/786571964 or @JanisKrum's "There's a plan on the Hudson . . ." at http://twitter.com/jkrums/status/1121915133.

The Twitter stream

All the action on Twitter, appropriately, lives front and center on your screen. This stream of Twitter updates doesn't have an official Twitter-sanctioned name. It contains your tweets and the tweets of those you follow in a chronological order, with the most recent tweets at the top.

This update stream goes by several names including stream, timeline, or sometimes feed (not to be confused with RSS feeds, which you can read about in Chapters 4 and 8). Some people who follow thousands of Twitter users call it a river — the tweet stream flows faster the more people you add to your list of friends and the more people you follow.

The stream only "flows" when you refresh your Web browser — it doesn't automatically display new tweets. Words like stream and flow most likely derive from the more dynamic moving displays on many third-party Twitter clients.

This is where the conversations happen; it's your home base for connecting with people and businesses on Twitter. By reading your stream, you can find new people to listen to (friends of your friends and connections) and a place to jump in and participate.

Each tweet appears in its own little rectangular box. If you hover your cursor over the box, a Star and an Arrow icon (or, if it's your tweet, a Star and a Trash Can icon) pop up on the right side of the tweet. These icons act like function buttons:

- ✔ **Star:** Clicking the star button adds that tweet to your Favorites list (which you can get to by clicking Favorites on the sidebar). When you mark something as a favorite, you make it easier for yourself to find that tweet in the future.

- ✔ **Arrow:** Clicking the arrow sets up the tweet entry field so that you can reply to that user with an @reply.

- ✔ **Trash Can:** This icon appears next to only your own tweets. Not surprisingly, clicking it lets you delete the tweet from the feed. (*Note:* If you're not seeing a Trash Can icon next to your own tweet, odds are Twitter is working on something. Occasionally, the Trash Can icon disappears, and you have to wait to delete a tweet — all the more reason to make sure that you don't tweet anything you don't mean to tweet!)

- ✔ **Coming attractions: Retweet?** Ryan Kuder (@ryankuder), a popular Silicon Valley entrepreneur on Twitter best known for live-tweeting his layoff from Yahoo! in 2008, recently noticed and captured screenshots of a possible fourth interaction icon in development at Twitter: RT (www. ryankuder.com/2009/05/is-twitter-making-it-easier-to-retweet). You can use the RT icon to repeat the tweet you're reading in Twitter lexicon, to *retweet*. It makes a lot of sense that Twitter would be experimenting with such a feature, as most Twitter clients offer it, and Twitter has historically adapted its product to popular user behaviors.

Tweeting to One Specific Person: @Replies

That little Arrow icon on the Home screen is the force behind one of Twitter's most powerful conversational features: @replies. Taking its format from a syntax used in text chat rooms, @replies is a tweet that, although public and visible to all Twitter users, is directed specifically to one Twitter user. Twitter has ramped it up by automatically detecting when an @ symbol is placed directly in front of a word (with no space in between) and adds a link to the Twitter user who has that word as his or her handle. More than just a way to direct a tweet to one person, @replies can also help you find new people to add to your network when you see one of your contacts conversing with someone you don't know and decide to check that person out.

This spring Twitter changed how @replies are collected by making the @replies link into an @username link that tracks *all* mentions. Anytime your @username appears in a tweet, it gets collected here. Some heavy users don't like this setup because it can get cluttered fast if you're lucky enough to get mentioned a lot. Even though the page is now considered the Mentions page, most Twitterers still call them @replies, so we use that here.

If you hover your cursor over the tweet that you want to respond to, the Arrow icon appears, which you can then click to reply to that tweet. Clicking the Arrow icon makes the user's Twitter handle appear in the "What are you doing?" window, and the words "What are you doing?" change to "Reply to" followed by the username of the person you're replying to, and the Update button becomes a Reply button. Twitter then associates your reply with the original tweet in the Twitter system. The person can see what tweet prompted your reply by clicking the In Reply To link at the bottom of your tweet to him. This In Reply To link is helpful, especially when you're responding to people who are frequent Twitter users and may have already put out more tweets since the one you're replying to — it lets them see specifically what you're responding to.

Here are some tips on how to make the most of your Twitter Mentions page (like the one shown in Figure 3-2), which you can open by clicking the @username link (with your own username) in the sidebar:

✔ **Send @replies anytime.** You can send an @reply to someone by just typing the @ symbol and, without a space, his or her username (for example, @geechee_girl). Then type your message and click Update. (See Chapter 5 for more on replying.)

If you just do your reply manually (as opposed to clicking the Reply icon on a specific tweet that you want to reply to), your reply won't be linked to any particular tweet. This may be exactly the case — @replies actually do initiate a conversation as much as they act as actual replies. But if you really want to reply to a specific tweet, you're usually better off clicking the Reply icon.

✔ **Read (or don't read) other people's @replies.** Some more conservative Twitter users prefer not to read @replies that don't concern them. In the Notices tab on the Settings page, you can opt to

- • Not display any @replies

- • Display only @replies directed at other Twitter users in your network

- • View all @replies from your contacts

If you don't really care which @replies you see, try the last option: Seeing what your friends and followers are talking about with other Twitter users can help you get more value out of the service and is one of the very best ways to discover new people to add to your network by jumping into conversations.

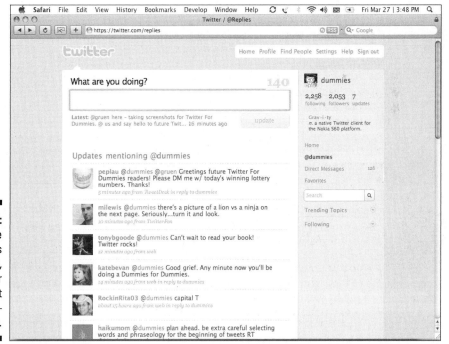

Figure 3-2:
The @mentions screen, where your ego can get a boost — or not.

Because of the recent shift to collecting mentions on the @username tab, it's interesting to note that the preceding settings apply only to tweets that begin with an @username, not those where the @username appears anywhere else in the tweet.

✔ **Join a conversation.** If you see that one friend or colleague on Twitter has responded to someone in his or her network who wants to know where to get the best pizza in Boston, and you have a recommendation, you can share it. You just have to click the Twitter handle that your friend is @ replying to and throw in your two cents. By starting conversations with friends of your friends, you bring new people into your own stream.

Keep in mind that @replies are public tweets. So, unlike text that you send in an instant message program, which you may be used to, other people can always read your @replies, and they'll be stored by search engines. If you have something private that you need to tell someone, use another feature of Twitter, the direct message (which we talk about in the following section).

Shhh! Sending Private Notes via Direct Messages

Direct messages (DMs) let you send your contacts private notes through Twitter. Just like regular tweets and @replies, they're limited to 140 characters. Unlike regular tweets and @replies, the only person who can see a DM is the recipient.

You can send a DM only to a Twitter user who's following you (but you don't have to be following that user), which is designed to prevent spamming and other unwanted messages by ensuring that people get direct messages only from people they actually want to follow.

The easiest way to see whether someone is following you and to send them a direct message while you're there is to simply go to that person's Profile page. You can get to the Profile page by either clicking that person's @username anywhere that you see it or by typing the username into the URL bar on your Web browser after Twitter.com (http://twitter.com/username). Then follow these steps:

1. **Look for the Message link in the right sidebar under Actions.**

   If the only action visible is to block the person, he does not follow you, and you can't DM him.

2. **Click the Message link.**

   The screen changes to a single text box over the user's Twitter background that is labeled Send Username a Message.

3. Write and send your message.

Compose your direct message in this box and then click Send.

You can also send a DM using the main Direct Messages interface:

1. If you're not on the Direct Messages page on Twitter, click the Direct Messages tab on the sidebar of any Twitter page.

The Direct Messages page opens (as shown in Figure 3-3), displaying

- The Inbox tab, which shows all the direct messages you've received over the course of your time using Twitter

- The Sent tab, which shows you all the DMs that you've sent

- A tweet input box that's specifically for DMs

Above the text field, you can find a drop-down menu from which you select the recipient of your DM. That menu lists only the Twitter users who are following you and hence can receive DMs from you.

2. Select a name from the drop-down menu.

Note: If a lot of people follow you, your drop-down menu doesn't contain every single follower's name. After recent Twitter changes, the list now appears to show you the list of people you've most recently been DMing with, which is a great solution.

Figure 3-3:
The Direct Messages panel, which lets you have private Twitter conversations.

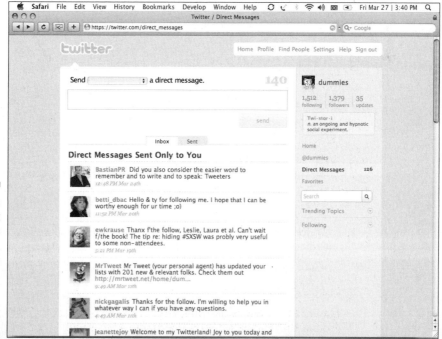

The only problem is that when a name doesn't appear in your Direct Message drop-down list, you may assume that it's because the person no longer follows you. The Direct Message interface can even mistakenly return an error message saying that a given person doesn't follow you. It's just not true. The only reliable way to see whether someone follows you back or not is to visit that person's Profile page. (These steps are described in the preceding list.) Laura has actually had people get sort of mad at her about this, which is ironic because she goes really far out of her way (following everyone back) to make sure that any reader can send her a DM.

3. **Type a message in the Send a Direct Message box.**

4. **Click Send to send the message.**

You can send DMs from any regular Twitter input source — text messages, third-party apps, or the main Twitter interface — by entering **d [username]** and then typing your tweet. For example, if you want to send a direct message to our Dummies account (@dummies) to ask when the next edition of *Twitter For Dummies* is coming out, you format the DM as **d dummies When's the next edition coming out?**

Sending DMs is easy. But proceed with caution! Many Twitter users have embarrassing tales of DMs that they accidentally sent as public tweets because they formatted the tweet incorrectly or sent it from the Twitter Home screen instead of from the user's Profile page (best bet) or the Direct Messages page. Double-check, just to be sure.

Playing (Twitter) Favorites

One of the icons that appears when you hover your mouse over a particular tweet is the Favorites star. It's basically Twitter's equivalent of a bookmarking tool, and twitterers often overlook it. When you mark a tweet as a favorite, it appears on your Favorites page (see Figure 3-4). You may want to mark a tweet as a favorite to:

✔ Save it for later.

✔ Acknowledge that it helped you or that you found it amusing.

✔ Mark it so that you can reply to it later.

✔ Remember it so that you can reference it in a blog post or article.

✔ Save it to quote later.

Figure 3-4:
Your favorite tweets are stored forever.

Ari Herzog (@ariherzog) pointed out that favorites are an untapped opportunity to collect testimonials and other tweets that might have value for your company. Innovation software company Brightidea (@brightidea) uses it to curate a great collection of Tweets about innovation, drawing upon Twitter search results for keywords related to innovation.

Our point is, don't limit yourself to using Favorites only as literal favorites. Use Favorites whichever way works best for you!

If you start using the Favorites icon on a regular basis, you'll soon have a large collection of tweets that you can gather data from for various projects or reference when you need to remember a particular joke or comment. You can also use it for bookmarking links so that you can visit it later — many of your best links and referrals will come from your fellow Twitter users.

One way to find more people on Twitter is to visit the Profile pages of your friends on Twitter and look at *their* Favorites, to see which tweets they liked the most. If your best friend marked a particular tweet as a favorite, and you're not yet following the person who posted that tweet, you may want to start following that person.

Searching favorite tweets

At the time we write this book, Twitter doesn't yet offer a way to search within your list of favorite tweets and hasn't announced any plans to do so. While your list grows, you may want to find some way to catalog your tweets. Some people use a spreadsheet in a desktop program such as Microsoft Excel or a Web-based one such as Google Docs. Some keep a record of their favorite tweets' permalinks (permanent link URL) pages and tag them by topic, using bookmarking services such as Delicious (www.delicious.com) or Diigo (www.diigo.com).

Indexing your favorite tweets takes a bit of hacking:

1. **To get to a tweet's permalink, find the tweet in your Twitter stream and click the small link below it that shows the time the tweet was sent.**

That link loads the tweet on its very own page, which you can bookmark for later because that page has a standard Web URL that always leads to that specific tweet.

2. **Add that URL to your favorite bookmarking service.**

Follow the directions that your bookmarking service offers for how to add a URL.

3. **If the option is available, tag the link so that you can search by topic later to find it again.**

After you have a system in place for keeping track of tweets that you want to save by using the favorite feature, you can then find them whenever you need them. You can also use the third-party application Tweecious (see Chapter 14) by tweeting the permalink to your favorite tweets and including the word favorites in the tweet where you do so.

Becoming a Renaissance Man via the Everyone Tab (RIP)

The Everyone tab used to lead to Twitter's Public Timeline, which contained all tweets from all twitterers everywhere. It's no big surprise that the Public Timeline was always pretty crowded and random, and that it became ever more so during the meteoric growth leading up to our publication deadline.

As we go to press, you can peek at the Public Timeline in two ways, neither of which appear anywhere in Twitter's interface. The original link (http://twitter.com/public_timeline) still works for now. Rumor has it that you can also still access the timeline by running a search with no terms in the search box (http://twitter.com/#search?q=Search — thanks @krystyna81 for this tip!) So although the true Public Timeline is gone, for old time's sake, we left this section in the book for you to play with and think about.

The timeline includes all Twitter users who haven't opted to protect their updates: people you follow, people you don't follow, and people who don't follow you. You can use the timeline to broaden your network, finding new conversations and topics, and generally expanding your presence on Twitter.

If you can get to the Public Timeline through the preceding links, it shows the most recent tweets from everyone who uses Twitter, in real time (like the page shown in Figure 3-5). It looks a lot like your own Twitter stream on your Home screen, but with more content to discover.

After you get to the Everyone timeline, spend a little time either scrolling from page to page and tweet to tweet manually or skimming for interesting conversations. (Refresh your Web browser to see the latest tweets.) If you find an interesting person or conversation, just click that Twitter handle to find out more about that user. You can also send an @reply to the tweet, which lets you just jump into the conversation, even if you don't yet follow any of the people in it. Or, if you like what you see, you can follow someone without replying to them — follow whoever looks interesting to you!

You can check in on the Public Timeline periodically, even after you start to grow your network into the triple digits and higher. Even people who have thousands in their personal Twitter network can find fresh ideas and interesting people on the Public Timeline once in a while, which keeps their Twitter experience the most varied and interesting it can be.

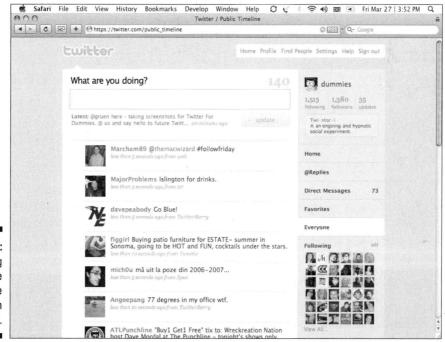

Figure 3-5: Looking at the Everyone timeline on Twitter.

Seeing Who You Follow

After you start using Twitter to its full potential, you may want to see a list of whom you follow. To see whom you follow:

1. **Log in to Twitter.**

   On any page in Twitter, you find the sets of numbers in the upper-right sidebar labeled Following, Followers, and Updates.

2. **Click Following.**

   A list of people you're following appears (as shown in Figure 3-6). Currently, Twitter sorts your Following list chronologically by when you started following them, with the most recent at the top.

3. **Scroll through the list manually, page by page.**

   This process works fine until you start to follow many more people. Without a way to sort or search — which Twitter still doesn't have (hint, hint, Twitter!) — finding out if you follow someone specifically can become tedious after you start following more than 100 people.

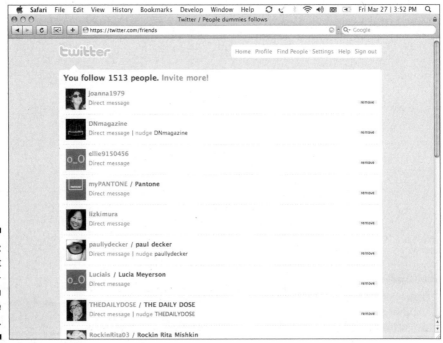

Figure 3-6:
Check out the twitterers whom you're following.

If you have a particular user in mind and you're not sure if you're follow-ing him, go that person's Twitter page. If you're following him, under his avatar, you'll see the "Following." If you're not following him, you'll see a Follow button, which you can click to follow him.

After you break the 100-following mark, you probably want to find another method for figuring out whom you follow. You can figure out whom you follow in a few ways, using third-party applications built on Twitter's API, which we cover in Chapter 9.

Figuring Out Who's Following You

You may also want to see who's following you on Twitter — maybe you want to find new people to follow, or you're just curious who's reading your tweets. You can pull up the list of your followers on any Twitter page. Find the sets of numbers in the upper-right sidebar labeled Following, Followers, and Updates, and click Followers.

Similar to the Following link (which we talk about in the preceding section), it brings up a list of people who are following you. Twitter sorts the list with the people who've started following you the most recently at the top.

Just like the Following list, you have to click through the Followers list page by page. Chapter 9 suggests some tools, such as TwitterKarma (http://dossy.org/twitter/karma) and FriendorFollow (http://friendor follow.com), that can show you both who you're following and who's fol-lowing you, which is considerably easier than scrolling through your follow-ers page by page.

If you don't want to have to constantly use a site such as FriendorFollow to keep up with your followers, you have several options:

- ✔ **Turn on e-mail notifications in the Settings area.** Click the Notices tab, check the Email When Someone Starts Following Me check box, and click Save. The e-mail notification authorizes Twitter to send you an e-mail alerting you about each new follower. Then, you can just click a link in the e-mail to that user's profile and see right away whether you want to follow them back.

- ✔ **Try to send a user who may be following you a direct message.** If she is following you, you're able to send that direct message. If that user isn't following you, you get a User Does Not Follow You error message (as shown in Figure 3-7). Then you have to decide whether you want to try to get that user's attention in another way. Be sure to check for the Action message on her actual Profile page when you do so, as the Direct Messages interface has been buggy in the past.

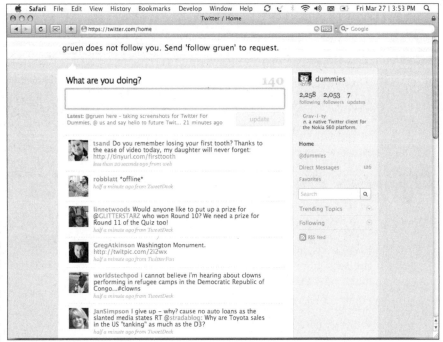

Figure 3-7:
A notifica-
tion of a
direct mes-
sage failure.

Looking at What You've Tweeted

You can see what you've tweeted in the past in a variety of ways. The first place to check is your own profile: Click the Profile link in the top-right corner navigation bar (or just click your avatar) to open your Profile page. Your Profile page, in addition to displaying your short bio and profile information, displays a feed of all your public tweets in chronological order. Just like the pages showing your followers and who you follow (which you can read about in the preceding sections), you can keep clicking the More button on the bottom of the page to see older posts.

Also, your profile is a publicly accessible URL. If your username is @dummies, navigate to http://twitter.com/dummies to jump directly to your Profile page.

If you're looking for a specific tweet, you can first look for it by using Twitter's search page (http://search.twitter.com). Do a search for your username — if it's a common name, you might want to include the @ — plus a keyword from the tweet. The tweet you're looking for is most likely in the search results. Figure 3-8 shows a Twitter Search results page.

Tracking trends

If you're interested in searching for more than just what you've tweeted about yourself, you can see what the rest of the world is tweeting about on Twitter's Search page and in the new Trending Topics part of the Home screen sidebar. Go to `http://search.twitter.com`, and below the Search button, you see a list of links to "trending topics." If a new movie is coming out, or the World Series is on TV, or a major news event is happening somewhere in the world, you're likely to see it as a trending topic. Sometimes the trending topics can introduce you to topics of conversation you didn't even know about.

If you protect your updates, searching by using Twitter Search doesn't work because the tweets aren't indexed in the search engine. It's a small price to pay for privacy.

You can also search for specific tweets by using Google or another search engine. In our experience, Google tends to update its index against Twitter.com very often and also offers advanced search terms so that you can really focus the search. Additionally, Google's search interface makes it possible to see who else is talking about your tweets, in addition to the tweets themselves.

Google does such a good job of indexing Twitter that it remains (at this writing) the best way to find out whether someone is on Twitter or not. At Google.com, run a search for Firstname Lastname Twitter, and usually you can find out right away whether a person is a tweeter. Bear in mind that very famous people who appear to be tweeting may be fan pages or other hoaxes, though — unless @DarthVader actually does exist, in which case, be very afraid!

Your public tweets are indexed by search engines. You can delete your tweets on Twitter by clicking the Trash Can icon, but if you don't do it within a few seconds, Google and other search engines, as well as Twitter's own search tool, have already indexed those tweets. So, sometimes tweets are forever. On one hand, this indexing is good for your visibility online. Because Google and other search engines index your tweets, those search engines can bring more people to your Twitter profile, which can then possibly bring those people to your Web site. On the other hand, you need to be cautious: Don't say anything on Twitter that you wouldn't want your mom, your boss, or your child to stumble across later on the Internet while searching for something else. Also take great care with names, as tweets about a person may actually show up closer to the top of search results than mentions of her name on other types of Web sites.

If you imagine that someone whose opinion you value is looking at what you write, you can avoid getting in any trouble. Twitter is so easy to use that it's equally easy to slip up, and because of its conversational nature, you can sometimes forget that it isn't a private room, and that it isn't an "inner monologue." A Ketchum PR executive famously upset his client — FedEx — when he tweeted a snide remark about Memphis on landing there for his meeting with them. Ooops! Remember the context you're tweeting in (he was on a client visit) and also remember that people may assume that you're talking about them when you're not. You also may not be thinking today about what may be findable weeks, months, and years from now.

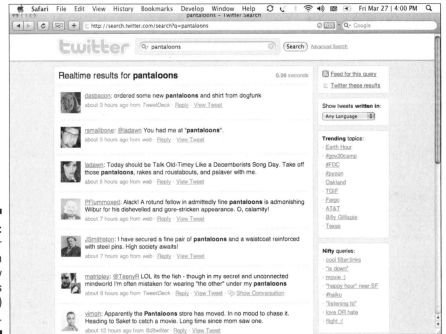

Figure 3-8:
Twitter
Search
(formerly
known as
Summize)
results.

Chapter 4

Using Twitter Wherever You Think Best

*T*witter's a great tool for providing friends, family, and followers with updates on what's going on in your life. But, as you've probably noticed, life occurs in a lot of places, not just on the computer. Don't worry, though, because Twitter's got you covered. The folks at Twitter have designed their application so that you can use it in multiple ways.

In this chapter, we go over all the ways that you, as an individual, may want to use Twitter, and we also give you some pointers for maximizing the application, based on your needs.

The User Multi-Face: Interacting with Twitter Every Which Way

If you want to get the most out of Twitter, you need to figure out how you prefer to access the service. Some people use the Twitter Web site or the Twitter Mobile Web site, text messaging, or any number of third-party services built by using Twitter's application program interface (API). You can use widgets, gadgets, browser plug-ins, and in short, a huge array of ways to interact with Twitter at your convenience and on your terms. This is a big reason for Twitter's popularity.

Like most users, you probably started by logging into Twitter.com and using the basic Web interface, shown in Figure 4-1, to manage your Twitter stream and communicate with your contacts. It's simple, no-frills, and convenient: Most of what you need is right there in the sidebar or in the top toolbar, and roughly half of all twitterers (probably more now with Twitter's extraordinary recent growth) use Twitter.com to access the service. But what happens if you need more functionality, mobility, versatility, or you just want more bells and whistles?

Figure 4-1:
The Web interface, which is just one of the ways you can use Twitter.

Some Twitter users prefer not to access the service through a browser window, need a few more organizational options than the Web page affords, or just want to share Twitter on an external Web site or blog. You can find plenty of options out there for doing all this and more.

Text messages (SMS delivery)

You can fairly simply opt into receiving Twitter via text messages (SMS delivery). First, you have to set up a mobile device so that Twitter knows where to send your tweets:

1. **Click the Settings link at the top-right of your Twitter Home screen.**

   The Settings page opens.

2. **Click the Devices tab.**

3. **Enter your mobile phone number in the text field, check the box granting Twitter permission to send you a text message, and click the Save button.**

   You're given an alphabetical code and instructed to text this code from your phone to 40404.

4. **Send the code from your phone as a text message to 40404.**

   You'll receive a text message from Twitter confirming that your device has been verified and SMS alerts have been enabled.

5. **Refresh the page until you see your cellphone number listed.**

   Now, you can choose to have text-message notifications on, off, or direct messages only. You can also opt to have them turned off during a specific time (say, while you're usually sleeping or at work).

6. **Turn on SMS device updates for your Twitter account and then click Save.**

   In the Device Updates drop-down list, select On if you want to receive tweets as text messages on your phone or direct messages if you would like to receive only your direct messages. Then click Save.

7. **(Optional) Select a sleep period when you prefer not to receive updates and click Save.**

   If you're enabling device updates, but you don't want them coming in 24 hours a day, under the heading Sleep, select the Turn Off Updates During These Hours check box and select the hours during which you don't want to receive updates on your phone. Click Save when you're done.

8. **Choose whose device updates you want to see.**

   Click Home and then click Following (or just go to www.twitter.com/ friends) to view a list of the people you follow. When device updates are on for your account, you'll see toggle buttons next to each person on your following list.

Make sure that your cellphone carrier has an unlimited text-messaging plan — or that you're willing to pay for a lot of extra texts — before setting Twitter device notifications to On. Twitter doesn't charge for texts, but your carrier might! Laura has unlimited texting even though she doesn't receive any text updates from Twitter, because she loves to use the text commands to add people, send tweets, and send direct messages.

You don't automatically receive device updates from everyone you follow on Twitter. You have to manually turn these device updates on for each individual. To check and see whether any given individual is set to device updates ON or OFF:

1. **Go to that user's profile on Twitter.**

   You can access a user's profile by clicking the user's @username in one of his tweets.

2. **Just under their avatar photo look for the device updates status.**

   The red dash and OFF means you won't get this person's tweets as SMS messages even when SMS device updates are turned ON for your account. The green check and ON means that you will.

3. **Turn an individual's device updates on or off.**

   First, enable all device updates on your phone. Then on Twitter.com, select your Following link (www.twitter.com/friends), and you can toggle Device updates On and Off for many users at a time right on one page.

   Of course, you can also control this setting using SMS on your phone. Send an **on username** message to turn Device updates on and **off username** to turn them off.

If you forget who you've set to receive mobile device updates from, you can always go to the list of people you're following by clicking Following (see Chapter 3 for more instructions) to find that information. It's listed underneath the person's username. If you turn device updates off, you won't be able to view it, but the information is still there and will reappear when device updates are turned back on for your account.

RSS feeds

You can receive updates from Twitter via an RSS (Really Simple Syndication) feed, much like you would for any blog or news Web site that you follow.

An RSS feed delivers the content to you so that you don't have to constantly be logged into the Web page. You just need a way to see the feed: Most people use something called a feed reader. You don't have to know much about technology to get one of these and set it up. You can choose from many feed readers out there, but we recommend Google Reader (http://reader.google.com). You already have one of these accounts if you use Gmail, Picasa, iGoogle, or other Google-owned services. Follow Google's pretty easy instructions to get started with Google Reader. Then come back to Twitter and set up your RSS feeds.

Subscribing to RSS feeds

If you want to set up an RSS feed for your direct messages or all your followers' tweets, simply repeat the steps to get your @replies RSS feed, clicking the link for your direct messages page or Twitter Home screen in Step 2. Now, you can read Twitter from your RSS reader alongside blogs and news outlets, and you don't have to be logged into any service to stay on top of who's talking to or about you.

What can you see with a Twitter RSS feed? You can set up a feed for your @replies so you never miss a message, one for your DMs (direct messages), or one for the people whom you follow. After you get your RSS feed reader set up, you just have to look for the feed symbol in your browser's URL entry field (see Figure 4-2), click it, follow the instructions, and the feed shows up in your feed reader.

Figure 4-2:
An RSS button, which varies by browser.

The feed symbol is universal, not unique to Twitter. If you see one on a Web site, that means you can add its content to your feed reader.

To get your @replies RSS feed:

1. **Click the Profile link in the upper-right of any Twitter page.**

   Your Profile page appears.

2. **Click the Mentions tab in the right sidebar (which is marked with @username).**

   Your Mentions page appears.

3. **Scroll to the bottom of the page and click the orange RSS button.**

   You can also click the RSS logo in your browser. This logo is usually all the way to the right in the text field where you enter URLs, but it may differ, depending on which browser you use.

   Clicking this button (or logo) automatically prompts you to add the feed to the feed address into Google Reader if you have it set up. If you use an application other than Google Reader, you may have to copy and paste the RSS feed's URL into your reader.

Desktop clients

You can access Twitter through one of the many downloadable desktop applications that third-party developers have created using Twitter's API. We cover these desktop clients more thoroughly in Chapter 7. Some of the most popular applications are Twhirl, Twitterrific, and TweetDeck (shown in Figure 4-3).

Figure 4-3: You can get your Twitter info by using TweetDeck.

Basically, a Twitter client allows you to use Twitter from your desktop without having a browser open. Many of these clients also offer features that Twitter doesn't, including the ability to thread tweets and track conversations, create groups, filter content, open simultaneous accounts, delete direct messages, and more.

These services work by talking to Twitter to get the information they need. So, they don't work if Twitter isn't working; they rely on it to gather and relay the data you see and use.

TwitterFox

A third-party application created for Twitter is TwitterFox (`http://twitterfox.net`), which is a plug-in that you can build onto your Mozilla Firefox Web browser. *Plug-in* just means that the application gets installed right into the browser and runs from there. It won't run on Safari or Internet Explorer, and you can't use it if you don't use Firefox.

Although most plug-ins and add-ons made for Twitter are safe to put on your computer, always be careful any time you install something new. A good way to tell whether an application is okay is to ask your friends on Twitter whether they use it. Most active Twitter users are happy to provide tips and recommendations.

Mozilla approves plug-ins that have been submitted to its developer program. Plug-ins that are proven not to be harmful are endorsed by Mozilla.

Widgets and gadgets

Twitter and other sites offer widgets (or, as Google calls them, gadgets) that let you embed information from a service such as Twitter onto other sites so that you can share Twitter more easily. Sometimes, widgets come in the form of HTML code that you can copy and paste into a MySpace profile or blog template. Other times, they come in the form of an application that you have to install on a social-network platform, such as Facebook. You can use dozens and dozens of official and unofficial widgets for Twitter. Using free widget-building tools, anyone can build a widget using any RSS feed as the content supply, so there's no telling how many thousands of Twitter widgets actually exist.

Twitter has an official page where you can find the code for an embeddable widget, complete with step-by-step instructions for installing it. Just go to `http://twitter.com/downloads`.

You can find an official Twitter application for Facebook, too, which means that you can make your Twitter updates show up as your Facebook status updates, or you can display a badge of your tweets on your Facebook profile. You can find the Twitter application for Facebook at `http://apps.facebook.com/twitter`.

The Google gadget works on Google Desktop, as well as the iGoogle personal home page product. You can install the Google gadget by clicking the download button at `http://desktop.google.com/plugins/i/twitter.html`.

Putting Twitter on your site

You might want to go a bit beyond run-of-the-mill widgets if you're hoping to put Twitter on another Web page seamlessly. If you have technical expertise or access to a good Web developer, you can build your own widget or plug-in for your site that uses the Open Twitter API. You can find details on building a widget at http://apiwiki.twitter.com.

If you're not a computer programmer or developer, you probably won't ever touch the Twitter API directly, but you will be using it — without even knowing it — every time you use a third-party application. We mention Laura's startup project www.oneforty.com a handful of times in this book because its mission is to help those new to Twitter find the very best and most useful applications, services, and tools within the Twitter ecosystem. When it launches, please let us know whether it's helpful to you.

Going Mobile: The Key to Happiness

In our opinion, the key to Twitter happiness is mobility. You should be able to use Twitter anywhere, anytime, and any way that you want, including on your phone. You can get this mobility via SMS (which we talk about in the "Text messages (SMS delivery)" section, earlier in this chapter) or on the Twitter Mobile Web site at http://m.twitter.com. Twitter Mobile is missing a few of the regular, Web-based Twitter site's features (for example, you can't see your favorites or a list of your followers), but you can use it pretty much as you do the normal site.

If you have a higher-end phone, such as the iPhone or BlackBerry, you can try out a few downloadable Twitter apps. Apple's iPhone has a nice interface for Twitter, and you can find several options in the iTunes App Store that you can download to make Twitter on the go even easier. Some of these apps (such as Twinkle and TwitterFon) are free, some (such as Tweetie, which you can see in action in Figures 4-4 and 4-5) cost a few bucks, and some (such as Twitterrific) have both free and paid versions.

BlackBerry users have fewer applications at their disposal, including the extremely popular TwitterBerry (shown in Figure 4-6). BlackBerry users also have a challenge — the device's specialized browser can't display all the content on Twitter, such as photos and some links.

If you have a Windows Mobile phone, we recommend an application called ceTwit if you don't have a touch screen. If you do have a touch screen, look into an iPhone-like interface client called PocketTwit (made by Google Labs).

The open-API difference

Twitter's open API fuels its flexibility, and that flexibility is a big part of what keeps Twitter users loyal through all its growing pains. The API is so customizable that you can create a completely new service for Twitter on a whim, based on what you want to do with it — which is a big plus, especially if you plan to mold Twitter to fit a specific company goal or make it a big part of a marketing campaign or promotion. If you can't find an existing application that works with Twitter to make it do exactly what you need, you can either make one yourself or hire someone to do it. Full customization is rare on the Web, but with Twitter, you can mold it to work anywhere you need it to: at work, at home, or even while rock climbing.

Everyone pretty much swears by the apps they love the best, and no user group is more enthusiastic than the iPhone crowd, whose debates over Twitterfon (free), Tweetie ($2.99), and Twittelator Pro ($4.99), among others, can keep a conversation going through several pints of beer at a tweetup.

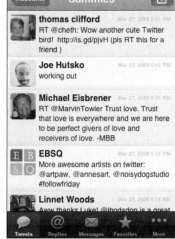

Figure 4-4:
You can read your tweet stream with the Tweetie iPhone application.

These mobile Twitter apps barely scratch the surface of what you can find out there, and new ones are created fairly regularly. There's no real consensus on which is the best. Try out a few to see which ones you prefer. Again, once www.oneforty.com launches, we hope to have much better answers to your perennial Which app is best for. . . ? questions.

Figure 4-5:
You can
post new
tweets
by using
Tweetie.

Figure 4-6:
Twitter-
Berry, a
Twitter
BlackBerry
application.

Part II
Joining Your Flock on Twitter

The 5th Wave — By Rich Tennant

And me without a Twitter account.

In This Part . . .

After you set up a Twitter account and know how to find everything Twitter-related that you might need, you probably want to know and find the people you want to communicate with.

In this part, we show you how to find the people you may know outside of Twitter on Twitter, locate people who share your interests, and identify other personalities and brands that you may want to connect with using Twitter.

Chapter 5

Tweeting It Up

*O*ne of the neatest things about the Twitter experience is that your conversations, your followers, and your ability to interact with them extends far past the Twitter.com interface into other platforms and even into the real world due to the Twitter community's tendency to plan both formal and spontaneous events. But equally important to accessing your Twitter account from virtually anywhere is understanding how to interact within the community.

In this chapter, we go over the nuts and bolts involved in discovering, managing, and interacting with the people you follow on Twitter and the people who follow you. Additionally, we give you some hints about how to play well with others within the twitterverse so that you can start having conversations right away!

Finding People to Follow on Twitter

A key part of getting the most out of Twitter is knowing where and how to find people whose Twitter streams are of interest to you.

You can pretty easily find people to follow on Twitter: You naturally browse to people's profiles when you think that something they say is interesting or relevant to you. But, when you start accumulating updates from the people you follow, you'll quickly realize that you need to figure out who's worth following. That process can become complicated because of the large size and diversity of the Twitter ecosystem.

Avid users have countless theories and strategies about the best ways and reasons to follow others. That's the beauty of Twitter: You can make it up as you go along and create your own criteria for building up a Twitter stream.

Twitter is a very personalized experience. No two people use Twitter in exactly the same way, and no two people follow a given account on Twitter for exactly the same reasons. Quite literally, no two people experience the same Twitter because everyone is consuming different streams, and publishing to, and interacting with different sets of readers.

Twitter is not a single village, as the term *Twitterville* implies. When Laura wrote "Twitter is my Village," (`http://pistachioconsulting.com/it-takes-a-village-to-understand-twitter`), she meant that each twitterer's personal community on Twitter functions like a village. Even if Twitter goes heavily mainstream, you'll still be able to shape your experience there by selecting who you listen to and interact with.

While you become better at your entire Twitter experience, you're continually developing and changing your own guidelines for building your following and follower bases. Luckily, Twitter is built to allow for these changes, so you don't have to miss a beat.

Whether you're looking for business associates, news sources, friendly conversation, or anything else, Twitter can help you surround yourself with people and companies that can enrich your stream.

Look who's talking

When you want to start looking for people to follow, see whether anyone's already talked back to you. If you've already posted some tweets, people may have replied to you. (If you haven't yet tweeted, what are you waiting for? Dive in and start tweeting!)

When someone wants to address you directly on Twitter, that user does so by replying to you. They simply put the @ symbol before your Twitter handle at the beginning of a tweet — that's all it takes to reply. If you're following that person, the tweet shows up in your Twitter stream. If you're not following that person, you can still see any tweets that mention you on the Mentions tab in the sidebar (it's the tab with @ followed by your username on it).

If you're completely new to Twitter and you've only posted a handful of tweets, you probably won't have any mentions yet. That's okay! You have plenty of other options for finding people to follow (see the next sections).

Searching for people

You can best search for people on Twitter by using one of two methods: Twitter Search (`http://search.twitter.com`) or the People Search function (`http://twitter.com/search/users`). You can also reach Twitter's People Search page (as shown in Figure 5-1) by clicking Find People in the upper-right corner of your Twitter screen's toolbar.

Figure 5-1:
Search
for Twitter
users on
the People
Search
page.

Another, lesser-known way to find people on Twitter is by simply using the Google search engine at `www.google.com`. Because Google indexes every public tweet, you can use it to find twitterers by interest or by name. To use Google to find twitterers that you might want to follow, either search their firstname lastname and the word Twitter or do a slightly more specific search this way:

1. **Type your keywords or the username you're looking for in the text box.**

2. **Add** site:Twitter.com **at the end of your search query.**

3. **Click the Search button.**

   See what pops up! Figure 5-2 shows the results of a search for Lance Armstrong.

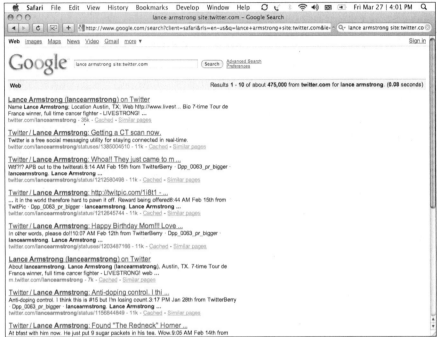

Figure 5-2:
The Google
results of
a Twitter
user search
for Lance
Armstrong.

You probably want to conduct people searches and keyword searches periodically to make sure that you continue to cultivate your Twitter experience's richness and value with new voices. Although Twitter is great for reconnecting with old friends and keeping up a conversation with existing business associates, it's also a fantastic way to reach out and find new people and companies to listen to.

A great way to get started following people on Twitter is to import your contacts from your Web-based e-mail account (like Yahoo! Mail or Gmail). We cover this in detail in Chapter 2.

Inviting people personally, through Twitter

Another option for inviting people to Twitter is to do it personally, directly to their individual e-mail addresses. You can find this tab (Invite By Email) on the Find People page (as shown in Figure 5-3), and it gives you a way to hand-pick people from your e-mail address book. You can also text Twitter at 40404 at anytime with the words **invite yourfriend@yourfriend.com** substituting in your friend's e-mail address, of course.

Keep in mind that Twitter doesn't offer you a chance to customize what the e-mail says. The person or company you invite gets a generic e-mail that mentions your Twitter handle and some basic information about how to sign up for an account. If you have people you want to invite to Twitter whom you think may not respond well to a generic e-mail, you can use the method described in the following section to invite them, instead.

Figure 5-3:
The Twitter
Invite
By Email
screen.

The main drawback to any of the invitation options in Twitter's Web interface is that none of them offer a custom message option. If you know people whom you want to invite, and you think they'd respond better to a private or more personalized note, just shoot them a normal e-mail that includes a link to the Twitter main page (www.twitter.com) and a note about why they might benefit from signing up and joining in. It's often more effective to e-mail them a link to an article that is going to help them understand what uses of Twitter they may find valuable. Twitter is definitely a minute-to-learn, lifetime-to-master type of system.

A community leads

Twitter users have come up with an interesting way of recommending people to follow — something called FollowFriday. It uses a community-driven system called hashtags, which we cover in Chapter 9. Our friend Micah Baldwin (@micah, pronounced *Me-ha*) started it, and he has this to say about it:

In January of 2009, I sent a simple tweet: "I am starting FollowFridays. Every Friday, suggest people to follow, and everyone follow him/her. Today its @jeffrey and @dannynewman." After a suggestion to add the hashtag #followfriday and four folks retweeting it, FollowFriday was born.

After a few months, more than 100,000 tweets with more than 300,000 recommendations are sent each Friday (it actually begins on Thursday U.S. time because it's Friday overseas!) and it's growing each week.

*FollowFriday mirrors what happens in the real world. One person suggests a book to read, or a restaurant to go to, or a person you should meet, and if you trust them, you take their word. The concept is very simple: Write a tweet listing two or three people you follow that you think others should follow as well, and provide a bit of an explanation. (**Remember:** It's only 140 characters,* so be brief both with your recommendations and with your explanations!) For example, "@pistachio @micah @gruen are three people that make me laugh every day. #followfriday." That's it!

If you're new to Twitter and you're looking for people to follow, you can search for #followfriday at http://search.twitter.com to see people who have been recommended, or check out sites like http://followfridays.com and http://topfollowfriday.com to see frequently recommended Twitter users.

FollowFriday is exactly what makes Twitter great. It gives you the ability to participate, it's easy, and you can share people you're proud to know (even if it's just on Twitter) with other people. After all, Twitter is about sharing information and experiences with people you're proud to be associated with, in a very easy, participatory way.

Why Fridays? Fridays seem to work well because it's the end of the week, and people have the time to think about whom they would like to recommend. Plus, FollowTuesday just doesn't have the same type of ring, now does it?

Opening up your stream

By default, Twitter shows you all the tweets sent by each of the users whom you follow. But sometimes, during the setup process, users accidentally limit their feeds to include only tweets that aren't replies — it's a neat feature, but not always desirable.

To configure your Twitter stream so that it shows you all the Twitter conversations that include @replies written by the people you're following:

1. **Click Settings in the top-right navigation bar.**

   The Settings page opens.

2. **Click the Notices tab (see Figure 5-4).**

   You see an @Replies section, with a Show Me drop-down list.

3. **Select Show Me All @Replies from the Show Me drop-down list.**

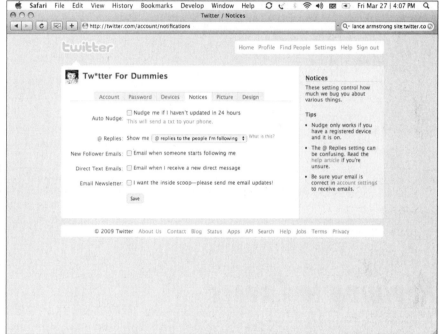

Figure 5-4:
On the
Notices
screen, you
can choose
which, if
any,
@replies
appear in
your stream.

By setting this option, when your friends post public @replies to other Twitter users whom you aren't following, you still see those tweets.

Give yourself a little time to get used to the flood of information and figure out which @replies you want to see. You'll soon find that your friends not only have valuable things to say, but their friends do, too. At that point, you can start to join the conversation, and broaden your circle of friends.

If you want your stream to be a little less crowded, you can opt to show No @Replies, which makes Twitter suppress any @replies from your stream. You won't see any @replies at all if you choose this option. A third, middle-of-the-road option is to select @Replies to the People I'm Following. What this means is that, if you're following both John and Mary, and John sends an @Mary tweet to Mary, you'll see that tweet (even though it wasn't directed to you) — which allows you to join in the conversation because you can see what your friends are talking about. At the moment, these settings only filter tweets that start @username, not those that contain @username within the message.

How to Follow People

Mechanically, following people on Twitter is dead simple. After you navigate to a person's Profile page, click the Follow button just below his avatar. And, you're done! Give it a shot:

1. **Browse to http://twitter.com/dummies.**

2. **Click the Follow button.**

   The button changes to the word Following. Cool!

Alternately, you can post this message from SMS or any Twitter interface by typing **Follow username** or **F username**.

Following people on Twitter is straightforward. On the most superficial level, you just have to pay attention. Twitter is full of thousands of great conversations going on all around you. If you open yourself up to them, you may find that hundreds of excellent people are thrilled to meet you.

Replying to Tweets

So, what happens when you receive an @reply, and you want to respond — or if you just want to respond to any tweet, for that matter? Hover your mouse cursor over the right side of the tweet in question when you see it in your stream on Twitter's Home screen, and images of an arrow and a star appear (as shown in Figure 5-5).

Clicking the Star icon bookmarks that tweet as a favorite — which we cover in Chapter 3. But clicking the Arrow icon sets up the Twitter entry field so that you can reply to that individual tweet. When you send your response, it says In Reply To below the tweet and includes a live link to the standalone page (also known as a *permalink*) for the tweet you responded to. Figure 5-6 shows a typical Twitter @reply.

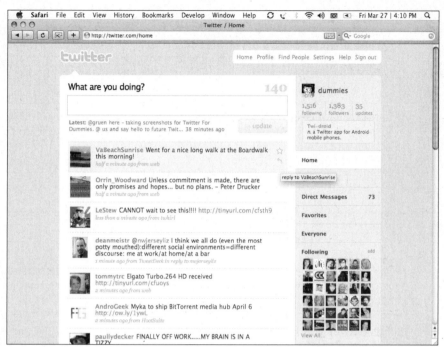

Figure 5-5:
Don't miss
the Reply
arrow!

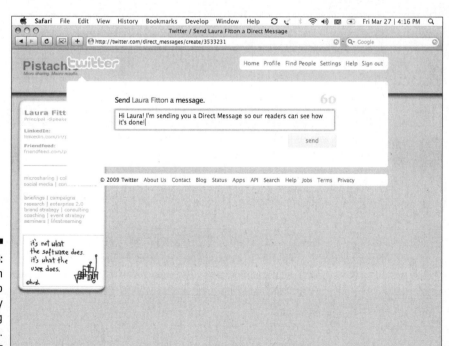

Figure 5-6:
You can
respond to
tweets by
using
@replies.

You may find these permalinks helpful because Twitter is not great at threading tweets together by conversation. If you're familiar with a set of @replies and the links associated with them, you can much more easily navigate the conversation later. When you know how to access the individual page for each tweet, you can also link to that tweet directly if you choose to respond to it in a longer format outside of Twitter, such as a blog post.

You can reply to any tweet that you can see, and the procedure is the same, whether you're following the person or not. But, assuming your Twitter account is public, your @replies are public, too. If you want to use Twitter for private messages, the protocol is a little different, as we talk about in the section "Direct Messaging," later in this chapter.

Go ahead and jump right in

Given the casual and conversational tone of Twitter, you can pretty easily jump into an existing conversation on Twitter, and (unless you're trying) you don't look like you're barging in. Twitter users are aware that this is a public forum and contributions can come from anywhere and at anytime. Start by clicking one of the usernames involved in the conversation, or enter one or both usernames manually in the Update window. (*Remember:* The format for addressing a Twitter user is `@username`.) Then chime in by saying something relevant to their discussion.

Don't rush to be conversational to the point that you end up being irrelevant. If the conversation is about something you don't know anything about, hold off. But if it's about a movie that you've seen or a business theory that you've put into practice, pipe up!

It may take a few tries with a few different people to get the ball rolling. Don't be discouraged if you send out a few @replies and don't get responses; some Twitter users, especially relatively new ones, don't always pay close attention or respond to @replies either from people whom they're not following or those who don't seem particularly perceptive to them. Many people on Twitter, however, respond very quickly to new voices in their Twitter stream because, for many on Twitter, the point is to be conversational.

Be patient about expecting replies to questions that are easily answered using Google or other resources. Also please be patient with people that a lot of people talk to. Demi Moore, for example, does a great job of conversing with the hundreds and hundreds of people who write to `@mrskutcher` every day, but if she tried to answer everyone, she would have no time to be with her family (or for that matter, to be beautiful and entertaining in her films!). To see how busy her @mentions tab is, just search `@mrs kutcher` (`http://search.twitter.com/search?q=%40mrskutcher`).

Direct Messaging

Private messages on Twitter are called direct messages (DMs). Like any other kind of tweet, they're limited to 140 characters in length. You can't send a DM to someone unless that Twitter user is following you — likewise, only your own followers can send you DMs.

What do you do if you want to get in touch with someone privately on Twitter but that person isn't following you? New Twitter users are often tempted to send @replies to that person saying "tried to DM but you don't follow" or something of the sort. Some Twitter users don't mind receiving those kinds of tweets, but many others see them as rude or as blatant attempts to get new followers.

So, if you're trying to get in touch with someone who doesn't follow you, you have some options:

- ✔ **Check the user's Profile page.** See whether he has made available some other form of contact information — a Web site URL, an e-mail address, or a blog. You can often find this info in a user's short bio section.

- ✔ **Conduct a Web search.** Try searching for the user on your favorite search engine.

- ✔ **Tweet a polite question publicly to the user.** While the you-don't-follow-me approach is a little obnoxious, most twitterers will make a reasonable effort to respond if you respect their time and make it clear why they should answer you. Send a message to @username expressing why you're requesting their time and attention, and ask that they respond privately. Just try to differentiate between the ability to reach out to someone and the right to demand a response.

Direct-messaging shorthand

When you're truly connected, you start to find going to the Direct Messages page every time you want to send someone a message a bit tedious. Thankfully, the folks at Twitter have come up with a shorthand. To send a DM without going to the Direct Messages page:

1. **Click in the What Are You Doing? window.**

2. **Type d, followed by a space, and then the username of the person to whom you want to send a direct message.**

3. **Type a space after his username and then write a message.**

   The update should have this form: d dummies Hey, there!

4. **Click Send button to send the DM.**

We cover other shorthand tricks in Chapter 7.

One word of caution if you plan to send direct messages from a phone or by typing **d** and the username of the recipient: On a small keyboard, you can very easily make a typing error, such as misspelling the username, accidentally posting a letter other than d, pushing two d's, or something else. Look twice before you send your message to make sure that it's truly private and not a public tweet by accident, especially if it contains personal information that you don't want the whole Internet to know (such as a phone number or address).

Should I @ or DM?

When you try to decide whether to respond to somebody on Twitter by using a public @reply or a private DM, you should consider the following criteria:

- ✔ **Questionable content:** If your mother, grandmother, boss, or kid were looking over your shoulder at what you just started typing, would they be in any way embarrassed or disapproving? If the answer is yes, perhaps a direct message is in order.

- ✔ **Volume:** If you're a power user who posts to Twitter many times a day, every tweet goes into your followers' streams and contributes to the noise. You should be sensitive to this fact. If you tweet often, give your followers a break and save those one- or two-word responses, such as "@pistachio LOL" or "@dummies How?" for a direct message.

- ✔ **Sensitive information:** If you're supplying contact information, addresses, phone numbers, or other personal information that you don't want just anyone on the Internet to have access to, it's the right time for a direct message. Keep in mind that not everybody has the same standards regarding privacy and openness on the Web, so if you're sharing any information pertaining to anybody else's contact information or whereabouts, err on the side of caution and use a DM.

If you haven't protected your tweets, remember that whatever you write is indexed for all time. So, think twice!

Encouraging More Followers

Twitter is a very receptive environment for forging connections with new friends and contacts, so amassing a list of followers is relatively simple. Typically, you gain followers in the natural course of using Twitter, but here are a few guidelines to follow:

✔ **Be real.** Being genuine goes a long way, and you're likely to gain followers without even trying.

✔ **Be interesting.** You don't have to fascinate with every tweet you type, but do try to tweet about things more relevant to the world at large than what you just ate for lunch or the heinous traffic on your morning commute. Talk about your interests, instead. Talk about what's in the news. Or talk about what you think *should* be in the news.

✔ **Be involved.** The more "into" a topic you are, the more people will respond to your enthusiasm. Say that you're really into classic cars — don't talk just about your own fascination with them, but try to help other people on Twitter who might have questions on the subject. Get into heated conversations and debates, too. Without being too authoritative, position yourself as someone who has some valuable information on your chosen issue to see an increase in your number of followers.

Plenty of influential people use Twitter, from celebrities like Ashton Kutcher (@aplusk) and Britney Spears (@britneyspears) to politicians like Democratic Congresswoman Claire McCaskill (@clairecmc) and dozens more. Heck, now that Oprah Winfrey (@Oprah) tweets, it's almost proof enough in and of itself just to mention her.

If you're lucky enough that @Oprah posts a tweet with your @username in it — usually after you @Oprah her, and she notices and responds — you're going to be barraged by new followers who've seen your username in connection with that famous person's. But the most popular Twitter users have hundreds of thousands of followers and hundreds of people @replying to them, so don't count on a response from a famous twitterer as a way to get your foot in the door when it comes to Twitter influence.

It's also just rude to use someone like that. If you wouldn't interrupt the person next to you in line at the store with your question, it's probably not nice to interrupt someone with a lot of demands on their time with it. Conversation is two-way and most effective when it's generous to the listener, not selfish for the speaker.

Some Twitter users try to lure followers by offering contests, giveaways, or other incentives to reach certain pseudo-milestones, such as number of tweets or number of followers. This approach is a little bit cheesy and can look like you're desperate for new followers. In our opinion, you can have a better time on Twitter if you just allow your network to grow organically.

Regardless of how you get people to follow you, make sure to keep your Twitter interactions genuine. What you post on Twitter and contribute to the conversation, along with your ability to listen, determines your authority more than any follower count ever could.

We can't stress the importance of listening enough. The more you listen and hear what people have to say, and then respond thoughtfully, the more you can find out about people and the more well-rounded your experience (and the experience of your followers) becomes. Listening is the golden ticket of Twitter — make sure to do it every day that you log in. And log in often.

Chapter 6

Who's Using Twitter

*B*ecause Twitter is so easy to use, Twitter opens doors and grants you all kinds of accessibility to people you might never have had access to before. It's become an effective tool for reaching out to people, companies, and even celebrities, both on- and offline.

Have you ever thought, "I wish I could talk to someone higher up the ladder and get a real solution to this problem!" or even "I'd love to be able to tell this person or that company what a good job they do, but I don't have their contact info!"? Well, Twitter can help you bridge that gap.

You may be surprised to see which companies, people, and brands have jumped onto Twitter. In this chapter, we cover some of these well-known Twitter users. You can take a look through this chapter to see whether the person or company that you want to find is already here.

Tweeting with Regular People

After it gained a foothold among the digital-media enthusiasts at the South by Southwest Interactive Festival in 2007, Twitter quickly became a playground for techies and geeks. But over time, people from all walks of life have discovered Twitter and embraced it. Twitter allows a user to communicate effectively with one person or many, and the benefits can work for anyone.

Twitter has become a quick and easy way to stay connected to family, friends, and coworkers. People at all levels of all sorts of business can use Twitter to easily interact with customers and potential clients and get real-time engagement and feedback.

You'll probably want to use Twitter to talk to people whom you know in real life, such as your family and friends, as well as to meet some like-minded people. But you can also meet some very unconventional people on Twitter. Sometimes, the unconventional twitterers are the most interesting. On Twitter, you'll encounter everyone from celebrities (see Figure 6-1) to local religious leaders and great-grandmothers who blog. You never know who you may find from day to day, which is part of Twitter's charm.

Figure 6-1: Martha Stewart has her own Twitter account.

But the biggest asset of Twitter is the sheer mass of everyday people who want to share their thoughts, spread the news, and network. You can probably discover at least one new thing from someone on Twitter every day that you log in.

Plus, as superficial as a stream of 140-character messages may seem, the Twitter community has evolved into a real way for real people to connect in the real world, too. You can easily set up meetings and events through Twitter on fairly short notice, so many twitterers find themselves turning their online connections into offline friendships and business relationships fairly often. Both introverted and extroverted people can really benefit from this environment.

So, what noncelebrity people can you find on Twitter? At first glance, you may think that everyone on Twitter is in the technology or marketing industries in some way. The core-base of twitterers who formed Twitter's initial user group still tweet away, and they're still some of the most prolific users. But you can also find thousands of people tweeting who are just like you, your mom, or your best friend from high school — in fact, your mom and your best friend from high school may already be on Twitter.

Just because a Twitter user isn't one of the most prolific people on the service doesn't mean that person isn't worth your time. Some of the most interesting twitterers post less than others, waiting to add their two cents until they think they have something worth saying. Keep an eye out for those people and follow them as they become visible to you — you sure can get more value out of following them than following someone who posts 20 times a day about their dog.

Regardless of whom you know on Twitter, you may want to set a few boundaries. Twitter works on the Internet, after all, and even though the Twitter community has tended to be a trustworthy one, it's growing rather fast now. Also remember that Google indexes your tweets, so the whole Internet can see what you say. Exercise caution! Don't blurt out sensitive information — say, your home address or phone number — in public tweets. Save those for e-mail or direct messages.

Building Company Relationships with Twitter

Many companies have found value in Twitter as a way to build awareness of their brand name, strengthen relationships with customers, provide better and more immediate customer service, and boost sales. Companies' presences on Twitter range from individual Twitter accounts belonging to CEOs and employees, to corporate accounts for the brand run by teams of marketing or PR representatives.

Here are some of the most famous examples of companies that have gotten some positive buzz for their presence on Twitter:

- **Zappos.com:** This online retailer was founded in the dot-com boom and is based in Las Vegas. It has fully integrated Twitter into its corporate structure. Not only does the company monitor and use Twitter for customer service and feedback, but CEO Tony Hsieh encourages Zappos. com employees to participate on Twitter to keep the world posted on what's going on in the company. (He even has an account for his cat, El Gato, who is @el_gato.)

Of nearly 1600 Zappos.com employees, more than 400 are on Twitter, (`http://twitter.zappos.com/employees`) actively tweeting to one another, about their own lives and work, and, in the process, Zappos.com. Hsieh himself often responds to Twitter users if they tweet him about a problem or specific need. Hsieh and the rest of Zappos.com make sure that they're engaged with their customer base, both current and potential. Their dedicated microsite `http://Twitter.Zappos.com` features Twitter searches for every brand they sell, collected tweets about Zappos, and an amalgamation of every employee's tweets and profiles.

✔ **Comcast:** After serious issues with negative connotations to their brand name, this cable company took Twitter by surprise (although they had been actively listening to Twitter for two months when they did) and established the Comcast Cares account (`@comcastcares`), run by Frank Eliason, the company's director of "digital care." Frank now has a team of employees on Twitter who handle customer service, helping as many as they can and backed up by the ability to escalate problems directly into Comcast's executive customer service department. How this will scale remains to be seen, but Frank's team is extremely dedicated and inspiring and has attracted substantial press coverage and goodwill toward the company.

✔ **Dell:** This computer manufacturer has also had some branding issues. At one point, customers filled a popular anti-Dell Web site with negative feedback and derogatory remarks. The company countered with a strong social media program that now includes real people behind active Twitter accounts, such as `@RichardAtDell`, offering customer service support and Twitter-only discount deals (DellOutlet) that led to over a million in sales. Dell, which also maintains a Twitter-focused microsite at `www.dell.com/twitter`, is engaging with customers in several innovative ways thanks to Twitter's ability to enable real-time interactions and on-the-ball responses.

In fact, companies in all kinds of industries are using Twitter effectively. Here is just a tiny sampling of some companies that do business related to food, drink, and nightlife:

✔ The Roxy Theater (`http://twitter.com/theroxy`)

✔ 21st Amendment (`http://twitter.com/21stamendment`)

✔ Flying Dog Ales (`http://twitter.com/flyingdog`)

✔ Elanas Pantry (`http://twitter.com/elanaspantry`)

✔ Pangaea Organica (`http://twitter.com/pangaeaorganica`)

✔ Templeton Rye (`http://twitter.com/templetonrye`)

These retailers tweet:

- Seventh Generation (`http://twitter.com/seventhgen`)
- GiftGirl (`http://www.twitter.com/giftgirl`)
- Comcast (`http://twitter.com/comcastcares`)
- Network Solutions (`http://twitter.com/netsolcares`)
- Baby Fish Mouth (`http://twitter.com/bfmwear`)
- Second Life (`http://twitter.com/secondlife`)

These publishing companies have Twitter accounts up and running:

- Grand Central Publishing (`http://twitter.com/grandcentralpub`)
- Little, Brown and Company (`http://twitter.com/littlebrown`)
- MEP Publishers (`http://twitter.com/meppublishers`)
- Septagon Studios (`http://twitter.com/septagonstudios`)
- Yale Press (`http://twitter.com/yalepress`)

If you're looking for travel info, check out these Twitter accounts:

- Booking Buddy (`http://twitter.com/bookingbuddy`)
- Global Base Camps (`http://twitter.com/globalbasecamps`)
- HotelChatter (`http://twitter.com/hotelchatter`)
- Seat Guru (`http://twitter.com/seatguru`)
- Smarter Travel (`http://twitter.com/smartertravel`)
- Travel Rants (`http://twitter.com/travelrants`)

For a sampling of resorts and hotels on Twitter, check out the following:

- Heavenly Ski Resort in South Lake Tahoe (`http://twitter.com/skiheavenly`)
- Luxor Hotel and Casino (`http://twitter.com/luxorlv`)
- Mandalay Bay Resort and Casino (`http://twitter.com/robert_hoffmann`)
- MGM Grand Hotel and Casino (`http://twitter.com/mgmgrand`)
- Treasure Island Hotel and Casino (`http://twitter.com/vegasdv`)

If you want some resources on financial matters, business, and budgeting, have a look at these accounts:

- Capgemini (`http://twitter.com/capgemini`)
- H&R Block (`http://twitter.com/HRBlock`)
- Lenderflex (`http://twitter.com/lenderflex`)
- LenderflexCares (`http://twitter.com/lenderflexcares`)
- QuickBooks (`http://twitter.com/quickbooks`)
- QuickenLoans (`http://twitter.com/quickenloans`)

Thousands and thousands of businesses large and small are using Twitter. For more information, you can read Pistachio Consulting's TouchBase blog (`www.touchbaseblog.com`) or browse the extensive Twitter for Business bookmarks that Pistachio maintains on the TouchBase link blog (`http://delicious.com/touchbaseblog`). Easiest way to keep up with both? Twitter, of course. Follow @touchbase to receive a tweet when either of these resources is updated.

Talking Politics with Actual Politicians

Politicians have been taking to Twitter as a means to connect with their constituents and their fellow politicians — as well as to give a more intimate look into their lives at a time when *transparency* is one of the most positive buzzwords around. The Democratic Party was the first to jump on the bandwagon, and many users started exploring Twitter in the midst of Barack Obama's tech-savvy and successful presidential campaign. But many prominent Republicans are now onboard as well, as evidenced by the hashtag #tcot, which stands for Top Conservatives on Twitter.

Government figures have to deal with privacy and legal issues that most other twitterers don't, so politicians may occasionally seem a bit on the quiet side when tweeting.

Here are some political groups and figures to get you started:

- U.S. Democratic Congressional Campaign Committee (`http://twitter.com/dccc`)
- U.S. National Republican Congressional Committee (`http://twitter.com/nrcc`)
- U.S. President Barack Obama (`http://twitter.com/barackobama`)
- California Governor Arnold Schwarzenegger (`http://twitter.com/schwarzenegger`)

- The Office of British Prime Minister Gordon Brown (`http://twitter.com/downingstreet`)
- Former Vice President Al Gore (`http://twitter.com/algore`)
- The White House (`http://twitter.com/whitehouse`)

Following Celebrities on Twitter

Many people are hearing about Twitter for the first time because they've seen it on entertainment news shows such as *Access Hollywood* or *The Soup*. Celebrities use Twitter, too! The celebrities who use Twitter do so for different reasons:

- **To connect with fans:** Bands such as Coldplay (`@coldplay`) announce tour and concert dates by using Twitter. Cyclist Lance Armstrong (`@lancearmstrong`) provides information about the race circuit and his charity efforts.

- **To get personal:** Basketball star Shaquille O'Neal (`@THE_REAL_SHAQ`) and celebrity couple Ashton Kutcher (`@aplusk`) and Demi Moore (`@mrskutcher`) use Twitter to offer an intimate — and often irreverent — glimpse into their lives.

- **To share interests:** Rapper MC Hammer (`@MCHammer`), who founded a Web video startup called DanceJam.com, uses his Twitter stream to help promote new artists, share his favorite music, and offer lively thoughts on the state of the industry.

- **To be real:** Singers Miley Cyrus (`@mileycyrus`) and Sara Bareilles (`@SaraBareilles`) tweet just like the rest of us — gushing in excitement over successes, complaining over tired feet and other mundane life moments that make theirs seem a whole lot more "real."

In many ways, Twitter functions as a sort of impromptu fan club for tech-savvy celebs both renowned and up-and-coming. In the weeks leading up to publication, Oprah Winfrey (`@Oprah`) and other world renowned household brands have started to sign up. Rumor has it that 1.5 million new people reached Twitter.com in the weekend after Ashton Kutcher appeared on her show and Oprah started to tweet.

Here are a few more Twitter accounts you may want to take a peek at:

- Jimmy Fallon (`http://twitter.com/jimmyfallon`)
- Tina Fey (`http://twitter.com/TinaFey`)
- Rainn Wilson (`http://twitter.com/rainnwilson`)
- 50 Cent (`http://twitter.com/50cent`)
- John Mayer (`http://twitter.com/johncmayer`)

- Jimmy Eat World (http://twitter.com/jimmyeatworld)
- Wil Wheaton (http://twitter.com/wilw)
- Soleil Moon Frye (http://twitter.com/moonfrye)
- John Cleese (http://twitter.com/JohnCleese)

People do start Twitter accounts using celebrities' names, and they often get a whole slew of followers who have no idea that they're not following the "real" celebrity — the person they think they're following. Impersonating someone on Twitter violates Twitter's Terms of Service, and Twitter has shut down accounts by impersonators. You can usually tell whether the person is legit by looking at the number of followers — if he has a large number of followers, the chances are good that he's for real, but even that isn't a guarantee. Of course, you may not care if the person is the real celebrity if you actually enjoy the person's tweets!

Signing Up for Syndicated Material

Plenty of Twitter accounts syndicate material from all kinds of online non-Twitter outlets: event listings, blogs, newspapers' Web sites, and so on. These accounts fall into a sort of gray area on Twitter: Most of them are quite welcome in the site's community, and, in the case of news outlets such as *The New York Times* (@nytimes) and CNN (@cnnbrk), make up some of Twitter's most-followed accounts.

Cable news outlet CNN has nailed it when it comes to using Twitter for more than just headline syndication, letting Twitter really enhance its broadcasts. Their newscasters not only use Twitter accounts to both interact with viewers and relay breaking news stories, but anchor Rick Sanchez (@CNNRickSanchez) fields questions from Twitter followers in real time on his on-air program, *Rick Sanchez Direct*. Interestingly, though, CNN's most followed account, @CNNBrk, was developed by a fan, James Cox (@imajes) who later worked cooperatively with CNN and eventually sold it to them for an undisclosed amount.

Here are some news and media Twitter accounts you can check out:

- BBC (http://twitter.com/bbc)
- Harpers (http://twitter.com/harpers)
- Marvel Entertainment (http://twitter.com/marvel)
- The New Yorker (http://twitter.com/newyorkerdotcom)
- NPR (http://twitter.com/nprnews)
- Wired News (http://twitter.com/wired)

Tweeting in Unison

Sometimes, users or organizations create a Twitter account so that the community can feed it with updates. These community-created Twitter accounts can be automated (through the use of a script or bot) or moderated. But either way, these co-authored accounts gather the content from many Twitter users, sometimes anonymously. This aggregated stream of tweets can incorporate anything from stories to poems to confessionals, and the rest of the Twitter community can subscribe and follow the results.

One of the first of these community Twitter accounts was 140Story (@140story), tiny stories told in 140 characters. Other Twitter accounts have popped up that aggregate tweets into short stories, like a giant Mad-Lib.

But no list of community Twitter accounts would be complete without SecretTweet (@secrettweet). Similar to the popular Web site PostSecret (@postsecret), SecretTweet gives Twitter users a place to share their deepest, darkest secrets on Twitter's public timeline without divulging their identities. Twitter users can get something off their chests and read the secrets of others. SecretTweet has been called everything from addicting to brilliant to sad.

Small Business, Big Community: NYC's @shakeshack

Small businesses wanting to use Twitter to build loyalty, take note. Here's what Jason Schwartz (@jschwa), the gentleman who implemented the @shakeshack bot (see figure), has to say about the Twitter community built by twittering fans of the Shake Shack, one of New York City's most social eateries.

The heart of Silicon Alley is designated by the ShakeShack, a burger joint in Madison Square Park. Lunchtime lines stretch around the Manhattan refuge for the fabled burgers and shakes. It is the favorite meeting place of NY-based tech startups to discuss business, social media, and how to push the medium forward.

To facilitate tweetups (impromptu meetings facilitated by Twitter), the @shakeshack bot was created. This is how it works:

1. *Someone (say, me, @jschwa) decides to head to the ShakeShack and tweets*

   @shakeshack I'm in line, come join me for lunch

2. *The @shakeshack bot then automatically retweets this message, saying:*

   Via @jschwa I'm in line, come join me for lunch

3. *People who follow @shakeshack see the tweet and join their colleague, who is likely close to ordering by the time they arrive.*

(continued)

(continued)

The `@shakeshack` *bot is regularly used to report the length of the line, organize snow ball fights, and as part of the networking fabric of Silicon Alley (a nickname given to the area of Manhattan where a concentrated number of tech startups are located).*

Hundreds, if not thousands of NYC area twitterers are now more aware of the Shake Shack,

and it's become a must-visit for Twitter enthusiasts when in NYC for meetings or pleasure.

For the curious and technically-inclined, the code for the `@shakeshack` bot can be found here: `http://smr.absono.us/2008/04/anatomy-of-a-twitter-bot`.

Part III
Twittering in High Gear

The 5th Wave   By Rich Tennant

"I don't care what your Twitter friends in Europe
say, you're not having a glass of Chianti
with your bologna sandwich."

In This Part . . .

If you're reading this part, you've probably already established a bit of a presence on Twitter and have some friends and followers. In this part, we kick it up a notch.

We go over the tools and tricks that can make your Twitter experience more efficient, more rewarding, and more accessible for you, such as third-party applications and mobile updating.

Chapter 7

Tricks of the Twitter Gurus

*T*he more you use Twitter, the more you'll notice how complex the potential uses of this deceptively simple service have become. Celebrities, companies, and all sorts of everyday Twitter users are discovering their voices on Twitter, creating a whole new culture in the process. Yet at the same time, each twitterer has a slightly different way of using Twitter.

In this chapter, we provide an overview of protocol, etiquette, and culture that have developed on Twitter. This chapter can help you figure out what tends to be more effective and what tends to not go over well on Twitter, plus ways to be efficient. Keep in mind, though, you're going to come up with your own rules and standards while you tweet.

Following Twitter Protocol

Many Twitter neophytes want to know what the rules are or whether Twitter has standard protocol and etiquette. Like many other social media sites, Twitter sprang from a close-knit group of early adopters who set the rhythm. Because Twitter was a favorite of Silicon Valley's new-media elite long before it broke into the mainstream, some insider jokes and conventions used can be confusing. Longtime users have certainly fallen into certain habits or sets of rules. But now that Twitter has become so popular and diverse, you can find plenty of wiggle room to do your own thing.

Like any other social-media company, Twitter has a Terms of Service (TOS) agreement that all members must adhere to or risk having their accounts suspended or deleted. You can access Twitter's terms at http://twitter. com/terms. You won't find anything particularly surprising in them: You must be at least 13 years old to create an account and use the service, you can't engage in abuse or harassment, you can't spam other members or participate in activities that break any laws, and so on. The terms are actually more liberal than most Web services' regulations; pornography and explicit language, for example, aren't banned.

Beyond the terms of service, Twitter etiquette is simple: Be genuine and non-deceptive and provide value. Other than that, just use Twitter how it suits you. This is primarily an unofficial protocol, but do keep in mind that Twitter keeps tabs on "deceptive" activity, too: Twitter can ban accounts that impersonate celebrities or companies if those accounts don't make it clear that they're unofficial or parodies. This policy is a contentious point in the Twitter community: Many members were upset when the @cwalken account, belonging to an aspiring comedian pretending to be actor Christopher Walken, was deleted from the system.

Beyond the simple regulations, you can't really use Twitter in a right or wrong way because no two people use it for exactly the same reasons. But some members certainly have their opinions:

- ✓ Some users complain when others tweet too often, whereas others complain that their contacts don't tweet enough. (This complaint is a little silly. Don't like the contents? Turn the dial. Unsubscribe.)

- ✓ Some users take issue with strings of @replies and wonder why those conversations weren't conducted in a private forum.

- ✓ You may encounter confusing, even conflicting, advice and back-seat tweeting from the handful of people on Twitter who aren't comfortable without rules. Don't take them too seriously; Twitter just isn't that rigid.

Be polite on Twitter, for the most part, but no more or less so than you're expected to be in the real world — just keep in mind that Twitter is a public forum. Twitter posts and feeds get exported outside of Twitter and onto Twitter-based Web sites, blogs, social-media sites such as Facebook, and aggregators such as FriendFeed. If you know you plan to, say, sync up your Twitter account with your Facebook account so that your tweets appear as your Facebook status message, keep in mind that you're branching out beyond the Twitter community and culture.

Although users love Twitter's largely rule-free nature, some generally accepted behaviors have evolved over time. You can ease your transition into the culture of Twitter by getting familiar with these behaviors before you first start out. Establish dedication and credibility early on, in part, by knowing your way around the following Twitter customs.

Language and abbreviations

Over time, any group of people that interacts regularly falls into its own "vernacular" way of talking. Twitter is no exception to that rule; in fact, it may be even more subject to it because of the 140-character limit. Twitter's lexicon has evolved over time to include unique words, phrases, and abbreviations that most regular users understand and recognize. But new users often find these references confusing.

Right off the bat, you see a lot of puns involving the word "Twitter," with the prefixes tw- or twi- added to the front: tweet, tweeple, tweetup, and so on. At first, it looks like baby talk — and indeed, it can get a bit over-the-top. Not all members are fans of corny terms such as tweeple. Others think the Twitter-specific language is fun, or an easy and obvious way to delineate something as Twitter-specific. Either way, whether you plan to use goofy Twitter-speak or not, it does help to know what this stuff means.

Many application and Web site names have adopted Twitter-speak words for products and services associated with Twitter or which tap into Twitter's application programming interface (API) to use Twitter data. For example, the word *twinfluence* was used casually to describe (no shock here) the kind of social influence that individual Twitter users had within the Twitter community. Eventually, the slang term was used to name twInfluence (www. twinfluence.com), an application that gets its data from Twitter and turns it into a report that estimates Twitter users' power and influence.

Plenty of eccentric people use Twitter, not to mention loads of subcultures and sub-communities. Just because you see an unfamiliar term doesn't mean it's part of the Twitter vernacular. For Twitter terms you should be familiar with, check out the glossary at the back of this book.

We purposely didn't include in this glossary some of the nonsense words that begin with the tw- prefix. Twitterers don't widely use them, many avid users actually find them rather annoying, and beginning to use them more often may be the first sign that you're a twitterholic! (For more on these tw- terms, see Chapter 7.)

Engaging others on Twitter

On Twitter, the name of the game is engagement. Whether you use Twitter for business or fun, you don't just want to sit back and watch the stream flow by — you want to genuinely interact with people. You have to know how to listen as much as know how to converse (this goes twice for businesses) — but it always boils down to engagement.

First and foremost, do not be shy about finding people who share your interests, even if you don't know them (yet). Use `http://search.twitter.com` to look for some of the most obscure keywords related to your work, hobbies, or passions. Then click through to the profiles of the people who wrote the tweets you find. You'll be amazed how good an idea you get of someone just by glancing at their last 20 tweets. Interested? Follow them. It's not like other social networks where you're really only expected to connect to folks you already know.

A great way to engage others on Twitter is to turn on the Show All @Replies option in your settings. If you have this option turned off, your Twitter feed doesn't display @replies directed to people who aren't in your network. If you turn this option on, you can see the whole conversation. The more tweets to other people you see, the more chances you have to "meet" new people, jump in, and engage.

While you sift through the Twitter conversation, don't be shy about clicking the usernames that you see (as in @replies) and writing to strangers offering your own opinion. It may take a few tries with a few different conversations before the chatting users include you in their conversation, but eventually they do.

But even if you don't @reply, your tweets still appear in search, and other Twitter users can spot them. If you have something interesting to say, people start to reply to your tweets. If you seek out and use relevant keywords and #hashtags, you will start to connect with others who share your interests. Your early days on Twitter will probably be pretty quiet when it comes to replies and conversation. All those twitterers are just getting to know you, after all. Don't worry; after a few of your tweets appear in the timeline and you add a few contacts to your network, people will begin to notice you.

Tweeting frequency

Twitter users tend to settle into a rhythm of tweeting frequency, often unconsciously, over time. Some Twitter users are considered noisy because they tweet so much, whereas others can come across as standoffish because they don't tweet frequently. So, how much is too much or too little? How often should you tweet?

A good rule when you're starting out is to post at least four or five tweets per day. You most likely find yourself tweeting much more often than that, but if you aren't yet fully comfortable with it, use that number to get started.

If you're using Twitter for your business, or you plan to link to your products or posts on your personal blog, find a balance between the number of tweets that promote yourself and the number of tweets that provide value. You might think of this balance as an actual ratio. For example, for every link of your own that you place on Twitter, send out at least five tweets that inform, engage, and converse. If conversation and engagement are your aim, you definitely want to keep a human voice in your Twitter stream at all times.

It's worth thinking about who you want to reach. People new to Twitter and only following a few get bowled over by frequent tweeters simply because it's all they see on their stream. A roaring chat with friends you already know is a fine use of Twitter, too, and would involve *many* more tweets a day than, say, a business user or someone just figuring out what they want to do with the platform.

Inserting Links into Your Tweets

Virtually all Twitter users incorporate links into their tweets on a regular basis — by one estimate, 23 percent of tweets contain links. You can insert links to Web pages, blog entries, or even other tweets. The toughest part of including these links is getting them to fit in the 140-character limit while leaving yourself room to say something about why you're sending the link out in the first place.

The *URL shortener* is a tool that was designed to manage exceptionally long URLs so that they would not "break" in e-mail and so that they're easier to copy and paste. Twitter and services like it have heightened the need to save space when linking. Sites such as TinyURL.com (`http://tinyurl.com`), is.gd (`http://is.gd`), bit.ly (`http://bit.ly`), and budurl (`http://budurl.com`) automatically shorten a link into a shorter set of numbers and letters that forwards to the original link and can cut the link's length down by as much as 70 or 80 percent. As of this writing, Twitter uses TinyURL.com by default on its Web site, so many of the links you post will be shortened for you but it's done after the fact, so you don't get to use the full 140 characters. Visit one of the other shortening sites for ways to shorten URLs in advance. Shorteners like bit.ly and budurl also track how your link did, showing you how many people clicked through or in some cases, retweeted your link, which is helpful for business and for seeing whether people like what you post.

Most important is to remember to include a short reason for the link (otherwise, your Twitter followers don't know why they should click it), such as a headline or a hook that tells them why they might want to click. This is a real art. Some of the most popular tweeters have large followings because they're good at this, and their stream is enjoyable to read. It's also nice to give credit to a fellow tweeter by typing **@username** if you're sharing someone else's tweets or links. Typing @ followed by a Twitter username automatically links to that Twitter account Profile page so that you can see more about who that person is. It's context.

If you want to link specifically to one specific tweet, rather than to a user's account, first click the day and time at the end of the tweet itself to go to the *permalink* page for that tweet. You can then copy that link into a tweet of your own.

Using Your Twitter History and Favorites

If you want to access your Twitter history after you use the service for a while, you may find it a challenge, especially if you're a frequent tweeter. But you can get your whole history from Twitter in a few ways:

- ✔ **TweetScan (www.tweetscan.com/data.php):** A service that can pull Twitter history for any username. Unfortunately, TweetScan only goes back to December 2007, and if you've been on Twitter since it first hit the streets in 2006, you probably want to go back farther. Joined since then? You can get your entire Twitter history.

- ✔ **Twistory (www.twistory.net):** A cool little application that imports your Twitter history into the Web-based Google Calendar app so that you can view your tweets like a diary. If you tweet a lot, you might feel overwhelmed by so many tweets crammed into such a small space.

- ✔ **Profile page:** You can use the old-school way of seeing your Twitter history by going to your Twitter Profile page and clicking the More button over and over again until you see the tweet you're looking for. This approach definitely takes some time, though. (And if you really just want the one tweet, searching (http://search.twitter.com) might be a lot easier!)

- ✔ **Aggregator:** If you're a new Twitter user, you can have an aggregator, such as FriendFeed (http://friendfeed.com) or SocialThing (http://socialthing.com), save your history. *Aggregators* simply combine your Twitter feed together with any feeds you might have on other social sites. Do you share photos on Flickr? Then there is a feed of your pictures. Videos on YouTube? Same thing. It's kind of like double posting, for insurance purposes.

You can also keep track of some tweets by marking them as *favorites* with the little star icon on the web interface. A drawback to favoriting tweets is that you can't search within them on Twitter, and Twitter's team hasn't said anything about creating a means to do this search.

Instead of using the Twitter Favorites feature, bookmark your favorites by using a tool such as Delicious (`http://delicious.com`), Shareaholic (`www.shareaholic.com`), or FriendFeed. You may find using an outside tool a little more inconvenient than the Favorites feature at first, but you can find the tweets that you mark in more than one way later. Some people even do Favorite Tweets Roundup posts on their blogs every few days, which you can do much more easily by using a bookmarking service, such as Delicious.

Your Feeds, My Feeds, Everyone's Feeds

We talk more about RSS feeds and what you can do with them in Chapter 8, but we want to introduce a couple of different feeds that you can access and subscribe to right from Twitter.com.

First, every Twitter account has an RSS feed associated with it. To access the RSS feed:

1. **Navigate to a user's Twitter page.**

   Our account, @dummies, is at `http://twitter.com/dummies`.

2. **Click the RSS Feed of @dummies's Updates link.**

   You can find this link near the end of the content on the right sidebar.

   Depending on what RSS reader you use, you see a page to subscribe to that feed.

3. **If you've protected your updates, you need to log into the API (see Figure 7-1).**

   You gain access to that user's feed.

Figure 7-1:
Logging into
the API to
access the
RSS feed of
a protected
user.

If you want to access one single RSS feed with the tweets of everyone that
you follow:

1. **Navigate to your Twitter Home screen.**

   Either click the Twitter logo in the upper-left corner or the Home link in
   the upper-right corner of any Twitter page, or if you're already logged in,
   navigate to `http://twitter.com/home`.

2. **Click the RSS Feed link.**

   You can find this link near the end of the content on the right sidebar.
   (Scroll down until you find it.) The RSS logo appears nearby.

   Now, you can access an RSS feed of updates for everyone you follow.

In fact, every page that has some sort of update stream has an RSS update
feed associated with it. Alternatively, if your browser supports it, you can
click the RSS icon inside the address bar in your browser to access the feed
for that page.

We go over the more interesting points of what you can do with Twitter feeds in Chapter 8, including porting them over to an RSS reader so that you can view a stream without having to visit Twitter.com.

Deciphering Twitter Shorthand Code

The more you use Twitter, the more you're going to want to find quicker ways to do things. Conveniently, Twitter has included a number of shorthand codes that you can use to perform almost any action directly from the What Are You Doing? box. These codes are particularly useful when you're working from a mobile phone by sending your tweets to 40404 (or your local shot code) using the Twitter SMS (Short Message Service) gateway.

As we talk about in Chapter 3, be careful when using shorthand code! Making a typo when you want to send a direct (private) message can send an update to everyone who follows you. It's smart to be particularly careful about sending sensitive information via direct messages, just in case. At some point, you might accidentally share something with everyone that you intended only a particular user to see. Best bet? Use the actual message link on a person's page to send them a direct message.

D – direct message

You can send a direct message right from the Update box by using the following form:

D *username message*

In this message, *username* is the username of the person whom you want to direct message, and *message* is any message that you want to send. So, if you want to tell us how great this book is, you type in the What Are You Doing? box:

D dummies I am really enjoying Twitter For Dummies! Thanks for the help!

Many users opt to have direct messages sent straight to their cellphones via SMS and/or e-mail, so you can frequently use direct messages to reach someone instantly even if you don't have a cell number or if you know that he's an active Twitter user who may not be online at the moment. Some make heavy use of this while traveling and at events and find it much easier to coordinate on the fly.

F – follow

No matter what application or interface you use to tweet, you can quickly add a twitterer to your feed just by sending an update to Twitter. Say that you decide to follow the updates of Evan Williams (@ev), Twitter's cofounder and CEO. Just send this message to Twitter:

> **F ev**

Alternatively, you can type the word **follow** to do the exact same thing:

> **follow ev**

When you add someone using the follow or f command, you both follow them and opt in to receive their individual device updates (only when your account is set to receive device updates). When you follow them using the Web site Follow button or most Twitter clients, you connect only via the Web site, not also via SMS device updates.

@ – reply

We cover how to reply to users in Chapters 3 and 5, but the @ symbol is really a shorthand for referencing another Twitter user. The difference between this command and all other commands is that there is *no* space between it and the username of the person you want to reach. Want to say something to Leslie? Write

> **@geechee_girl hiya!**

Twitter makes sure that the message ends up in Leslie's Mentions tab.

On/Off

The commands On and Off control whether or not your entire account will receive device updates (SMS texts on your phone). You can use the On command to turn device updates on for your account. To turn them Off, you can use the Off command twice:

- ✔ **To silence updates to your cellphone:** Send Twitter the update **off**.

- ✔ **To silence updates and direct messages to your cellphone:** Send the update **off** a second time. You will not receive any device updates until you turn them back on using On.

Receiving SMS updates on your phone . . . from everyone

Getting Twitter updates as SMS messages right on your phone has its advantages and disadvantages. For one thing, it lets you choose to remain much more closely up-to-date with a small subset of your Twitter connections, which can be cool. Web celebrity iJustine (@iJustine) does this to find her real friends among the people she follows.

But what if you tried following the device updates of every single person you're connected to on Twitter? The command is simply

follow all

If you're following a large number of people who update frequently, your mobile phone might never stop beeping, vibrating, or doing whatever it does when it receives a text message. Definitely don't try the Follow All command unless you already have unlimited texting.

Fav – favorite a tweet

If something someone just tweeted made you laugh (say, our @dummies account), you can favorite that tweet by sending an update to Twitter:

> **fav dummies**

If you're receiving updates on your cellphone, sending **fav** by itself adds the last update you received to your Favorites tab on your Home screen.

Nudge

Do you have a friend who hasn't updated in a while? Send her a message asking her to let everyone know what she's doing:

> **nudge *username***

Nudge is a funny little feature, in that it works only for people who receive their tweets as SMS updates, and quite possibly only for people who have specifically signed up for your device updates. Look at the Twitter Profile page for anyone that follows you. Sometimes message and nudge links are both visible; other times, only message. If you can't see nudge, the person obviously can't be nudged. But frequently you can see nudge and still nothing at all happens when you click it.

Plenty of active users of Twitter — probably most — have never used nudge. So, don't sweat it if it doesn't make sense to you.

Stats

If you ever want to know how many followers you have and how many users you're following, send the update **stats.** If you're online, Twitter displays a message at the top of the screen letting you know. If you sent **stats** from your cellphone, Twitter sends you a text message with your stats in it. Obviously this makes a lot more sense than viewing stats on the Web page, where they are, of course, already displayed. Stats was a little more meaningful with Track because it also reminded you what words you were tracking.

Get

The Get command allows you to quickly view the last update from a user. Want to see Michael's latest tweet? Send to Twitter

get gruen

Leslie, Laura, and Michael had a particularly good laugh at this one — nobody really "gets" our dear @gruen, but we do love irony.

Whois

If you want to get someone's profile information quickly (say, Laura's), use the Whois command:

whois pistachio

Twitter sends you a message that contains the user's proper name (Laura Fitton), how long she's been on Twitter (since April 2007), and her current bio from her Profile page (http://twitter.com/pistachio).

Leave

Leave seems like it would be the opposite of follow, but it's not. At least, not quite. **Leave username** simply turns off the individual's device updates, those text messages that some Twitterers receive on their phones, it does not unfollow that person on Twitter.

On/Off username

Not to be confused with On/Off (see the earlier section), **On/Off username** turns device updates on and off for individual users. Like follow, On will also connect you to people on Twitter.com so that you're following their updates. Like leave, the Off username command stops device updates, but it doesn't unfollow the username account.

In other words, **On/Off username** has no unique functionality that is different from Follow/Leave.

Invite

Do you want to invite someone to Twitter? Send the Invite command, followed by her e-mail address or mobile phone number:

> **invite friend@example.com**
>
> **invite 212 555 1212**

Twitter sends either an e-mail or SMS to that person to let her know that you've invited her to use Twitter.

Quit and Stop

Quit and Stop discontinue all service between Twitter and your cellphone. They opt your cellphone number out of Twitter altogether. If used, you'll literally have to log into your Twitter account and redo the steps to add your cellphone to your account.

These commands are probably not the best options to quiet your phone. They're handy though if you accidentally lock your phone into a separate account by sending **join** to 40404 after you already have an account.

Codes may come, and codes may go . . .

Because Twitter is a living application, it has commands that come and go. Of note, you may still see some older Twitter users lamenting the loss of the Track feature.

For a recent list of Twitter commands, browse to Twitter's Help forums by clicking the help link at the top of every Twitter page. At time of print, `http://help.twitter.com/forums/10711/entries/14020` has the most accurate list of Twitter commands.

The Track series of commands enabled users to receive updates containing a keyword the user was tracking, even if they didn't follow the person posting the update. For example, if you were a *Battlestar Galactica* fan, you'd send the update **track Battlestar Galactica** to get every mention of that show, no matter who mentioned it, sent to your Twitter Home screen.

Unfortunately, Twitter removed the Track feature, but you can still get the scoop by using search in a similar way:

1. **Browse to Twitter Search.**

   You can scroll to the bottom of any Twitter page and click the Search link or just go to `http://search.twitter.com`.

2. **Enter the search term you want to track in the text box and click Search.**

   A screen appears, showing the results for all mentions of the term you want to track. You have the option of subscribing to an RSS feed for the search terms — a great idea if you're a business user and want to monitor mentions of your name, products, brands, or categories.

Remember, search offers advanced features to fine-tune what you want to keep track of. From the Search home page, click Advanced Search and add parameters like sender, recipient, optional keywords, required keywords, timeframes, and even "emotional sentiment" of the tweets you want to see.

Chapter 8

Twitter Minus Twitter.com

*Y*ou can easily get attached to Twitter simply because once you really get started, you're bound to discover many interesting and useful things it can do for you. You can literally take Twitter — and the information, ideas, and friends you connect with on Twitter — everywhere. Mobile applications and text messages give on-the-go users the ability to update their timeline and access their network. E-mail and RSS feeds also allow you to pipe your Twitter stream into your favorite RSS reader or e-mail, or onto your mobile device. Because the Twitter platform is so flexible, you can almost do everything you want with Twitter without needing to visit Twitter.com.

Look around the Web, and you'll see Twitter has become a staple on popular social-networking sites and a standard sidebar feature on many blogs. Because of the many ways that users can access and share Twitter on the Web, you can discover it in all sorts of useful places, from tweets about specific neighborhoods on RentWiki (www.rentwiki.com) to live widgets on major media sites like ABC.com during President Obama's 2009 State of the Union address.

In this chapter, we show you how you can use Twitter without having to browse to Twitter.com. When you realize how you can access Twitter from anywhere, you're bound to discover ways to make it even more useful to you.

Tweeting with Your Cellphone

Many twitterers use the service almost exclusively on their mobile phones. You can use Twitter on your mobile device in three ways:

- ✔ SMS (text messages) to and from 40404 (or your country's short code)
- ✔ Twitter's mobile Web site (`http://m.twitter.com`) if you have a Web browser on your cellphone
- ✔ Downloadable applications for smartphones such as the BlackBerry or iPhone

Literally dozens of applications come out for Twitter every couple of months. For more information, and to find the latest Twitter tools, check out Laura's startup Twitter directory and marketplace oneforty (`www.oneforty.com`).

Via text messaging

Although text messaging (or SMS) is the most basic way to access Twitter via your cellphone, you need to first make sure that your cellphone plan encompasses unlimited texting. Otherwise, your monthly bill may end up skyrocketing. Check before you enable SMS updates!

After you make sure that you can afford your mobile texting plan, you can easily use SMS to update Twitter on the go. (Turn to Chapter 2 for instructions on how to associate your cellphone with your Twitter account.)

One caveat: The maximum length for a standard text message is 160 characters, but Twitter's maximum is 140 characters. You have to manually verify that you aren't going over the Twitter limit because otherwise, Twitter cuts off your SMS tweet at 140 characters.

In addition to sending tweets as SMS messages from your phone, you can receive your contacts' tweets on your phone via SMS. Setting this up takes a little more work. First, think long and hard about how noisy you want your phone to be each day. Most Twitter users find that they can handle between 10 and 20 peoples' tweets being sent to their phone before the constant incoming text stream becomes overwhelming. Luckily, even power users like iJustine (@iJustine) have discovered that they can take advantage of SMS tweets to their phone by being really selective about whose actual tweets they get via SMS. It's not all-or-nothing.

To receive tweets from your contacts on your cellphone:

1. **Open your own Home screen and, under Device Updates on the right sidebar, click phone to activate your phone notifications.**

   Now you can subscribe to receive SMS tweets from any or all of the people that you already follow on Twitter.

   Don't confuse *notifications* with following, though. *Following* means you follow their updates generally via Twitter. Notifications are a more intimate connection where you get their every tweet as an SMS text on your phone. With notifications ON, you also get all your DMs via SMS.

2. **Make a list of people whose tweets you really want to receive directly as SMS messages on your phone.**

   These people can be anyone — friends, family, influencers, clients — whatever works for you.

3. **Go to each of those Twitter users' profiles and select (toggle) the updates on or updates off radio buttons to turn their notifications on or off.**

   You can also send a tweet to turn individuals' message notifications on or off (see Chapter 7).

Via smartphones or PDAs

If you have a smartphone, BlackBerry, or PDA that has Web capabilities, you can use Twitter's mobile Web site, `http://m.twitter.com`, or a number of other third-party mobile Web sites like Hahlo, pretty much the way you use Twitter.com on your computer. You can also download applications that allow you to use Twitter as an application on your phone. You can find several popular applications — these are just a sampling of what's available for various devices:

- ✔ **For iPhone:** Tweetie (`www.atebits.com/tweetie-iphone`), Twittelator (`www.stone.com/Twittelator`), TwitterFon (`http://twitterfon.net`), Twitterrific (`http://iconfactory.com/software/twitterrific`).

- ✔ **For BlackBerry:** Blackbird (`http://dossy.org/twitter/blackbird`), TinyTwitter (`http://tinytwitter.com`), TwitterBerry (`www.orangatame.com/products/twitterberry`). Considering how popular BlackBerry phones are for tweeting, it's disappointing how weak the apps are. Laura uses a combination of TwitterBerry (for her read-only account), texting (to send most of her tweets), `http://m.Twitter.com` (to drop by friends' pages or check replies), and `http://search.twitter.com` (to check trends, do searches, and so on).

✔ **For Windows Mobile:** PocketTwit (`http://code.google.com/p/pocketwit`), TinyTwitter (`www.tinytwitter.com`), TwitToday (`http://dalelane.co.uk/page.php?id=1047`), Twitula (`http://cid-eda3c1275909727a.skydrive.live.com/self.aspx/Public/MobileApps/Twitula35.CAB`), Twobile (`www.infinitumsoftware.com/twobile`).

Play around with the applications' options a bit until you find one you like best. They're all a little bit different, and they have varying advantages based on how you use Twitter, how often you tweet, how big your network is, and so forth.

Using Twitter through Your E-Mail

When someone new starts following you, Twitter sends you an e-mail that contains a link so that you can check out that user's profile right away to see whether you want to follow him back. These e-mails save quite a bit of time and hassle — you don't have to try to remember who followed you and when.

If you don't have the time or the need to follow back your new followers right away, use whatever options your e-mail client (or Web service) provides to search, file, or tag certain messages received. Setting up a mail filter to segment those notifications outside of your normal e-mail inbox can be really useful. Those e-mails then wait for you to process more efficiently in *batches,* many at a time, when it's convenient for you.

You can also set up your Twitter account so that direct messages are sent to your e-mail inbox:

1. **On your Home page, click Settings at the top of the screen.**

   The Settings screen appears.

2. **Select the Notices tab.**

3. **Next to Direct Text Emails, check the Email When I Receive a New Direct Message check box.**

Even if you're receiving direct notifications through Twitter and your mobile phone, you may also want to get them by e-mail. Most modern e-mail applications, including Webmail software, allow you to search through your mail. By always having a copy in your e-mail inbox, you can much more easily retrieve and find a direct message that you receive. Otherwise there is no way to search your direct messages, which can be a problem.

Although Twitter can send you e-mails, it has no mechanism that allows you to send updates, replies, or direct messages directly via e-mail. (But they do provide a link in the e-mail that you can click to open pages at Twitter.com [or mobile Twitter] where you can send Twitter info.)

To work around this limitation, some developers have used the API to come up with e-mail clients for Twitter. Two of our favorites include Topify (`www.topify.com`), shown in Figure 8-1, and Twittermail (`www.twittermail.com`), shown in Figure 8-2. Both of these Web applications enable you to interact with users and update Twitter directly from your e-mail address.

As with many third-party Web applications, Topify and Twittermail ask for your Twitter username and password. If you don't think you can trust a site with your credentials, just don't use it! Luckily, OAuth holds the promise of letting you give third-party applications limited permission to function with your account without giving away your password and the ability to access everything about your account.

Figure 8-1:
Topify offers enhanced Twitter notifications and e-mail-based replies.

Figure 8-2:
Twittermail
looks like
Twitter, but
integrates
Twitter with
your e-mail
inbox.

Swimming Your Twitter Stream with RSS Feeds

If you want to keep tabs on your Twitter network without logging into Twitter.com, you can use *RSS* (Really Simple Syndication) to pull in your Twitter stream like it's a blog. Really Simple Syndication is a format for delivering dynamic Web content — blogs, news stories, and multimedia — in a standard, easy-to-read format (called *feeds*). RSS isn't a Web site or a Web page: It's a raw data feed for the content on a Web page or Web site. You often find RSS on blogs and news sites, but any site that has live and updating content, including Twitter, can use RSS.

Most modern browsers (such as Safari, Firefox, and later versions of Internet Explorer) have RSS reading capabilities built in, but you likely want to use a dedicated application or Web site to handle your feeds because then you can go back later and search them, refer to them, catch up on many at once, and more.

An RSS reader, such as Newsgator (`www.newsgator.com`) or Google Reader (`www.google.com/reader`), aggregates RSS feeds, which you can then read. Within these applications, you subscribe to an RSS feed, which allows you to access your favorite Web content within a single destination and keep up with frequently updated sites.

RSS is a fundamental part of Twitter because it allows users to share and access timelines from virtually anywhere on the Web, as well as through desktop applications and mobile devices. Each user's timeline has its own RSS feed, which you can read via an RSS reader.

By the way, the gentleman credited with inventing RSS is on Twitter! Say hello to Dave Winer (`@davewiner`).

Grabbing RSS feeds

If you have a smartphone that has RSS capabilities, you can use that smartphone to get Twitter while you're on the go. To grab the RSS feed for your Home screen, click the RSS button in the bottom-left of the status window and follow the specific instructions for your RSS reader. If you hover over the RSS icon in your browser (depending on which browser you use, the location of this icon varies), it also displays the feed address. You can then add the feed address to your RSS reader of choice, such as Google Reader or Bloglines.

You can obtain an individual RSS feed address for your Home screen (the Twitter stream of all your friends), the Everyone page (the public timeline of all Twitter users), and your *@username* page — but not for your Direct Messages page. To read direct messages, you have to rely on e-mail, text messages, or another method.

Also, Twitter Search has RSS capabilities built in. You can pull any search that you perform on Twitter Search into an RSS feed directly from the site.

Sending RSS feeds back to Twitter

Twitterfeed (`http://twitterfeed.com`) is a third-party application you can use to send RSS feeds to Twitter so that each item in the feed "posts" as a tweet. It turns out you can accomplish a lot by using this application:

> ✔ **Announce new blog posts.** If you have a blog and want to promote each new post by using your Twitter account, you can have Twitterfeed pull in the RSS of your blog and send the title of the post and a link to Twitter (posting it as a tweet from your account). You may find this feature particularly useful if you update your blog frequently.

✔ **Create and share a *link blog*.** At Pistachio Consulting, we maintain a link blog of some of the best articles we can find about the business use of Twitter. We use www.delicious.com/touchbaseblog to track, tag, and share these articles, and we direct the RSS for that Delicious account to @touchbase on Twitter (along with a feed to our http://www.touchbaseblog.com posts, too). That way, business users of Twitter can easily access up-to-date case studies, articles, best practices, and ideas simply by following a Twitter stream.

✔ **Re-tweet hashtags.** If you're running an event and want everyone who plans to attend that event to be able to send a message to everyone else, search that hashtag on http://search.twitter.com and then grab the RSS feed from those Twitter search results page and feed it into the event's account. Now everyone at the event can follow your single event account to see all the hashtagged tweets being shared. *Note:* This will work for any search term. Be creative!

✔ **Translate tweets automatically.** This one is advanced, but if you want to reach an international audience by sending your tweets in another language and you're comfortable playing with advanced tools like Yahoo! Pipes (http://pipes.yahoo.com/pipes), you can actually pull in a Twitter stream, automatically translate it into a number of different languages, and then publish the stream to its own language-specific Twitter account by using Twitterfeed. Just be sure to mention on that account bio that it's automated, or native speakers will wonder why the writing is so awkward!

Limit the number of times that you have to feed send messages to Twitter so that you don't send too many tweets and irritate your followers. You should also mention in the bio for the account if it is heavily — or completely — automated. See the Pistachio Consulting account @touchbase (for our blog and link blog) for a good example of being upfront about RSS-fed Twitter accounts.

Using Third-Party Services

Twitter itself is extremely basic: 140-character updates, nothing more. But the entire world of Twitter is much more complex because its founders created a way for developers outside of the Twitter team to develop tools for their service.

Twitter opened up its service by creating an application programming interface (API), which allows third-party developers to have access to some of Twitter's code. Both users and developers reap the benefits of this API in the form of fun new toys that let Twitter do even more cool stuff.

APIs: The key to twittering off of Twitter.com

An *application programming interface* (API) is basically a set of programming instructions and standards that developers can use to access a software application such as Twitter. When a company like Twitter opens their API, they allow other developers to look at their application's code and make new products that complement or expand the original application. These new creations are called *third-party applications.*

If you're new to Twitter, or to Web apps in general, you may wonder whether APIs raise security concerns. Developers who use Twitter's API can't access private data, such as your password or direct messages. But you still need to be cautious: Some third-party apps do ask that you log into Twitter by using your username and password. Before you hand over your information, make sure that the app in question is reputable; thankfully, no one yet has had to deal with a major scandal in which a Twitter app turned out to be a password-stealing scam, but some very real security breaches have occurred, and you should always be very careful about giving any password to anyone. With your password, a third-party application could look at your DMs.

If you're concerned about allowing third-party services to have your username and password, good news is on the way. In February 2009, Twitter started beta testing open authentication (OAuth). Using OAuth allows you to authorize a third-party Web site or application to essentially log in as you and perform actions on your behalf without ever having your username or password. Flickr, Basecamp by 37Signals, Facebook, and other online services already allow you to use open authentication. Full rollout of the feature is expected by mid-2009, and it will eventually become mandatory for all applications.

Arguably the best-known third-party applications built on Twitter are designed to make keeping up with your network easier. You can easily follow your network on the Twitter Web site when you have only 50 followers, but after you start getting followers into the hundreds, you can have some serious difficulty keeping track of your network without a little help.

Your options for third-party applications that help you use Twitter grow and change constantly; here are some of the current favorites:

- Twhirl (www.twhirl.org)
- TweetDeck (www.tweetdeck.com)
- Twitterific (http://iconfactory.com/software/twitterific)
- Digsby (www.digsby.com)

Twitter provides a short list of third-party applications right on its Web site at http://twitter.com/downloads. The Twitter fan wiki also attempts to index the growing ecosystem of applications, services, and other sites built on the Twitter API, but finding the best ones remains a problem that Laura's startup www.oneforty.com hopes to solve.

Third-party applications such as Twhirl and Twitterific provide more complex, customizable ways to sort through your Twitter network, stream of friends' tweets, @replies, and direct messages, as well as update your tweets. Some avid Twitter users choose their third-party apps based on those apps' compatibility with other social-media services that some twitterers also use, such as FriendFeed (`www.friendfeed.com`) and 12Seconds (`http://12seconds.tv`).

Most of the downloadable third-party applications that you can use to view Twitter on your desktop require an additional download called Adobe Air, a free program that many of the applications are built on. Generally, when you choose to download an app that requires Adobe Air, Air also downloads automatically.

We cover these third-party tools in depth in Chapter 9.

Sharing Tweets All Around the Web

Twitter's a far-reaching service, but you can also pull your Twitter presence out onto the rest of the Web by using social-networking widgets (some of which are powered by RSS) and a few other nifty tweaks.

Social networks are those sites online where people can go to meet and stay in touch with new and old friends and colleagues. Twitter itself is a social network. Some of the social networks you may use already include MySpace, Facebook, Ning, FriendFeed, and LinkedIn. And — you guessed it — you can put your tweets on social networks.

If you're a MySpace user, for example, Twitter makes a badge (or widget) that you can embed right onto your Profile page. Twitter offers a Badges page at `http://twitter.com/badges`, where you can go to customize the look and feel of your badge for each network. This page also gives you instructions about how to embed the badge code, which is also compatible with blog templates on platforms such as Blogger and WordPress so that your blog readers can see what you're up to and connect with you on Twitter, as shown in Figure 8-3.

After you put the badge code into your social-networking Profile page, Twitter updates the badge each time you send a tweet. You can use a badge to quickly and easily share Twitter with people outside the service, letting them know your status and what you're up to on a daily basis.

Facebook, the most popular social network, doesn't let you embed code onto profiles. You can, however, install the Twitter app on Facebook (`http://apps.facebook.com/twitter`), which lets you choose to either display a badge on your profile or have your Twitter updates set as your status message on Facebook. Because some people on Facebook get confused when they see a lot of tweets out of context, it's not a bad idea to only share some of your tweets with your Facebook friends. You can share your tweets by using a special tag (see the Facebook Twitter app for instructions) in your tweets to designate which ones to also re-post to Facebook.

Figure 8-3:
You can put the Twitter. com widget on a blog.

Services such as Ping.fm (www.ping.fm) and HelloTxt (www.hellotxt.com) allow you to send the same tweet or update to many social networks, such as MySpace and Facebook, in addition to Twitter, all at the same time. This service saves you the trouble of logging into each site separately, but it can get impersonal and alienate your followers. Use these services with caution!

Auto-Tweeting

Auto-tweeting is exactly what it sounds like: automated tweets. You can auto-tweet by using one of a number of third-party applications built for that purpose. These third-party applications use the same API as the Twitter readers (which we talk about in the section "Using Third-Party Services," earlier in this chapter), but these auto-tweet applications apply the API for a different purpose.

Some auto-tweet applications, such as TweetLater (www.tweetlater.com), allow you to schedule tweets in advance. Mostly, marketers use these applications, and some Twitter users don't like them because they undermine the spontaneity of Twitter by having things pre-scheduled (which, in our opinion, defeats the purpose of the "What are you doing?" question). However, you may find TweetLater useful if you're going on vacation or plan to be off the grid for some other reason. You can schedule a post or two while you're away from your computer, just to check in and remind your Twitter network that you may be out of touch. It's also useful for businesses, announcements you know about in advance and can plan for, or special projects like Laura's tweeting her great-grandmother's diary as @ggpratt.

Services in the section "Sending RSS feeds back to Twitter," earlier in this chapter, are also essentially automatically tweeting for you.

Chapter 9

Embracing the Twitter Ecosystem

*T*witter is a useful tool on its own, but by design, it remains extremely simple, even stark, in its functionality. The folks who created it wanted to make Twitter a platform for users to build on, improve, and enhance, so they opened up Twitter's *API* (application program interface), or code, to the public. Enterprising and creative software developers, as a result, can create applications that work with Twitter to offer even more compelling features and ways to make use of the dynamic system.

Twitter itself is constantly evolving and changing — from design facelifts to new features to changes in how the back-end technology works. The Twitter team pays close attention to how people interact with the system and what those users want to do with it. Because the long-term success of Twitter depends completely on a healthy base of users generating a regular stream of content, the management obviously wants to do their best to keep Twitter on its toes.

As a result, Twitter is a living application and community, extending far beyond what Twitter itself controls. Conventions and third-party tools have popped up to fill in functionality that Twitter may have missed, chosen not to implement, or intentionally left for other developers to handle.

You can find a rich toolset online to enhance and personalize your own Twitter experience. In this chapter, we introduce many of the third-party tools that enrich the service. We'd like to note, though, that it's very hard to capture the vast and dynamic Twitter ecosystem in these few, and static, pages. The daunting challenge of writing a book chapter to direct people to the best tools and services is a significant reason for the very existence of Laura's startup oneforty inc. (www.oneforty.com).

By the time you read this book, dozens, if not hundreds, of new mashups, services, applications, and other tools and products will be built out onto the Twitter ecosystem. Please check out www.oneforty.com and the book's official Web site at www.twitterfordummies.com for up-to-date guidance on how to find the best and latest tools.

Finding Interesting Twitter Talk with Search Tools

With so many conversations going on every day on Twitter, how can you manage to find the ones that are relevant to you? You can use search applications to manage your interactions with Twitter; you can track people and topics, find data about what's trendy and buzz-worthy up to the second, and more.

You can search Twitter many, many ways, but here are three noteworthy things for you to know:

✔ Twitter Search (formerly called Summize and now finally integrated right into the pages at Twitter.com)

✔ TweetScoop and TwitScoop

✔ Hashtags

Twitter Search

Summize, a powerful search engine that trawls through the enormous volume of public tweets in real time, emerged in 2008 and soon became the go-to tool for searching Twitter. The powers that be at Twitter noticed. Seeing the value in Summize's application, Twitter acquired Summize and began a slow process of incorporating it into Twitter itself, renaming it Twitter Search. So although the Summize name is a thing of the past, Twitter Search is a powerful and important part of the Twitter experience. Just as this book went to press, Twitter formally rolled out its search functionality displayed right on Twitter.com with the rest of your account. Search is still also available at its own Web address, http://search.twitter.com, as shown in Figure 9-1, or by clicking the Search link at the bottom of your Twitter Home page.

Twitter Search isn't static: It keeps searching for your query, even after you click the Search button. When Twitter Search finds a new search result, a link appears at the top of your Twitter Search results telling you how many new matches for your search term have appeared since you last hit the Refresh button on your browser. This may not seem like a big deal, but it's extremely useful when news is breaking, or you're following a live event. Just click a trending topic to see what we mean. *Note:* Search as embedded into Twitter. com is static. You have to hit Refresh to see whether any new results have come in.

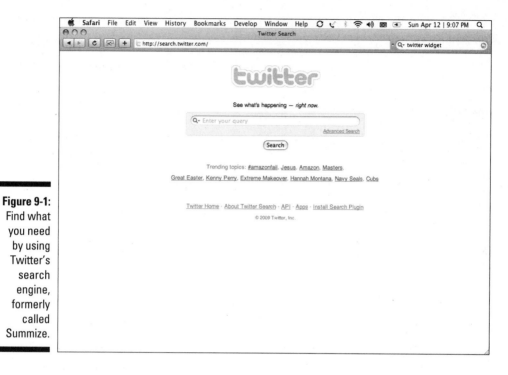

Figure 9-1:
Find what
you need
by using
Twitter's
search
engine,
formerly
called
Summize.

Something else that makes Twitter Search so useful is how specific you can get with Advanced Search. You can fine-tune searches by usernames, locations, or keywords. Keep in mind, you're better off using only a couple of advanced search settings at a time, or you may find no results at all!

Here's more on how to use advanced search:

1. **From the Twitter Search page, click the Advanced Search link located below the text box.**

   A new page appears that contains a fill-in-the-blank interface to help you search for the information and people you want to find.

2. **In the Words panel, fine-tune your search by word.**

   You can specify that a search match all or none of the words in your query, the exact phrase you input, Twitter hashtags (which we talk about in the section "Hashtags," later in this chapter), or even set your advanced search defaults to all or one of 18 different languages. (*Persistent* off to the right of the Languages drop-down menu just means that the language you select will remain your Advanced Search default until you select a new one.)

3. **In the People panel, specify whether you want to search by user.**

   You can search tweets that come from or reference a certain username.

4. **Enter information if you want to search by location or distance, as well as by date, in the Places panel.**

   For example, you might search only tweets of users who enter their location as a given city.

5. **In the Attitudes panel, select whether you want to search for "positive" or "negative" tweets, or search for tweets that ask a question.**

   These options search for natural language clues about the tweet that imply whether it's positive or negative.

   If you use Twitter to improve customer relations for your business or a client, the Attitudes panel search can really help you find certain types of feedback. It's not perfect, of course, but it can make rooting out negative or positive feedback much easier.

6. **In the Other panel, specify whether you want to search for tweets that have links.**

   You can also limit how many results are returned per page.

7. **Click the Search button, which appears both at the top and bottom of the Advanced Search page.**

   Your search results appear.

Here are a few tips to keep in mind about search:

✔ Remember search is a living thing. Having fine-tuned a useful search, many times you'll want to do something with it, like watching it over time, subscribing to it, or sharing it with others.

✔ Keep the search window open to watch as new results come in or subscribe to the RSS feed for the search to monitor it longer term.

✔ You can also share the search results by selecting the Twitter These Results option on the search page or by copying and pasting the search URL from your browser bar. (*Hint:* Shorten that URL, or it will be difficult to tweet.)

TwitScoop

Time and again during news events, (earthquakes, wildfires, politics, accidents, deaths) as an extension of popular culture (TV shows, sports, movies, celebrities, fashion) and for emerging information of any kind, Twitter shines as a powerful way to find out what's going on in almost real time. TwitScoop (www.twitscoop.com) is one of many applications that display what trends are rising and falling. TwitScoop does this both at a Web site and as a feature built into popular Twitter client TweetDeck (`www.tweetdeck.com`).

Built into TweetDeck, TwitScoop, shown in Figure 9-2, helps you track keywords and trending topics, which can be really useful and is mandatory if you're using Twitter to keep tabs on your brand. You can access TwitScoop by clicking the button with the small bird icon in the TweetDeck toolbar (which is a row of icons along the top left of the application). A new TweetDeck column dedicated to trending topics and the information related to them loads.

On the main Web site that is behind the TweetDeck application, you'll find trending topic and keyword tracking in a browser interface. From the TwitScoop home page (`www.twitscoop.com`), shown in Figure 9-3, you can see tags, tag clouds, popular hashtags, and other words that are trending on Twitter. You can also use a handful of widgets to embed a list of trending topics on your Web site or blog.

TIP

Trending topics let you know how popular something is by tracking keywords and hashtags. For example, if you're running a meeting or conference, tell attendees to mark their tweets with an agreed-upon hashtag and then follow the conversation by tracking that hashtag on TweetScoop in TweetDeck or on the TwitScoop site. Twitter also offers a Trends tab now, which gives you a short, unsorted list of popular topics in real time.

Figure 9-2:
TweetDeck can run a TwitScoop column.

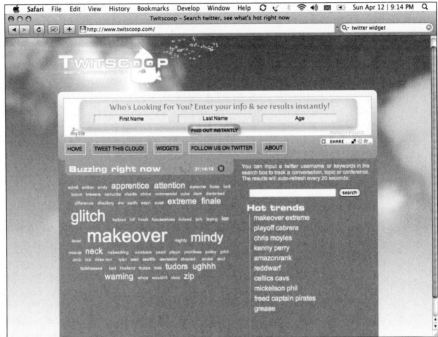

Figure 9-3:
TwitScoop
shows you
a tag cloud
and hot
trends.

Hashtags

Hashtags have become a part of the culture on Twitter for many avid users. Basically, *hashtags* are a way to delineate a keyword for other Twitter users to organize discussions around specific topics and events. Originally, the Web site #hashtags (www.hashtags.org) automatically tracked and displayed these hashtags. But Twitter occasionally turns off the portion of its application program interface (API) that hashtags.org uses, so you can't always search it reliably.

Not all Twitter users like hashtags: Some users think that hashtags make the Twitter stream clunky. Admittedly, seeing tweet after tweet go by containing hashtags, such as #GNO, #TCOT, #journchat, and other codes, can seem noisy and disjointed if you don't follow or understand those hashtags. You can always unfollow a heavy hashtag user if it really bothers you, but don't hit the trigger too quickly: You can probably get used to hashtags, along with the rest of Twitter's quirks, before too long. The ability to tag tweets is extremely powerful. It's something people are just starting to figure out, and they have a very interesting future.

As a concept, hashtags make it possible to quickly filter tweets by topic, event, or other content by using an easy abbreviation that doesn't take up too many of a tweet's 140 characters. People at the same event or meeting, or who are discussing the same topic, can use the same hashtag. Later on, if you want to review the information related to that event or topic, you can simply search for the hashtag on Twitter Search to find all tweets that reference the same code. (Figure 9-4 shows the results of a search for #dummies.) Sure, you can search by keyword, but the # in a hashtag is a signal for others that it is *the* keyword to use so that they can easily find, read, and share all tweets for a certain topic or event.

What that means is that a hashtag that catches on forms an instant *community* around it. Most of these communities are short-lived. Others become ongoing conversations, recurring real-time events, or even entire movements.

Hashtags are handy for note-taking and conversation during events, especially if organizers say something like "include #ourevent in all your tweets" (where ourevent is a unique label for that event.) People tweeting about it just type that #ourevent tag in each tweet to contribute to the combined flow of tweets that all can watch and respond to. More and more, talks and conference panels in the tech and media industries display the search results for the official hashtag, creating a shared billboard of ideas, notes, questions, and other information. People not present at the event can also participate in the discussion by searching the hashtag stream and following along with the presentation or speaker, just like they were there. From how the hashtag is included in the tweet, you can often discover other attendees at the conference that you might want to meet or talk to (although sometimes the people tweeting from offsite are so engaged, you might actually think they were in the room with you).

Say that you're organizing an event or want to start a discussion or debate on Twitter, and you want to establish a hashtag for that Twitter conversation. Here are some tips for creating an effective hashtag:

- If you want to avoid confusion, check Twitter Search for the hashtag that you want to use to make sure that someone else hasn't already claimed it.

  For example, people use the popular #wishlist hashtag for everything from software feature wish lists to requests for birthday presents, so searching for it brings up a fairly cluttered stream.

- Make sure everyone at your event or discussing your topic is aware of the proper hashtag in advance.

  After you choose your hashtag, make a note of it on your event page or blog post — or, of course, by tweeting it out — so that people responding to it can use the same hashtag.

Figure 9-4:
The results
of a search
for the
hashtag
#dum-
mies.

Expanding Your Twitter World by Using Clients

Twitter's open API means that enterprising and creative software developers are constantly creating applications, mashups, and entire services that feed off of the Twitter platform. For example, Figure 9-5 shows the desktop client TweetDeck.

Many of these third-party applications are *Twitter clients,* programs designed to let you update Twitter on your desktop or mobile phone, instead of having to use the Web interface or text-messaging. Many of these applications auto-load tweets from your Twitter followers. This is nice, because on the Web site, you have to actually click the Refresh button on your browser every few minutes to see what's going on. Each of these applications have different ways of displaying, organizing, searching and letting you interact with tweets, making them a very diverse crop of applications. There is definitely a competition afoot to become the preferred way for most Twitterers to engage with Twitter. Whether a few clear leaders emerge or whether people continue to interact with Twitter dozens of ways remains to be seen.

Figure 9-5:
Put Twitter
on your
desktop
with a
client
such as
TweetDeck.

Desktop clients

Many Twitter clients for your Mac or PC take the form of a software download that you install and run from the desktop. Most of these clients are based on a programming standard called Adobe Air. Adobe Air doesn't come preinstalled on your computer, so if you don't have it already, you'll be instructed to install it when you download a Twitter desktop client. Adobe Air is a free program; so, in fact, are many of the Twitter clients that we talk about.

Anybody with a decent amount of programming know-how can create a Twitter client, but here are a few that stand out from the crowd because they're particularly easy to use and offer the features that most Twitter users want:

✓ **Twhirl (www.twhirl.org):** Based on Adobe Air, you can install Twhirl on any computer that runs a Mac, Windows, or Linux operating system. It has a slim, attractive, and unobtrusive window interface (as shown in Figure 9-6), which many avid Twitter users like. Importantly, Twhirl can switch back and forth between multiple Twitter accounts, which is handy for those users who keep separate personal and professional ones, or who run Twitter accounts for clients. It also works with several social-networking services, such as aggregator FriendFeed, open-source microblogging application Identi.ca, and video-chat company Seesmic (which owns Twhirl), so you can use many of your social tools in one place. The interface is semi-customizable, fairly easy to get the hang of, and currently free to use.

In spring 2009, Seesmic rolled out a beta version of its Twhirl replacement Seesmic Desktop. The new client offers many new features, an easier way to work with multiple Twitter accounts, and can subscribe to Facebook contents.

✔ **TweetDeck (www.tweetdeck.com):** This free Twitter client, based on Adobe Air, is compatible with Mac, Windows, or Linux systems, just like Twhirl. If Twhirl isn't hardcore enough for you, you're in luck — TweetDeck is for the power Twitter user. The main selling points of TweetDeck are the ability to form specific groups of your contacts, integrated Twitter search, and multiple-column interface. Beyond that, you'll find many of the same features as on Twhirl, including the ability to get content from more than one social network (Facebook, for example). TweetDeck is almost too functional for some casual Twitter users, but if you use Twitter frequently, you can't easily beat seeing trending topics in a column or performing a detailed Twitter search right from your desktop. TweetDeck and Twhirl increasingly vie for the top spot as most popular desktop Twitter client, but it's worth noting that approximately half of Twitter use seems to happen right at Twitter.com.

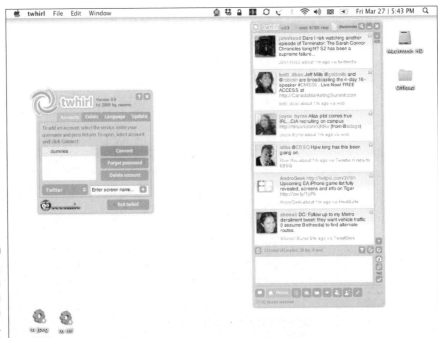

Figure 9-6:
Twhirl has a stylish interface design.

Adobe Air

Most consumer applications, such as Microsoft Word or Adobe Photoshop, need to be written separately for each operating system that they run on. At Microsoft, for instance, two separate teams work on two versions of Microsoft Word: one for Windows, the other for Macintosh.

For smaller companies or independent developers, particularly those that are writing light-weight applications, coding two (or three) versions of the same application can be a huge investment of time. Enter Adobe Air.

Adobe Air is a piece of software you install on your computer that lets you run applications built for the Adobe Air set of standards. Like the programming language Java, Adobe Air aims for the "write once, run everywhere" ideal. That means developers can reach a larger potential audience than if they had to re-create their product over and over to work on different platforms. Many Twitter third-party desktop applications (notably, TweetDeck and Twhirl) are written for Adobe Air. Some software developers actually joke that the main reason to learn to program for Adobe Air is to build a new Twitter client.

Because these applications run on any machine that can run Adobe Air, they function exactly the same across platforms. Anyone who has tried to jump from using Microsoft Word on a Mac to using Microsoft Word on a PC (or vice-versa) can appreciate the beauty of this. Because of Adobe Air's ease of distribution and networking features, programmers often write desktop-based social-networking and messaging clients for Adobe Air.

Installing Adobe Air is not that hard — often, if you try to install an application that requires it, you're instructed to install Adobe Air first. It may even automatically download itself and install on your computer if you give it permission. Just follow the onscreen instructions or go to www. adobe.com/products/air/.

✔ **Spaz (www.funkatron.com/spaz):** A newer Twitter desktop client (shown in Figure 9-7). It's an Adobe Air app that offers many of the same features that Twhirl and TweetDeck do, but Spaz has these added bonuses:

- **Skinnable:** You can customize Spaz by applying what techies call *skins,* frequently by using Cascading Style Sheets (CSS). Skins change the look and feel of the application. Creating and sharing custom skins is a popular thing for programmers to do. Don't worry too much about what this means to you; it just means more choices and options if you want them.

- **Open source:** You may have heard the term *open-source software* and wondered what it meant. Open-source software just means that the code underlying the application is shared with others so that other developers can change it to create new features, build applications for it, or otherwise improve upon it. The makers of Spaz have opened its code to the masses so that developers can change it to fit their needs.

Figure 9-7:
You can
customize
the desktop
client Spaz.

✔ **Twitterrific (www.twitterrific.com):** A Twitter client made for the Mac OS X desktop operating system, with mobile versions for Apple's iPhone or iPod Touch available in the iTunes App Store. Twitterrific is shareware: You can download a free version, but if you choose to support the developers by purchasing the application, you'll avoid the ads on the regular version, and it costs less than $15. And many people swear by Twitterrific's interface and customer service. Twitterrific has the standard gorgeous and streamlined interface most often associated with Macs (as shown in Figure 9-8), as well as the ability to manage more than one Twitter account. But, unlike many other Twitter clients, you can't track other social networks within its interface.

✔ **Digsby (www.digsby.com):** A Windows-only desktop client that combines together many instant-messaging, e-mail, and social-networking accounts, in addition to Twitter — Facebook, LinkedIn, MySpace, AIM, and Yahoo!, to name a few. Figure 9-9 shows the Digsby home page. A version is in the works for the Mac operating system, but it has yet to be released as of this writing. The interface is similar to a universal instant-messaging client such as Pidgin (www.pidgin.im) or Trillian (www.ceruleanstudios.com), but Digsby comes with social networks built in, too.

If you're not on a Windows PC, you can sign up to be notified when they publish a Mac/Linux version of Digsby by going to `www.digsby.com/signup/maclinux`.

Try out a few of the Twitter desktop clients in the preceding list. But if none of the most popular Twitter clients appeal to you, never fear. You can find many Twitter desktop clients out there to choose from. Use Google or another search engine to search for desktop Twitter client, because more and more emerge every day. Again, we're building `www.oneforty.com` to make all of this easier.

Another way to see what clients are popular? Simply look at the end of tweets from people you trust to find out what they use — tweets are *source* tagged with the name of the source client or application that sent them.

Figure 9-8:
A
Twitterrific
desktop
interface.

Figure 9-9:
You can
keep up
with your
Twitter
account
by using
Digsby.

Mobile clients

The most basic way to use Twitter on a mobile phone, smartphone, or PDA is by text messaging (SMS). You simply have to add your mobile device to your Twitter profile, sending tweets to the 40404 short-code, and consequently having them associated with your username if you enable Phone as a delivery option on your Home screen sidebar.

You can also use SMS as a convenient way to receive tweets on your cell-phone because the phone delivery option sends you the tweets of any user for whom you have turned on Notifications. You also receive your direct messages, although not your @replies at the time of writing. But getting so many text messages can be expensive if you don't subscribe to an unlimited texting plan. Because SMS also costs Twitter money, Twitter might eliminate the SMS service in the future to cut costs or begin charging for SMS to offset those costs. To prepare yourself for that possible situation, you may want to invest in a mobile Twitter client.

You can take the easy road if you have a smartphone or PDA that has a decent Web browser and a data plan from your cell carrier. Visit `http://m.twitter.com` for the mostly-functional mobile version of the site.

Or, download one of the following mobile applications and see how amazing Twitter can be when you take it on the road:

- ✔ **For an iPhone:** You can use the Twitterrific (www.twitterrific.com) iPhone app, as well as other apps such as Hahlo (http://hahlo.com) and Tweetie (www.atebits.com/tweetie-iphone). You can find them by searching in the iTunes App Store.

- ✔ **For a BlackBerry:** Your choices are limited, but most BlackBerry users prefer an app called TwitterBerry (www.orangatame.com/products/twitterberry).

- ✔ **For a Java-enabled phone:** TinyTwitter (www.tinytwitter.com) is an excellent choice out of many options. One of the more stable Java applications for the mobile phone, TinyTwitter gives you all the functions that other mobile Twitter clients do, yet it doesn't take up a huge amount of space if your phone doesn't have a lot of room on it for extra applications.

- ✔ **For Windows Mobile–based smartphones and PDAs:** You can find several options out there, but none of them are all that great. Here are several clients for Windows Mobile that you might want to check out:

  - • **Twobile (www.infinitumsoftware.com/twobile):** Users swear by its stability, especially on the often-unstable Windows Mobile operating system. But some users do have issues with the fact that, like the Digsby desktop client (see "Desktop clients," earlier in this chapter), Twobile doesn't display avatars, making it more difficult for you to tell at a glance whether your favorite people and companies on Twitter are talking. If you want a stable option that experiences few crashes, Twobile (shown in Figure 9-10) fits that bill, but the list interface has its problems.

  - • **ceTwit (www.kosertech.com/blog/?page_id=5):** A bit better on the design front than Twobile. It does have avatars associated with the tweets that come through, and you can easily use it, especially if you have a touch screen phone. It doesn't look as pretty as some desktop Twitter clients, but it's fully functional and reasonably stable. Users have reported, however, that it's more crash-prone than Twobile.

  - • **PocketTwit (http://code.google.com/p/pocketwit):** A new contender, which comes from Google Labs, for the touch screen Windows Mobile market. Its slick, fully functional interface (shown in Figure 9-11) operates much like most desktop clients and looks gorgeous. It's still in *beta* (early testing release), so it has some occasional freezes, and you have to be ready to download regular updates. But if you want your mobile client to look and operate just like your desktop client, this one can do the job.

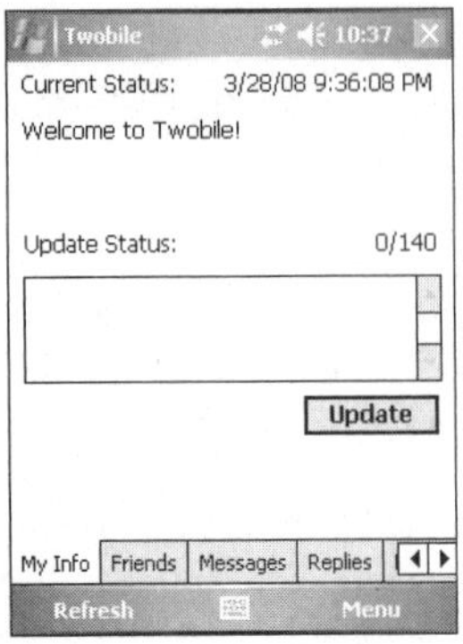

Figure 9-10: You can use Twobile on your Windows Mobile device.

You can use a site called the Twitter Fan Wiki (http://twitter.pbwiki.com/apps) to find out more about Twitter clients, both mobile and desktop. Active Twitter users have written up their favorite Twitter applications and provided links that can point you to the download sites. There are several other directories, but none of them, even the fan wiki, is remaining very current or user-friendly with the fast pace of innovation within the Twitter ecosystem. We sincerely hope to fix that with www.oneforty.com. We'll let you know on www.TwitterForDummies.com how that goes.

Figure 9-11: PocketTwit is a new Windows Mobile device client.

Keeping Your Tweets Short with URL Shorteners

One of the main issues with Twitter is space. The 140-character limit makes it easy to run out of room before you finish what you want to say. Sometimes, you want to show your Twitter network a link to a Web page that you find fascinating or amusing, to a blog post that you wrote or an article about you, or to just about anything on the Web. But those URLs can be quite long, often well over 140 characters themselves.

URL shorteners are extremely easy Web-based applications that take long URLs from Web sites and make them shorter by turning them into coded small URLs that forward the reader to the original linked page. The URL shortener permanently assigns the link to that shortened URL.

Twitter uses TinyURL (`www.tinyurl.com`) as its default URL shortener. If you enter a whole, unshortened URL in the Update window on your Home screen on Twitter.com, Twitter automatically shrinks that URL to a more manageable size by using TinyURL. You don't have to do a thing.

If you're looking to save as many characters as possible, you can use a URL shortener that promises to make your URL fit into the smallest of spaces on Twitter. To use one of these shorteners, copy the URL from the address bar of the Web site that you want to share, and then paste that URL into the input field at the URL shortener site of your choice.

Some URL shorteners offer added services, such as a way to track who's clicking your link in Twitter, how often it's being clicked, and other statistics that you can use to gather data on the effectiveness of your (or your client's) Twitter account:

- **bit.ly (`http://bit.ly`):** Tracks clicks over time, clicks on other shortened versions of the link, where clicks are coming from, key information from the target page, and retweets of the link (even if they use a differently shortened URL)

- **BudURL (`http://budurl.com`):** Tracks the IP address of visitors and how many times your link was clicked

You can find many options by doing a Google search for the term **URL shortener**.

Although new applications come out frequently, bit.ly (`http://bit.ly`) remains our favorite of the URL shortener crowd. bit.ly, shown in Figure 9-12, offers a complete tracking service that lets you see where the URLs you shorten and share are going, and what kind of results they're getting. This application's tracking includes location and metadata, two huge pieces of information that can help you target your audience in a more refined way.

bit.ly also integrates with TweetDeck, and you can set bit.ly to remember your Twitter handle(s). So, unlike other URL shorteners, bit.ly catches your tracking data for you no matter what Twitter interface you use when you post. In Figure 9-13, you can see bit.ly tracking results (how many people clicked and when) for a link that was shortened in bit.ly and then tweeted.

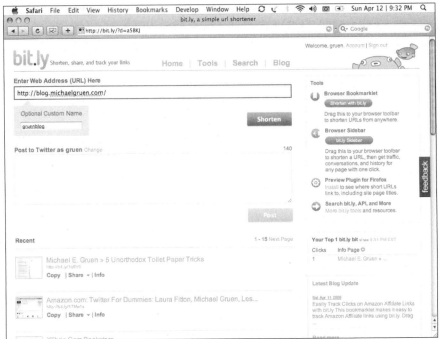

Figure 9-12:
The bit.ly
interface.

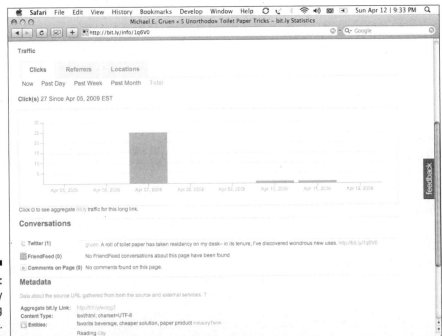

Figure 9-13:
Some bit.ly
tracking
results.

Getting All Your Online Activity in One Place by Using Aggregators

Aggregators are sites that bring all your social-media activity into one place, pulling in your accounts from sites such as Twitter, MySpace, Facebook, YouTube, Flickr, and so on. An aggregator gives you one stop where you can see all your social profiles and all the updates from your friends and colleagues on those services, without having to spend a lot of time clicking from Web site to Web site so that you can keep up with what's going on.

The most buzz-worthy aggregator right now is FriendFeed (`http://friendfeed.com`), shown in Figure 9-14. FriendFeed can pull in accounts from any social network, any blog or Web site that has an RSS feed, photo-sharing sites such as Flickr, social music sites such as Last.fm, social bookmarking sites such as Digg, and more.

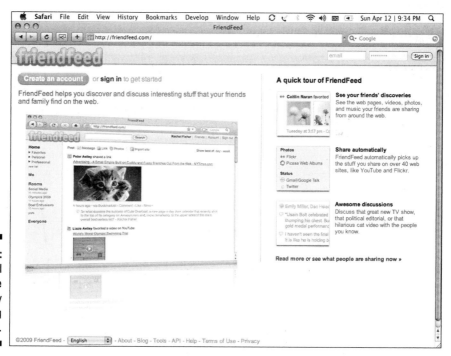

Figure 9-14: Combine all your online activity by using FriendFeed.

Not everyone loves FriendFeed, especially at first. It's pretty complicated. It has some issues with user interface, although a new one just launched as this book went to press. You may find figuring it out a bit difficult. Some people find that putting so many accounts into one place just makes things noisy, and it gets too hard to follow meaningful conversations or keep up with friends. But many active twitterers love FriendFeed because it handles vast amounts of data from both you and your contacts with ease. It also works with Twhirl and Seesmic Desktop, so you can see it right on your desktop Twitter client.

You can find plenty of other aggregators out there, and you can use many of them much more easily (and they look prettier) than FriendFeed, even though they don't necessarily have the hardcore community that FriendFeed does. We kind of like Strands (www.strands.com) but you can also use SocialMedian, SocialThing, Plaxo, Spokeo, and many more. Facebook itself now pulls many third-party services into its News Feed, making that News Feed function very much like an aggregator.

Using Trending Topics to Stay on the Twitter Cutting-Edge

When you use Twitter, you can see topics *trending* (becoming popular) in real time. Twitter Search offers a short list of the top ten or so trending topics by tag word on its main page http://search.twitter.com. TweetDeck offers a column for a tag cloud in its desktop application.

You can most easily keep up with trending topics and popular tag words on Twitter — assuming that you don't have TweetDeck doing it for you — by going back to the Twitter Search home page.

You can also use a service called Twellow (www.twellow.com) to search the latest trending topics and popular tag words. A *tag word* is the same as a hashtag or keyword. It's just a word that people are using frequently to discuss a certain topic or issue.

Trending topics also appear at a service called TweetGrid (www.tweetgrid.com), and on sites such as the Twitter Trending Topics RSS Feed (http://twitter.trends.free.fr). You can also follow the user @TrendingTopics (http://twitter.com/trendingtopics), a bot that claims to track and report live trending tag words on Twitter. Twitter also recently added a Trending Topics button that expands into up-to-the-minute trending keywords and topics when you click it (as shown in Figure 9-15).

Why should you care about trending topics? You can use them to gauge the popularity or success of anything from a specific person to a political theme to a marketing campaign. They can also help you figure out what the Twitterati find newsworthy. Trending topics give you real-time statistics on public appeal.

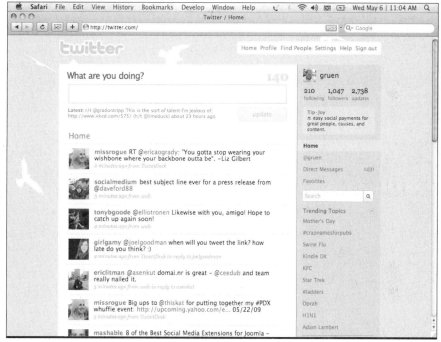

Figure 9-15: You can check out Twitter trends with the Twitter navigation bar.

Playing with Twitter Games and Memes

Hardcore Twitter users are a playful bunch. They've been known to turn the service into a wacky social gaming platform on occasion, such as when Internet sensation Ze Frank organized Color Wars (as shown in Figure 9-16). In the Color Wars, Twitter users joined teams designated by color in a summer-camp-inspired game, and those teams proceeded to complete tasks such as online scavenger hunts and Photoshop challenges.

Figure 9-16:
Color Wars!

You can use Twitter for creative games, as well. TwitStory is a game in which people create a story tweet by tweet, all collaborating on the outcome by adding individual lines. You use other people's tweets, rather than your own, to build the story, fitting unrelated lines together like a puzzle. You can read how TwitStory #3 came out on its creator's blog at `http://andypowe11.net/blog/?cat=10`.

Web sites for Twitter games are popping up. One of the first of these sites is Twoof (`http://twoof.doof.com`), which lets you play interactive games with your Twitter friends. Individuals have also tried to amass people to play a Twitter-enhanced game of Battleship by using the hashtag `#twitships` (`http://www.squidoo.com/battleships-board-game-twitter`), but the game does not appear to be active.

In addition to games, many Twitter users like to use its potential to spread virally, from one person to another, to create *memes* — trends that flow through the Twitter stream with many people participating. Sometimes, users create hashtags to spark discussion, such as `#favoritehappysong` or `#favoritefallfood`. When Twitter users see the hashtag go by in their

Twitter stream, they voice their own opinions, answering the implicit question and tweeting it out with the hashtag attached. You can have fun going back to visit these games in Twitter Search later, and you can also use them to find out a little more about your Twitter connections.

One popular meme that doesn't seem to ever die out is the Overheard meme. You may have noticed a lot of tweets containing OH and wondered, "What's the deal with Twitter and Ohio anyways!?" OH just abbreviates "overheard" and is usually followed by something funny or awkward or even quite horrible. The twitterer is sharing it as if to say, "Can you *believe* this?!" Hear something funny or crazy in real life and want to share it? Just type OH and then put the quip you heard in quotes. Most of the time, you don't use any names, keeping the OH anonymous — it's funnier out of context. Some OH tweets are racy or raunchy, but most are just average things people say that seem funny at the time.

With all the creativity on Twitter and its general fun-loving nature, you may well create your own Twitter game or meme — either just for kicks or even as a marketing strategy. Don't be shy!

Tag Clouds

TwitScoop, Cloudlet, trending topics, and hashtags all have something in common: They all can generate a Twitter *tag cloud,* a visual display of words where the relative size of the word corresponds to how many times it has been mentioned. Tag clouds provide an easy visualization of what's going on in the twitterverse in real time. Words that twitterers are using a lot will appear in the tag cloud, and the more mentions a word gets, the larger, darker, and bolder its display will be as well. It's another, often quite visually appealing, way to see what is really going on.

You may enjoy watching tag clouds. Applications such as Wordle (`www.wordle.net`) even let you play with tag clouds a little so that you can generate graphical representations of whatever your topic is (as shown in Figure 9-17), which you can then use on slides and Web sites. Tag clouds are an interesting way to present what topics and keywords around your subject are interesting to the group at large and can give your presentation or blog entry a little more punch and relevance.

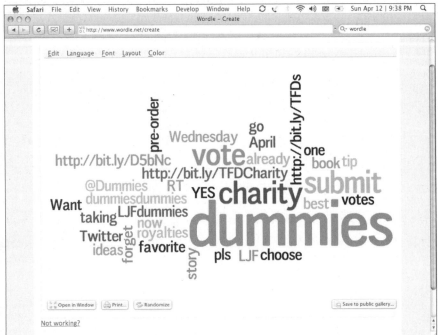

Figure 9-17:
This
Wordle-
generated
tag cloud.

Keeping in Contact with Visualization and Listening Tools

Sure, building connections and influence on Twitter is a great objective, but there is even more value in the Twitter experience when you take the opportunity to tune into what people are saying about you, your company, and your favorite topics. Also, a finely attuned listening program will greatly enhance your ability to build connections and influence on Twitter in the first place.

You can find plenty of tools available that let you track your social media presence. These tools allow you to set it and forget it — you can still find out what's said without actively trawling through Twitter. Many of these tools are free, though you can pay for some tools that come with additional business features like analytics and better organization of search results.

In the following sections, we really only skim the surface of what's possible. But no matter which service you use, make listening a priority for yourself on Twitter. Keeping an ear to the tremendous firehose of information about consumer sentiment and even world events helps and can definitely bear fruit and make effective use of your social media engagement time invested.

Gmail as keymaster

If you don't already have a Gmail address, you really should. Gmail is emerging as a very convenient key to your social media identity, and having a Gmail account is your pass to many valuable, free Google applications and services like Google Alerts. Gmail is free, and as an e-mail service has some of the best spam-blocking, tagging, and message search going.

Your Gmail address is also the key to your Google profile URL, which means that

`PistachioConsulting@Gmail.com` reserves this Google profile for the company: `www.google.com/profiles/PistachioConsulting`.

Remember, you don't have to use your Gmail address as your main e-mail to benefit from having a Gmail account. But you may find more and more uses for it once you test the waters and do a few things with it.

Google Alerts

Setting up some basic Google Alerts, while not a Twitter-specific listening tool, is something every individual and company should do as a minimum social media listening program. The Google Alerts tool trawls the Web, looking for new blog posts, Twitter tweets, and news stories that mention whatever keywords you want to follow, then delivers those posts, tweets, and stories to your Gmail inbox (as shown in Figure 9-18).

To set up a Google Alert:

1. **Log into your Gmail account.**

2. **In the top toolbar, click More.**

   A drop-down menu appears.

3. **Select Even More from the menu.**

   The More Google Products screen appears.

4. **Click the Alerts link, which has a bell to its left.**

   The Google Alerts screen appears.

5. **In the Search Terms field, enter the topic, keyword, name, business name, or phrase that you want to monitor.**

   Doing a Boolean search, such as putting quotes around two words to keep them together, can help you fine-tune your Google Alert results.

6. **From the Type drop-down list, select what kind of search you want to do.**

   We recommend Comprehensive at first, to cover all your possible search bases. If you find it is simply returning too many results for your brand, name, or keywords, you can always scale it back later.

7. **From the How Often drop-down list, select how often you want Google to trawl for results.**

8. **In the Deliver To field, enter your Gmail address.**

   Google delivers the Alerts to this address.

9. **Click the Create Alert button to activate the Google Alert.**

10. **Repeat Steps 5 through 9 for additional Alerts.**

    You can create as many Alert searches as you need.

BLVDStatus

BLVDStatus (www.blvd.status.com) is a new tool that works to help you track who is talking about you on the Internet (see Figure 9-19). It helps you pay attention to people who are using your name, your company name, a brand name, or any keywords you choose. This kind of monitoring and listening tool is a valuable way to keep track of how you, your company, or your product is perceived.

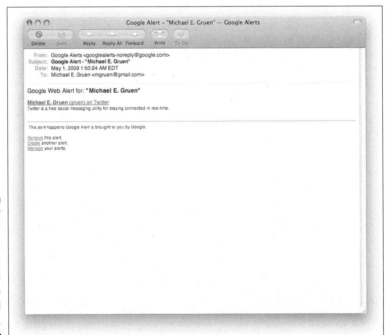

Figure 9-18:
You can have Google Alerts delivered directly to your Gmail inbox.

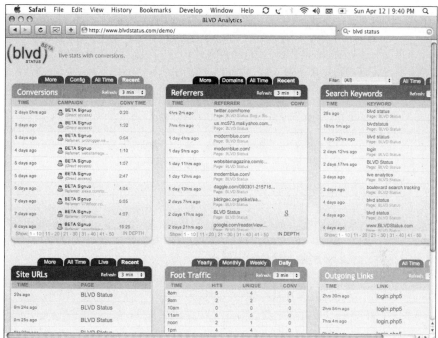

Figure 9-19:
The
BLVDStatus
Stats page.

What does BLVDStatus have to do with Twitter? It's one of the few listening tools out there that lets you incorporate tweets as well as conversations about you found other places on the Web, such as blogs, into something called *conversion tracking*. Conversion tracking means BLVDStatus will help you see which tweets about you led to visits to your site and then go deeper to filling out a contact form or ordering a product. It helps you see real results from your online involvement, and it takes you to a level a bit deeper than a simple Google Alert.

BLVDStatus displays these results in an attractive and easy-to-read set of *widgets* (colorful squares full of information you ask for, sorted how you wish to see it). The most interesting things about BLVDStatus is that it offers a free version that is valuable, offers real results you can customize, and is comparable to a larger, paid tracking company.

Twitter Search

Twitter's own Twitter Search (http://search.twitter.com) allows you to figure out how people are interacting with you and what they're saying about you on Twitter. You can track all mentions of your name, whether or not those mentions have an @ in front of them, by setting up a search and then bookmarking that search for later. If you leave the search tab open, its results automatically refresh every few moments. We have several book-marked searches set up for our names, company names, and for any topics we are currently working on. You can also subscribe to the results of any search using RSS (see Chapters 4 and 8).

To set this kind of inclusive Twitter search:

1. **Go to Twitter Search (`http://search.twitter.com`).**

2. **In the search box, enter your search terms.**

   If you want to get fancy and you know how to use search strings, you can search terms like this:

   -from:dummies dummies OR dummys, replacing "dummies" with the term for which you want to search.

3. **Click the Search button.**

   Your search results appear. Figure 9-20 shows the results for the example Dummies search string.

4. **Bookmark the search using your favorite bookmarking feature, program or Web site.**

5. **Repeat Steps 2 through 4 for as many search terms as you want to track.**

Radian6

We recommend Radian6 (`www.radian6.com`), a paid monitoring service, for a large corporation that needs to track multiple campaigns on a national or international scale, or for a company that doesn't have the manpower to set up and track multiple free searches on a variety of tools. Figure 9-21 shows the Radian6 Web site.

Radian6 offers some functionality that free search monitoring services don't, such as tracking, graphs, analysis, and the ability to assign specific tweets to team members for followup. Radian6 offers the results in an easy-to-interpret, aesthetically pleasing, real-time package. It also offers superb real-time cus-tomer service, if you need assistance.

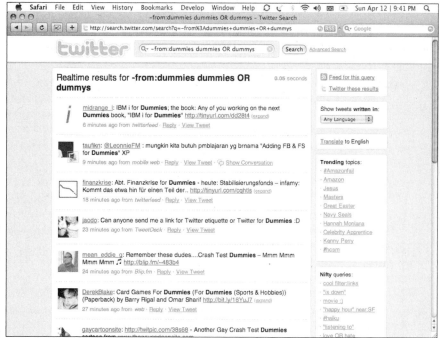

Figure 9-20:
Twitter
Search
results for
a Dummies
string.

Figure 9-21:
You can
download
Radian6
from its
Web site.

Knowing Your Network with Follower and Following Tools

While your Twitter universe grows and grows, you probably want to find the best way possible to keep up with your followers and who you're following. Twitter itself falls short in this area. For some reason, Twitter doesn't offer a way to search your follower or following lists (which you can see in Figure 9-22). It also doesn't offer a way to sort your followers alphabetically or navigate in any way more efficient than the slow page-by-page scan.

You can quickly find out whether someone is following you back by trying to send that user a direct message. If you're on the Twitter Web interface's DM update screen, that twitterer's username appears in the drop-down list only if he follows you back. If you're on a desktop client, you can try to direct message that user — if he doesn't follow you, you get a message telling you so.

Figure 9-22:
Twitter lets you see who's following you (left) and whom you follow (right).

Networking is by far one of the most powerful uses that anyone can make of Twitter. But, finding interesting people, maintaining your network, and digging in to really understand who you are connected to are not always straightforward. Here are some tools that will improve your networking experience on Twitter:

✔ **Find your followers.** You can use sites such as Twitter Karma and FriendorFollow to check and compare who follows you and whom you follow, and to keep up with those people you want to add to your follow list. You can use these kinds of services to check out your followers and to double-check that you're following the people who are important to you:

• **FriendorFollow (http://friendorfollow.com):** Came onto the Twitter scene more recently than Twitter Karma, and its interface is a little bit easier to understand. The FriendorFollow interface tells you who your mutual follows are, whom you follow without being followed back, and who follows you without you following them back. You can then pick and choose whom to follow and whom to stop following. FriendorFollow connections don't automatically opt you into individuals' device updates, so it's okay to use the tool to connect to many people, even if you have device updates turned on for your account.

- **Twitter Karma (www.dossy.org/twitter/karma):** Offers you a way to see whom you follow, who follows you, and which users both follow you and are followed by you. You can also use Twitter Karma to add followers, as well as remove users whom you no longer want to follow. But Twitter Karma tends to select Notifications On as the default setting when you add a new follower from Twitter Karma's interface, so be sure to double- check that user's profile if you don't want to receive her notifications by text message.

✓ **Find new people to follow.**

- **We Follow (www.wefollow.com):** User-generated Twitter directory launched by Digg Founder Kevin Rose at SXSW in April 2009. Associates up to three hashtags with each twitterer who lists themselves in the directory and then presents the most followed individuals and accounts for each category. Because the results are searched by follower numbers, it's a particularly good way to find the top celebrities, musicians, journalists, politicians, and so on who are using Twitter at any given time.

- **Twellow (www.twellow.com):** Structured like a Yellow Pages for Twitter, allows you to find new followers based on category, name, location, or trending topics. If a Twitter user has been active long enough to have a few tweets on the record, as well as a bio, you can find him on Twellow. If you search for yourself on Twellow, you can claim your profile, meaning that you contact Twellow and prove that you are you in order to get editing privileges for it, and then tweak it to categorize yourself so that others can find you based on your interests, services, or professional categories.

- **Twitter (http://search.twitter.com or your Home screen):** We'd be remiss not to remind you here that you can find new people to follow on Twitter itself in three useful ways. Twitter's people search function is ironically the weakest. Even to find a specific individual that you know to be on Twitter, you're often better off searching Google for his first and last names and the word Twitter. Twitter also offers a list of suggested users, and while there has been some controversy around who gets to be on that list and who does not, it includes some pretty interesting accounts and is worth browsing. But to *really* fine-tune your interests, periodically search Twitter itself for tweets about topics close to your heart and unique amongst your interests. You never know who you might find. Click on a user's name in any tweet he's written and peruse his last page or so of tweets. You get a surprisingly good feel for who they are as a person that way. It's very cool.

- **100TWT (`http://100twt.com`):** This site simply combines the streams of the 100 most-followed Twitter accounts. So while it overlaps heavily with the Suggested Users list, it does a nice job of letting you skim random tweets from the Twitter heavyweights in a combined screen. Poke around from time to time, and you may notice some cool ideas coming from equally cool people.

✔ **Find users by location.** TwitterLocal (`www.twitterlocal.net`) used to use Twitter's XMPP feed to show what users were in what locations. Because Twitter has its XMPP feed switched off for the time being, TwitterLocal is offered only as a downloadable Adobe Air application you can use to view tweets by location. You can also try several other good sites for finding local twitterers:

- Hubspot's TwitterGrader returns lists of the top graded twitterers for given cities (`http://twitter.grader.com/top/cities`).

- Twellow's Twellowhood feature (`www.twellow.com/twellowhood/`) lets you find twitterers by city using a zoomable map.

- LocalTweeps (`www.localtweeps.com`) lets twitterers sign themselves up by tweeting their zip code publicly.

✔ **Back up your data.** Tweetake (`http://tweetake.com`) offers you a way to back up your Twitter data, including your follower and following lists, so that you don't lose the data if Twitter ever crashes. The initial backup takes quite a long time, so be prepared to wait a little while.

✔ **Find out when you lose followers.** TwitterLess (`www.twitterless.com`) and Qwitter (`http://useqwitter.com`) are two tools that alert you when someone stops following you. Depending on your outlook or your reason for using Twitter, you may want to know when you lose followers — but this information can also be quite the blow to your ego.

It's just not encouraging feedback, and it's a waste of energy to try to "determine" why someone left your stream. These tools are very much against the spirit of Twitter, where unsubscribing is really just a personal choice about the consumption of content, not a personal affront or rejection of the friendship. Laura has many business and personal contacts that don't happen to be interested in the way she uses Twitter. It's really no big deal. It's probably not even a good idea to use these quitting services, especially as some are set up to imply that a certain tweet caused the unfollow. Use with caution!

⮡ **Watch Twitter unfold, on a map of the world.** You can use a mash-up application called Twittervision (`http://twittervision.com`) that displays the activity on Twitter in real time on a Google map. When each tweet comes in, it's associated with the actual, physical location from which it came, as well as the specific Twitter user, on a live, constantly updating map. Twittervision is certainly not an efficient way to find new people to follow, but it can be entrancing to watch. We've heard that someone who viewed the display at the Museum of Modern Art stared for a very long time and came away pretty breathless, saying, "I've seen God." Far be it from us to pass judgment on anyone's sense of reverence. It's enough to say, you may find it kind of fun and mystifying to watch. Just don't expect "utility" from it, per se.

You can take it with you

Depending on how you use Twitter, having your own copy of your tweets, relationships, and conversations may be a mere nicety, or it may have some very real economic and or emotional value to you. Laura frequently mentions her children's milestones or captures meaningful moments in her life through her tweets.

One of the areas of likely innovation in the Twitter ecosystem is better publishing tools. You can take your unwieldy stream of tweets and extract out a few key moments, perhaps embellishing them with the videos and photos you linked to, or visual display of the conversations you were having at the time. Personal scrapbooks or *annual reports* (see Nicholas Feltron's work) could be a really nice thing to have personally.

For a business, this kind of recordkeeping has even more obvious value — having the data in a format that you can search, parse, and analyze will come to be a business necessity as more and more types of business interactions take place on Twitter. We become what we measure, and measuring effectiveness will be a crucial reason to be able to get a copy of your Twitter data.

Part IV
Knowing Why We Twitter

In This Part . . .

In this part, we ask the big questions: Why are you on Twitter? As a business, how can you use Twitter to build and stabilize your brand? As a not-for-profit, what can you do to make people evangelize your cause? What should you say? Whom should you talk to?

We answer these question and more in this part, and we promise we won't put you through an existential crisis.

Chapter 10

Finding Your Tweet Voice

*I*f you let it, Twitter can conveniently become an integral part of your day-to-day life. Twitter is available almost everywhere — you can update your Twitter feed many ways on many platforms. Wherever you have Internet or cellular coverage, you can more or less use Twitter. The mechanics are pretty easy.

But as you get up to speed and even "embrace the twecosystem," writing and sharing in only 140 characters at a time definitely takes some getting used to. It may seem a bit limiting at first, but over time that limitation changes the way you write and communicate. If you plan to use the service with some regularity, you'll probably want to think at least a little bit about how your updates compare with the image you want to convey.

In this chapter, we explore different approaches to using Twitter and how you can find your own unique voice.

Finding Your Voice, Whether for Business or Pleasure

When you first sign up for a Twitter account, you don't follow anyone yet, and nobody follows you. Updating your feed may seem a bit awkward. You're tweeting into the void, you have no idea who's really listening (if anyone), and you're almost certainly wondering what the heck the point of tweeting even is. Don't feel bad — most everyone's first tweet (see Figure 10-1) is a little awkward. But if you follow our advice, you should be able to get the hang of Twitter in no time!

Figure 10-1:
Michael's
example
first tweet.

When you start following users and other users start following you, you may want to think about what sort of things you want to share with your following. For many new users, one of the great debates is whether to use Twitter for business or pleasure, and we address that a lot in this chapter. You might have joined Twitter for either reason (or both). As you come to embrace the medium to its fullest, you will find yourself figuring out what kind of voice you want to use on Twitter. The answer, as with so many answers about Twitter, depends entirely on what you want to get out of the Twitter experience.

Part of determining your identity on Twitter involves choosing your username (which we cover in Chapter 2). If you choose a nickname or pseudonym for your username, you probably aim for Twitter personal use. If you use your business name as your Twitter handle, you likely intend to create a presence for your company. But if you use your real name as your username (which is probably the best way to go), it simply implies that you are who you say you are — and you can take your account in the direction that makes the most sense to you as you evolve. That's one reason why you probably want to use your real name or some variation of it.

Whatever name you pick, you can change it at any time on your Twitter account's Settings page. We explain how to make this change in Chapter 2.

No matter what you name your Twitter presence, you need a voice and personality that's uniquely yours. We go over some tips and thoughts on how to make your Twitter voice your own in the section "You as you on Twitter," later in this chapter.

Your business on Twitter

Can you use something as simple as Twitter for business? Absolutely! However, you can't exactly adopt the usual salesperson "Sell! Sell! Sell!" mentality on Twitter. To operate as a successful business presence on Twitter:

- ✔ Master the art of give and take.
- ✔ Figure out how to engage your Twitter base in conversation.
- ✔ Give your audience, clients, and customers a reason to read your tweets.

Twitter is a conversational medium, and for businesses to mesh well with user expectations, companies and businesses need to understand how to navigate the landscape as a brand. You can read about strategies and case studies in Chapter 11 (no bankruptcy pun intended).

If you're representing a large company (such as @JetBlue or @Starbucks), your Twitter presence might be a little more complicated because you're not representing just yourself, but your business — and for some companies, that may mean tens of thousands of people. That's a lot of responsibility!

If you're managing a Twitter presence on behalf of your company, we highly encourage you to start a separate account for yourself so that you can get used to the service. Before you start tweeting on behalf of your business, know what users expect from brands and businesses, and how customers like to be approached. Getting used to how businesses operate on Twitter can prevent you from making a serious faux pas down the road. That said, a lot of what makes the best business accounts great is their personality and humanity, so the case can also be made not to always have two different (business and personal) accounts.

In Chapter 11, we go over how businesses can best take advantage of Twitter.

You as you on Twitter

Although Twitter can be a powerful tool for business owners and employees, it's just as powerful for individuals who really have no intention of conducting any sort of business on it (although business might happen accidentally).

Twitter was originally popular helping individuals keep in touch with their friends and acquaintances via mini-updates. Many personal Twitterers still tend to use Twitter in this manner, updating a close circle of friends about thoughts and happenings in their lives. Over time, you can keep up with — and even make new — friends you might otherwise not contact often. Twitter removes many communication barriers.

A few things to consider for your personal Twitter presence:

- ✔ **Keeping your tweets private:** If it helps you feel more comfortable with your personal use of Twitter, you can set your updates to Private. (We show how to adjust that setting in Chapter 2.) Enabling the privacy feature ensures that no one, other than the users you authorize, has access to your updates. However, setting your updates to Private also prevents Twitter Search from picking up your tweets; it's a minor inconvenience that you may be willing to accept if you really feel strongly about protecting your personal updates from the world.

- ✔ **Introducing your business:** Regardless of whether you plan to build your business by using Twitter "just as a person," you might want to include some information about your occupation and company in your Twitter profile, and perhaps add a link back to your company's online presence. The *social capital* (trust, thought leadership, and more) that you earn within the Twitter community may lead to new opportunities for you and for your business. Also, your opinions and statements may be biased because of your job, so in the interests of transparency, disclosure is a good idea.

- ✔ **Making it personal:** You don't have to include any business information on Twitter if you don't want to. Twitter was built with personal connections in mind. Twitter is personal, so dress up your profile and adjust your settings in a way that makes sense to you and what you want to get out of your Twitter experience.

If you're twittering as an individual who works at a company, use a real photo of yourself as your avatar and put your company logo on the Twitter background that you use for your page. By using this setup, you let people know that you're affiliated with the company, but users don't mistake you for the company's official twitterer. Be sure you follow your company's regulations regarding what you're allowed to share. For example, many Apple employees can't reveal that they work for the company.

Mixing business with pleasure

Some of the most successful Twitter personalities have embraced Twitter by transparently sharing personal, professional, family, and other aspects of themselves all rolled together. This is nothing wildly new. We've always spent time with colleagues, clients, and our professional network at the golf course, out to dinner, attending charity events, and the like. Most networking events have a highly social component to them. It's simple: People like to do business with people they like.

Some find balancing your personal life and your professional life on Twitter tricky at first, but you can definitely do it. Give yourself time to discover what you're comfortable doing. We don't really know anyone who completely stops talking about work when out with friends — or vice versa — because work (whether we like it or not) is a big part of who we all are. Because Twitter is built for human communications, it can handle many facets of your life; you just have to find your own balance.

It's all about balance

Balance is important on Twitter, as in life, if you want to connect with people in a genuine, mutually beneficial way. Twitter is a pretty "what you give is what you get" kind of a place. Your true voice is often the best bet, unless you're really constrained for business reasons and need to rein it in. Accounts that are nothing but business (or worse, strictly business-promotional) all the time may have a pretty hard time growing much of an engaged base.

Want to be uber-personal all the time? There is absolutely nothing wrong with that, but it will influence the size and shape of your network. Don't be offended if it's not everybody's cup of tea. Present yourself the way you feel most comfortable.

If you cover both business and personal stuff on your account but aren't an official "for the business" twitterer, it can be good to go easy on how frequently you tweet about business-only stuff. We get asked for a specific ratio all the time, and it's really hard to say. As car ads say, "Your mileage will vary." Try a mix that's comfortable to you and then just see whether you're getting the results you hoped for. Also, please remember, the number of followers is much less important than the quality of the conversations. For long-term sustainable value, true engagement beats tonnage any day.

 If you're updating under your business handle (for us, it's @dummies), followers probably expect that nearly all tweets from that account will relate to that business. After all, they're following that account for business info! If you're really inconsistent, off-topic, or overboard personally all the time, and violate your followers' expectations too much, you may find your audience shrinking. Everyone needs to strike a balance, but most successful brand accounts stay relatively on topic. If you're an individual twitterer, followers probably want to hear about you and how you're going about your business. It's a subtle difference but an important point to establish yourself as genuine, and not a selfish peddler of goods.

Your goal should be to permit your followers to get a good understanding of what your business offers and come to trust you as who you are. Make the bulk of the content that you add to Twitter about you and the value that you provide (as a person and through your work). Think of some updates as "give" and other updates as "take": When you share or talk about things that are genuinely useful and helpful to customers, you're providing something they want. That sets the stage for occasionally promoting the goods or services that you sell, because you've earned the trust and attention of your readers. Just remember that promotional tweets that aren't framed from the perspective of your customer's needs too often come across as a "take" because you're asking for followers to buy what you're selling.

Want to know if the balance you strike is effective? Re-read your tweets at the end of the day or the end of the week and keep an eye on replies, re-tweets, the numbers of people clicking links you share, and, yes, follower growth. If you feel that your update stream comes off as too sales-y, then back off on the selling and stick to providing value. Twitter's about being a genuine individual. Over time, Twitter gives your followers a lot of information about you, who you are and what you represent. That builds trust, confidence, and interest in you. Be real.

Be yourself

Like with the individual and business-only accounts, be sure to give your name in your bio. Transparency about who you are and what you do can go a long way toward growing your Twitter foundation. And a good Twitter foundation is key to establishing a stable and growing Twitter network. Using your real name adds to your value as an individual.

Just as in other business interactions, you need to be genuine on Twitter and establish yourself as a trustworthy, multidimensional person.

At the same time, think carefully about how much of your private matters you want to share. Occasional mention of your love life, health, and other more personal stuff can be very funny, very humanizing, and very honest, but being really negative, self-indulgent, or tedious about the same will put people off. When you really need to talk about those things, it's very possible you'll find supportive people on Twitter. Having found something in common or someone who wants to help, you may even get into a more in-depth conversation with a twitterer via DM or leave Twitter altogether via e-mail, IM, or over your favorite beverage. You can also definitely connect with people on more public personal topics like sports, TV, books, movies, or politics without revealing all your deepest secrets.

As a person on Twitter, you might find value in talking about your business problems in the open. Many fellow twitterers are willing to give you advice about how to overcome a business challenge or situation. If you've spent time cultivating a network that works for you, you have many resources at your fingertips. Ask them!

Identifying Your Audience

Whether you're a business or an individual on Twitter, if you want to grow your Twitter network, it's helpful to think about your audience. If you haven't transplanted your existing social networks onto Twitter, it may be a good time to do that and to put a bit of time and effort into expanding your network.

Think about the kinds of people you'd like to talk to or the subjects you'd like to discuss through Twitter. Trying to build up business? Target your customers. Want to communicate with other avid cyclists on Twitter? Search keywords and look to see who tweets about major cycling events. Send updates that are relevant to whomever you'd like to reach or about the topics that interest you and engage yourself in that conversation. Yes, it's that easy.

When you start using Twitter, it's pretty hard to determine who your audience will be — your followers grow based on what value you can provide for other users. So, if you're trying to reach other cyclists to talk about racing, the Tour de France, or the latest in derailleur technology, start talking about it and search for other users already chatting about the subject. (You can find out about searching for users and topics in Chapters 5 and 9.)

You don't have to be one-dimensional in your Twitter chat — if you want to engage cyclists, you don't always and only have to talk about cycling. People understand that you have more to you than a single activity or idea (unless you're a company or targeted Twitter account, for which the implicit rules are a little different — see "Your business on Twitter," earlier in this chapter), so don't feel that you need to talk about only one thing to be of value to your target audience. Be yourself and talk about the things you like; but, if you want to engage other cyclists, just talk a bit more about cycling than anything else. That's all. Over time, your cycling network will grow.

Viewing your network

Although you have little direct control over who follows you, you can easily see what sort of user you're attracting. Browse through your list of Followers and click through to open some of their profiles to get a general idea of who's following you (on any Twitter screen, click the Followers link under your name in the sidebar).

When you look into who's following you, you might realize that you're drawing unexpected people as followers. Reaching people and businesses you never expected to reach is most likely not a bad thing. If you're a business, unpredicted followers could show that you're increasing your business's social reach, meaning a sign of successful Twitter use. If you're twittering as an individual, you're broadening your horizons — and other users consider you and your tweets interesting.

Diversifying your network

You can help guide who tends to follow you by talking about a myriad of topics. People aren't one-dimensional, and no one really expects you to be on-point all the time. Although you may have interests that you talk about more than others, getting a sense of what you're talking about and whom you're talking to can come in handy — it enables you to target your tweets to topics that are most interesting to your followers.

One of our favorite tools for understanding how often and what you're updating is TweetStats (www.tweetstats.com). This tool enables you to see who you're talking to, when you're talking, and what you're talking about — all in graph form. Figure 10-2 shows an example of the type of information TweetStats reports.

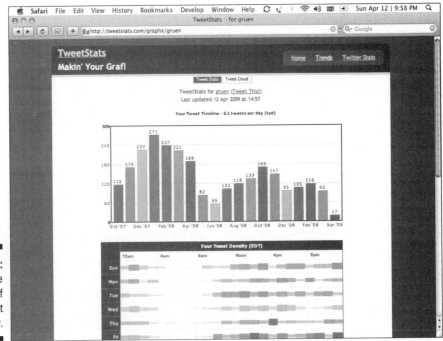

Figure 10-2:
You can see a graph of your tweet density.

Targeting specific networks

If you're targeting specific people with whom you want to interact more regularly, find a way to add value to the interactions for them. You can target these types of people by searching keywords and hashtags for that topic and seeing who uses them and who the real leaders appear to be. Once you're following a few key people within that interest area, look for whom they talk to, listen to, and value. For example, if you're a gardener, check to see who Martha Stewart (@MarthaStewart) follows and talks to about gardening topics. Click through any appealing @replies and consider following those people. You can also use this information to get a sense of what's important to any given twitterer and what types of information they like to receive. With Twitter, you can essentially browse not only the connections between people, but also between topics of interest. You can also easily drop into active ongoing conversations about specific themes. One or two key people can lead you to an entire subject matter landscape on Twitter.

In a very real sense, an individual or Twitter account that represents something can become the foundation for a community. Likewise, if you're trying to target a specific type of individual, go to the Twitter streams of those individuals and see what they're tweeting about. Join the conversation that they're having with other people and engage those other people, as well. Over time, if you're adding value to that conversation, then other people look to you as a person who's involved and relevant in that community, whether it's computer programming, baking cupcakes, or cancer research.

Measuring influence

While you start to gain a foothold within communities on Twitter, you might want to get a sense of what your network looks like and how far your updates travel.

As you read, please bear in mind that some of the less measurable results are the most important. The most important thing to measure is the thing you're actually trying to accomplish, not just numbers for numbers' sake. Are you meeting new friends? Finding new business leads? Sharing information widely about issues important to you?

Do your messages spread? In her keynotes, Laura argues that messages can be much more important influencers within Twitter than influential accounts and individuals, because good messages get repeated. A truly great message, even if it starts in quiet little corners of Twitter among people with small following networks, will echo and get repeated until eventually it reaches much of the network.

Twitter itself has a very primitive way of measuring your reach: You have following and followers counts. Although those numbers would seem to provide a good baseline for understanding how far your updates go and to whom, they don't say much about what types of people follow you and how influential those followers are. In response, the Twitter community has developed a number of tools to help gauge and measure influence and reach. Less ethical people aggressively boost their follower numbers, sometimes through questionable habits like following people just until they follow back and then dropping them to go follow someone else. Important lessons? Don't automatically trust an account with a really high number of followers. Don't build your network around high numbers at the cost of high relevance and high engagement.

Twinfluence (www.twinfluence.com), shown in Figure 10-3, and TwitterGrader (http://twitter.grader.com), shown in Figure 10-4, can help you figure out how you compare with other users, but even they use fairly arbitrary measures. You can also use these sites to determine who the popular users are in your geographical location.

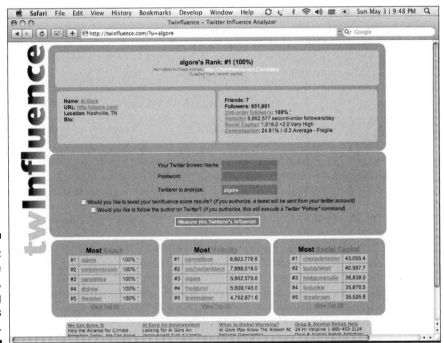

Figure 10-3:
Twinfluence stats, showing @algore's popularity.

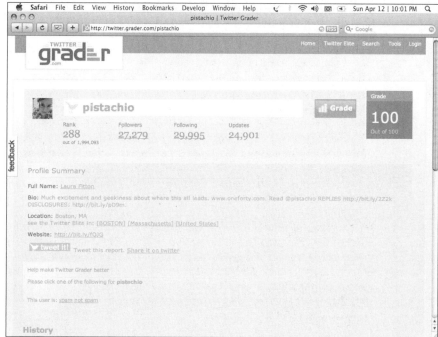

Figure 10-4:
Twitter-
Grader,
suggesting
the humble
@pista-
chio's
visibility.

For all intents and purposes, these numbers don't really measure influence or reach. The results you can get from these sites are so imprecise and subjective that they provide only a rough understanding of how influence flows through the Twitter ecosystem. First and foremost, use Twitter to communicate; and, although high follower counts may indicate genuine popularity, they can be gamed and don't necessarily indicate importance or quality. Laura goes so far as to say, "The most important, influential person in your Twitter stream is you; be proactive about your life."

Understanding your extended network

Twitter, by itself, can tell you only the number of people you follow and the number of people who follow you. As described in the previous section, those numbers give you just part of the story.

If 100 people follow you and communicate with you, then your actual extended network is much larger than 100 people because conversations relay messages and connect new people on Twitter. Say that Follower #86 has 1,000 followers. Whenever Follower #86 mentions your name, 1,000 people receive an update that contains your name. And you may find that kind of exposure quite useful. Twitter is an excellent way to "harness the power of loose ties" or benefit from friends of friends of friends who are more likely to know about things nobody in your social group knows.

If Boston-based Laura was trying to locate a venue in Nashville, Tennessee, to hold a Twitter marketing seminar, she might send an update that reads, "Trying to locate a good 700-person venue in Nashville to give a talk. A place to stay would be nice, too. Suggestions?" Because thousands of people read Laura's Twitter stream, chances are good someone lives in Nashville. If any of those handful wanted to connect Laura with a local business owner, they might ask their own networks, who may have an answer based on their own geography. In this sense, Laura's primary network gives her secondary access to all her follower's networks, as well.

It's pretty cool how friends of friends can end up becoming your direct friends, too. Say you're following five friends, and two of them are constantly communicating (via @replies) with some other person whom you don't know. Out of curiosity, you may start following that other person just to make sense of your friends' conversations. Because you're friends with two people that the other person talks to frequently, he follows you back. Now, all of a sudden, you have both a larger Twitter network and extended network.

Although finding new and interesting people in your Twitter network happens organically, the Twitter community has come up with a couple of tools to help grow your network in a way that's relevant to you. You can browse interesting tags for people in the Twitter directory www.wefollow.com that Digg CEO Kevin Rose (@kevinrose) started in spring 2009, or the service www.MrTweet.com (@mrtweet), a program that combs your Twitter network and recommends new people for you to follow. In our experience, Mr. Tweet is pretty accurate in automatically finding people who are relevant in scope to what you talk about and what your network looks like. Give it a try!

Keeping Your Tweets Authentic

Because of the frequency and personal nature of what people share on Twitter, any twitterer absolutely must be genuine and real, whether she's representing a business or tweeting as an individual. Joining Twitter as a private citizen is the route many users take, even if they have business to promote. Twitter is ideally suited for personal connection, and you can often more easily make yourself accessible and personable when you use Twitter as a person, not as your business.

Joining the conversation

You see the phrase "join the conversation" bandied about a lot on Twitter. If you're representing a business, you can get a dialog going very easily: Just search for users who have mentioned your products or the types of problems you solve and follow them. If you have something relevant to say, engage them in conversation using the mention they made as a starting point.

We go over how businesses should approach using Twitter in Chapter 11, so read through it to avoid any complications or Twitter faux pas. Singling users out and asking them questions may be appropriate for some products, but that approach may be completely inappropriate for others. Twitter's just another engagement point for your communications, marketing, and public relations, so know the rules of the road before you start driving too fast.

If you're representing a business, mentioning little-known facts or interesting things about what you do or sell can start a conversation. You can also talk about your staff; tell interested twitterers how you (or someone else) make what you sell; or take the easiest route of all and ask your fellow Twitter users what they think of your product or service, and how they think you can improve or expand.

Sharing links

By way of getting started, many new users start sharing links with a bit of commentary on their Twitter stream, as shown in Figure 10-5. For many users, sending a link provides a great way to get a commentary started about something you find interesting. Give it a shot and see what happens. Here are the basics for sharing links. (You'll probably want to use a link shortener most of the time, though. Review Chapter 9 for a refresher on how to do that.)

1. **Copy the link's URL and paste it in the What Are You Doing? box.**

2. **Type a comment about the link in the What Are You Doing? box (either before or after the link).**

3. **Post your tweet by clicking the Update button.**

   Usually after you post the tweet, Twitter shortens the URL for you using TinyURL.

Some users post a lot of links — some users like to use RSS or other tools to automatically update their Twitter streams with links to interesting articles that they're reading. Others just post links by hand.

Figure 10-5:
This update
comments
on a link and
includes
that link.

Linking to interesting articles changes the way that your Twitter audience perceives you. Remember, people follow you because you add value to their Twitter streams; but if you flood your stream with links that aren't relevant to your audience, you may start to annoy some of your following. By adding a link to a tweet that you post, you draw attention to the targeted Web page, photo or video, and you're implicitly endorsing it as a good use of your followers' time. Abusing that assumption will erode the interest and trust your followers have in you and reduce the effectiveness of your network.

If you do a lot of linking, review Chapter 9 so that you can track links like a pro. By using tools such as bit.ly (`http://bit.ly`), you can find out which Twitter users are linking to the same articles, which is a great way to start a conversation.

Image is everything

Your update stream is by far the most important part of your Twitter profile. However, your profile's presentation also needs to reflect something about you. In the same way that you wear a nice set of clothes to a job interview, you want to dress up your profile so that it reflects the image that you want to convey to the world.

Although you may have your update stream protected in your Twitter account's settings, anyone in the world can view your Twitter profile (at `http://twitter.com/`*yourusername*). Be sure that you're comfortable with the world seeing whatever you put in your profile.

Whether you're a business or a private citizen, your followers and potential followers react much more favorably if you include in your Twitter profile a photo of yourself and a link to something about you. People like to know who they're talking to, and when you present an image that reflects who you are, other people become willing to be honest and open with you.

If you're representing a large, iconic brand on Twitter, you can do your Twitter profile in your corporate colors. However, because Twitter's strength is in personal connections, you need to have actual people representing your brand's Twitter presence. Use a service such as CoTweet (`http://cotweet.com`), shown in Figure 10-6, to mark each tweet with its author, and in the 160-character bio on Twitter.com, let readers know who each set of initials belongs to.

Too many team members to list? You can show them off in your background graphic the way @CoTweet itself does. (*Note:* In the interest of full disclosure, Laura is an adviser for @CoTweet.) Check out Chapter 11 for more recommendations on the best ways for businesses to tweet.

Figure 10-6:
You can "sign" Tweets by author by using CoTweet.

Being genuine

Authentic people and businesses, using Twitter in a real and interactive way, can experience tremendous growth and return on investment from Twitter because they make real contributions and build up a rich base of trust, influence, and social capital. People respond much better to an authentic, human voice. They engage more closely because they feel comfortable responding, retweeting, and otherwise paying attention to the genuine voice. Bring some value to the twitterverse by adding your authentic contributions, whatever those may be.

For example, if you're tweeting about politics, whether you're a conservative, moderate, liberal, apathetic, or whatever, feel free to agree or disagree with someone — Twitter is, after all, a digital extension of real life, so if you want to engage in that type of dialog, be yourself. Don't try to come off as something you're not just to appeal to people.

If you're representing a business or tweeting on behalf of your company, you probably want to avoid politics, religion, sex, and other hot-button topics, so as not to offend your potential customers.

Your update stream speaks volumes about you. Twitter is a network built on trust and relationships, and being insincere jeopardizes the quality and effectiveness of your network, both on- and offline. You lose some of that hard-won trust that you've been building since you joined Twitter.

Even though you want to be genuine and real at all times, remember that you can easily forget to be nice to people behind the safety of a monitor and keyboard thousands of miles away. Treat others with respect, as you hope to be treated, and you can have a positive online experience. Try not to engage in arguments over petty things — this behavior gets you branded as a troll, and people start to avoid you and stop taking you seriously. (Get the scoop on trolls in the sidebar "Don't feed the trolls," in this chapter.)

Evangelizing your causes

When you're on Twitter as an individual, if you share a favorite cause or a local event in a way that makes it interesting to others, you'll attract those with common interests. They may get involved and show support, and the more fellow twitterers know about you and about the things you have in common, the more connections and ideas will flow in your network.

Don't feed the trolls

In Internet parlance, a *troll* is someone who intentionally posts messages to upset people — for example, making rude and insulting comments on someone's blog or replying to someone's tweets with personal attacks.

Because so many conversations happen so quickly on Twitter, sometimes about touchy subjects, users need to be on the lookout for others who insist on asking inappropriately-charged questions, saying questionable things to users, and otherwise being a poor citizen of the Internet. Because Twitter's a network based on trust, you can often easily identify trolls and block them. (We cover how to block users in Chapter 3.)

You feed the trolls by acknowledging their existence and allowing them to take control of the dialog. Just ignore them, and they eventually get bored and go away. (If you block them, you may reduce your chances of having to hear from them again, but that's a pretty aggressive move

if they're simply annoying. They can still view your public profile — assuming you haven't protected your tweets — and they can even still reply to you if they want, which will show up on your Mentions tab in the sidebar, but they have to make a real effort to do that, because your tweets won't show up in their timeline if you block them.)

On the other side of the coin, some people get a little intimidated by the thought of tweeting about something serious. Some people actually decide to not even try Twitter because they worry that they don't have anything interesting to say! We promise, whatever you feel like twittering about, someone, somewhere on Twitter, is into that subject, too. You might have to tweet for a few days or weeks before you connect with them, but after you find one person who "gets" you, the floodgates open — hundreds more twitterers start to hear what you have to say and want to share with you.

Don't be afraid to voice your support for social causes and charities. By tweeting about your cause, you both spread awareness about what's important to you (which may lead to more contributions for that cause or charity) and give your audience a better idea of who you are as a person.

So, if you're passionate about cancer research, domestic violence, or another cause and want to have a fundraiser for it, a Twitter update that you send about the fundraiser might get repeated and reach 50, 500, 5,000 or 50,000 people (or more) who are directly and indirectly connected to you. Spread the love!

Many have raised money for worthy causes right on Twitter. One of the first was Beth Kanter (@kanter) whose network sent a Cambodian woman to college in a matter of a few hours of Twitter conversation about it and links to a donation site. For more about Twitter and charity, see Chapter 15.

Keeping Twitter Personal . . . but Not Too Personal

Above all else, remember that Twitter is a public forum. Even when you're talking to your trusted Twitter network, your tweets are very much public, Google and other search engines still index them, and anyone on the Web can link to them.

You can adjust your settings to prevent search engines and the occasional passerby from viewing your updates by protecting your account. See Chapter 2 for details.

All the public exposure that Twitter offers can really help promote you and your business, but that exposure also comes with some responsibilities:

✔ **Use common sense!** Don't publicly tweet or @reply someone your address, phone number, or other personal details that you should keep private. Send that kind of information via DM (direct message) — or, even better, via e-mail, instant message, or phone. Keeping your personal details private protects both you and anyone in your care, such as your kids.

✔ **Use DMs cautiously.** Typing **d** *username* and then your message does send a private direct message from any Twitter interface. But trust us, if you made a typo or wrote **dm** *username*, you would not be the first person to accidentally post a private DM publicly.

To avoid accidental updates, make it a habit to use the Message button on a user's page, double-check your **d** *username* tweets before posting or use `http://twitter.com/direct_messages` to send DMs. You want to be extremely careful if you decide to send sensitive information by DM. Better yet, use an even more secure medium like e-mail or even encryption. *Never* send passwords, credit card numbers, social security numbers, or other valuable private data by Twitter (or even e-mail, for data that secure).

✔ **Maintain boundaries.** Try to be aware of how you are (or aren't) maintaining boundaries with the people you interact with frequently on Twitter. Especially before you agree to meet someone in person, take a look at how you've interacted in the past and make sure that you've kept your relationship clear from the start, whether it's for business or friendship.

Protecting personal details

Many people opt to not even use the real names of family members or children who don't use Twitter. Twitterers commonly refer to relatives, friends, and kids by nicknames or initials, just to give those loved ones a layer of protection. Use a bit of caution and ask permission before tweeting someone's real name (or any other information that we mention). Laura, for example, uses her daughters' initials S and Z, as shown in Figure 10-7. Twitter is a powerful influence on search engines, so casual mentions of unique names remain findable for a long time. If Laura even used their first names on her tweets (which all also contain her last name), they'd likely appear visibly in Google search results for their firstname lastname. Don't believe her? A Google search for Z Fitton brings up two recent tweets about her antics.

The same words of caution go for any number of personal details. Dive into information about your health or your private life in private conversation. Although being authentic and a little bit personal goes a long way on Twitter, everyone understands that you need a layer of privacy to keep you, your loved ones, and the details about them safe.

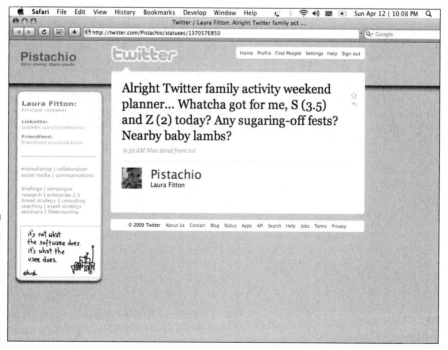

Figure 10-7: Laura (@pistachio) referencing her spawn in a tweet.

Things you probably shouldn't say on Twitter

You definitely want to keep some information to yourself when you're tweeting away:

- ✔ Your home address

- ✔ Your home or cellphone number

- ✔ Your kids' names

- ✔ Your financial information (such as credit card numbers, your yearly income, and anything else you wouldn't want the whole world to know)

- ✔ Vital health details (such as diseases you have or a diagnosis you just received — unless you're comfortable with the world knowing about it)

- ✔ Details about schools and other locations where you or people you know spend time — you never know who might drop in after seeing your tweet on a Google search

Maximizing privacy and safety

After you Twitter for a while, you've given away a lot of information about yourself. If you mention who you spend time with or that you always hang out at a certain cafe, someone can start tracking where you've been and what you're doing. We don't want to scare you — but whenever you post in a public medium, anyone could go through the information you've published, later on, and start piecing things together. Laura loves the unique charms of her neighborhood and street, but she keeps the details really fuzzy, preferring Boston as specific enough.

Chapter 11

Twitter for Business

. . . .

. . . .

So, you want to find out more about what Twitter can do for your business. In this chapter, we cover some of the essentials, explain what some other businesses have tried, and point you in the right direction to get started yourself.

The Business of Twitter

People often ask Laura, "What's the business use of Twitter?" Laura frequently answers with a different question, "What's the business use of e-mail?" It's not that the technologies are similar or play the same role; it's that Twitter has the potential to filter into every possible aspect of business as a versatile communications platform and problem-solving tool. Both technologies are extremely open communication platforms that have uses way beyond the marketing and customer-engagement layer. Twitter can impact pretty much everything, from the way enterprise software works to how project status is shared. It can fundamentally change communication and problem-solving, as well as match resources, accommodate HR challenges, and lower expenses. Most of the potential business applications of Twitter are just starting to become understood.

Twitter can have powerful effects on personal and professional networks. Sales professionals can use it to generate leads, journalists to locate sources, publishers to discover new content, or any business to create better relationships with customers. You can listen to and harness the massive flow of ideas and information passing through Twitter so that you can advance your business objectives.

You can use Twitter to create ad-hoc communities, organize and publicize live events, or extend an experience to a remote audience. You can sell directly — if you do it right — or you can just develop an inexpensive listening and conversation post among the very people whose problems your business solves. You can use Twitter to generate traffic to your business's Web site. You can use it to solicit feedback. It can even make your company and brands easier for users to find on search engines such as Google.

First, it helps to take a look at some ways Twitter might fit with your brand.

Putting Your Best Face Forward

Businesses can use Twitter to talk to their customers and potential customers, and generally increase brand recognition. Given that Twitter has so many potential uses that are so diverse, how can you get started?

You can probably guess that your profile is your business's face on Twitter. Even though many people use Twitter through a service on their phone or desktop, rather than through the Web page itself, assume that most everyone will at least look at your Profile page — if not the Web URL that you provide within that profile — before deciding whether or not to follow what you're doing on Twitter.

Dress nicely on Twitter: Fill out the whole Profile page when you set up your business's Twitter account and upload an avatar (in some cases, your company logo is appropriate, but in others an individual photo is better). Link back to your main Web site, and in turn, link to your Twitter account from your Web site. You need to verify that the business account is actually yours and promote the availability of the Twitter stream to all your customers. With a widget on your site, you can even tweet to your customers (keeping freshly updated content front and center) without them having ever even heard of Twitter.

Make sure that the Twitter Bio section, short though it may be, tells Twitter users about your business. Also, the content of your business's tweets needs to honestly, transparently show what you're doing on Twitter. Introduce the people behind your business's Twitter account — they're the people your Twitter readers and connections actually talk to, so let the individuals behind the keyboard shine through. (For more on polishing your profile, turn to Chapter 2.)

After you create a great Profile page, what do you do? Here are a few simple ways to get out of the Twitter background and into public awareness:

✔ **Listen.** Pay attention to what's going on around you on Twitter. Twitter users have fascinating things to say about pretty much everything, but more importantly for you, they may already be talking about you and your business. You're going to want to find as many ways as you can to tune in. From using Twitter Search to sophisticated social-media listening tools, (see Chapter 9) you can get useful information from Twitter in many ways. If you think of Twitter as a giant consumer sentiment engine, you can start to understand its potential. You can learn a lot by listening.

✔ **Balance.** For the average business Twitter account, you need to have a good ratio of personal (or conversational) tweets to business (or promotional) ones. This ratio depends, in part, on how much you interact on Twitter and what you hope to accomplish — not to mention the nature of your business and your target audience or customer base.

You may want to come up with an approximate numerical ratio that accomplishes your balance goals. You might want to decide, for example, that you can make only one or two of every ten tweets personal. Alternately, you can opt to put a particularly personal or original slant on promotional tweets, making them notably funny, valuable, or interesting to your readers.

If you have a more conversational Twitter account that you still want to connect to your professional life, make about half your tweets personal, fun, or off-topic, and the other half about your business. If you prefer to deliver business value all the time, set up your account to curate and cultivate links about events, essays, news, and ideas that are relevant to your field, in addition to promotional tweets so that you can still push your brand (without making that the only thing you do). Whatever you do, be useful. Offer value. You want to keep people engaged, which is what Twitter is all about.

✔ **Engage.** While you listen and talk on Twitter, be sure to also interact with other twitterers. Twitter is a communications tool, and although it's based on a one-to-many concept, it works best when you make friends and have real conversations right in the Twitter stream. Sometimes when you find people talking about subjects relevant to your business you can offer helpful contributions to their conversations! When it comes to business, public relations, and customer service (which we talk about in the following sections), you absolutely need to engage other people on Twitter.

✔ **Connect.** Use the ability to take conversations offline and into the real world via tweetups, events, and meetings to your business's advantage. Twitter makes finding ways to meet and engage with customers in real life easy, and therein lies its largest business value. Bring your business's conversations and connections beyond the 140-character limit.

Public relations

You can use Twitter as a fantastic public-relations channel, whatever kind of business you work for. It offers global reach, endless connections, networking opportunities, a promotion platform, and immediate event planning and feedback. Best of all, if you float your ideas out there in genuine, valid, and interesting ways, others can pick them up and spread them around. Many Twitterers — from individuals to large corporations — report scoring numerous press opportunities as a result of engaging other Twitterers and sharing on the Twitter platform.

Some traditional public relations firms may be intimidated by Twitter's potential to connect stories, sources, and journalists. Many of them don't yet see the opportunity, or they're thinking about it too narrowly. Twitter is just one more tool — albeit a powerful and efficient one — to add to your arsenal if public relations is important to your business. Twitter simply gives you a way to make what you do more accessible to people who might otherwise not hear your message.

You may have heard about Twitter in the first place in the context of a mainstream news story about an event of global importance that was first reported via citizen journalism on Twitter — such as the emergency landing of a commercial airplane in the Hudson River in January 2009. Indeed, Twitter is an exceedingly powerful tool for detecting breaking events. You don't always get in-depth analysis (at least, not until links to longer writings about the story begin to spread), but you do frequently find yourself way ahead of the game when a story breaks if you're on Twitter.

Journalists and PR practitioners are among some of Twitter's most avid users, and they do some pretty interesting things with it. On Monday nights, professionals from both sides of the field gather to talk about current stories, their professions, and the future of media, all by simply tagging their tweets with the word #journchat. Because #journchat is an agreed-on tag and a longstanding event, people know to point their search tools (or http:// search.twitter.com) at that word and watch the conversation scroll by.

It was Twitter innovator @PRSarahEvans who came up with the idea for #journchat, and the community she built catapulted her from obscure community college PR practitioner to an extremely well-known social-media innovator. John A. Byrne (@JohnAByrne) of *BusinessWeek* implemented a similar standing event (Wednesday nights, for those of you playing along at home) when he went onto Twitter one night to answer questions and encouraged the use of the #editorchat hashtag.

Because Twitter usernames are short and frequently easy to remember, they can be a powerful way to introduce people and pass along contact information. In an interview, a reporter was surprised how easily Laura could rattle off half a dozen sources whom the reporter might like to talk to. Armed with these Twitter handles, the journalist used the profiles behind those user-names to get a quick snapshot of those users' interests, abilities, and points of view, plus links to further detailed information about them and an easy way to make contact.

Here are some tips to make your Twitter-based public relations more user-friendly and successful:

- ✔ **Keep it real!** The be-genuine Twitter rule applies at all times, even when you're embarking on a publicity campaign (often *especially* when you're attempting to drive sales or awareness to your product, service, or site). Twitter's users can be very turned off by empty marketing banter.

- ✔ **Remember your balance.** Just because you want to see fast results doesn't mean that you should bombard your Twitter followers with *link spam* (numerous tweets that contain links to your business) or constant nagging about whatever you're trying to promote. Remember to space it out. On Twitter, overly aggressive promotions can slow your progress and reduce your audience. Tread with respect.

- ✔ **Give your idea wings.** Come up with a pithy or witty statement about your promotion that inspires people in your network to share and pass it along (to *retweet* the statement, or RT) to their own networks. Getting your message retweeted is much more effective than hammering your point home on your own.

- ✔ **Be genuinely helpful.** Watch for conversations about topics relevant to your company or product, and provide unselfish solutions, ideas, and help to those conversations.

- ✔ **Listen to feedback.** If someone asks you a question, answer it in your own public feed so that you can continue to generate organic interest in your promotion. Answer others who happen to tweet related questions, but make sure that your answers aren't selfish or too pushy. How can you tell? Watch for effectiveness. Do people click your links? Do they retweet your messages without you having to ask? Do they complain that you're being promotional, or worse, do they just not say much at all? Use trackable link shorteners so that you can see which of your tweets people are bothering to click or, even better, retweeting them-selves (and passing your messages along for you). Sometimes, you may need to tweet a little less frequently to avoid letting spamminess make you less effective.

- ✔ **Offer incentives.** We don't mean free giveaways or money, but value. Give people an unselfish reason to pay attention to you. It takes more than just promotions. Followers listen to you for the value you add, and if you consistently add insightful and worthwhile thoughts to their Twitter streams, they'll be there for you when the roles reverse and you need them.

Command and control is dead. Long live converse!

Many companies struggle to come to terms with how they might use social media because they are reluctant to let go of their old "command and control" models of corporate communications. What they need to realize is that they no longer "have control of the message" because anyone can publish — by commenting, posting on a message board, blogging, or yes, microblogging — complaints about the company in places that anyone can find them.

Twitter's content is very search-engine friendly. When a static Web page, a blog post, and an active Twitter account all contain the same keywords, the tweets will probably appear above the Web page or blog post in the search results for that keyword. Don't believe us? Try searching the word *pistachio* and the word *dough* on Google on your computer right now. Chances are good you're going to find Laura's Twitter profile (`http://twitter.com/pistachio`) and Boston-area PR practitioner Doug Haslam's profile (`http://twitter.com/DougH`) pretty close to the top of those respective searches.

Twitter provides all users access to influential journalists, bloggers, writers, and people from all walks of life. If you use it consistently and well, you can find powerful, inexpensive ways to share messages that help solve people's problems and gain visibility for your work.

Customer service

Big name companies, such as Comcast and Dell, use Twitter as part of an overall strategy to reinvent their reputations for poor customer service and turn things around for their brands.

How did they do it? Or, more importantly, how can *you* do it? Both companies set up Twitter accounts (@ComcastCares and all the Dell accounts listed at `http://dell.com/twitter`) as hubs for public customer-service responses. They got in the trenches of social media through Twitter and engaged their customer bases by facing criticisms and complaints head-on, and by showing a desire to help and respond quickly without making excuses or shifting blame. Better yet, Twitter users around the world can witness this transformation and watch the companies respond to others' complaints, improving the company image for even more people.

By listening diligently for mentions of their companies and quickly extending a helping hand, Comcast and Dell have generated substantial goodwill (not to mention, press coverage). Even when the products and services sold under those brands elicit unpleasant reactions from the public, having a real person reach out to help in a public forum can do a lot to prevent or dissipate consumer anger. Used artfully, one-to-one contact via Twitter instills a sense of hope that the people behind the company walls aren't leaving customers hanging. Presence and timely response on Twitter can make the difference between a firestorm of complaints and a quickly-managed situation.

Here's the caveat: No one has yet figured out whether Twitter-based customer service will still be such a great shortcut once Twitter grows even bigger and more popular. If the company's customer service system has fundamental problems, remaining in closer contact with consumers alone will not fix that. Customer service on Twitter allows businesses to catch consumers in their moments of frustration and help them right away. But Twitter alone can't fix back-end customer-service infrastructure problems such as overloaded call centers or poorly trained representatives who have no real power to help.

You don't need to be a huge company (and you certainly don't need to be suffering from a bad reputation) to create an effective business presence on Twitter. Twitter provides a great customer-service channel for small and medium-sized businesses, too. If you're at a small company, Twitter can broaden your ability to reach out widely and listen carefully at almost no expense (only some time and possibly tools) while saving you the cost of having an entire customer-service department. Having a Twitter account for your business can make your business more accessible, not to mention let you help people in real time who have real problems and see instant improvement in how consumers perceive your business.

Zappos (www.zappos.com), a sweetheart of the Twitter-for-business world, models an almost perfect implementation of the ideas laid out in *The Cluetrain Manifesto: The End of Business As Usual,* by Christopher Locke (@clockerb), Rick Levine (@ricklevine), Doc Searls (@dsearls), and David Weinberger (@dweinberger) (Basic Books). At Zappos, employees literally have a mandate to create delightful experiences for customers. The catchphrase? "Deliver happiness." Each employee who may come in contact with customers is encouraged and empowered to do whatever it takes to help. This policy holds true throughout the company's interactions, but the Zapponian culture of helpfulness absolutely shines through Twitter. Over 430 Zappos employees use Twitter, whether they're involved in customer service or not, and they all take a share in the "Deliver Happiness" mission.

When you first dive into Twitter for customer service, you may see negativity about your company, particularly at first. Keep going. The best part about Twitter as a customer-service channel is how you get feedback when a customer leaves satisfied. Many satisfied customers send out thank-you tweets that all their contacts see, which gives you instant good public-relations buzz — and that kind of buzz is priceless. Letting go of control (you don't necessarily have control anymore anyhow) of your brand and engaging publicly with dissatisfied customers can really get that goodwill going.

Networking on Twitter

Whether you do it via Twitter or an old-fashioned Rolodex, your business, personal, and career success depends heavily on a little thing called your network. If you're looking for ways to network more effectively — or you want to find interesting, valuable people efficiently — Twitter can help you build up a genuinely interesting, astonishingly relevant, and powerful network. Entire new horizons of opportunity can open up when you finally connect with the people that are right for you. Building a network comes naturally on Twitter. The platform makes it easy to interact and connect with people and businesses who share your interests and goals, and because of @replies and other links between Twitter networks and Twitter users, to randomly interact with and discover interesting new people along the way.

The more you interact on Twitter, the more your network increases. You can build almost any specific type of network on Twitter, too. Twitter offers access to all levels of people and businesses, from those seeking work or a better social life to CEOs and national politicians.

One of the most interesting phenomena on Twitter is the communication and collaboration that can occur while businesses network with one another in public. Twitter offers a level of transparency that erases normal boundaries and rivalries. Take, for example, the CEOs of competing companies IntenseDebate (`http://intensedebate.com`; `@IntenseDebate`) and DISQUS (`http://disqus.com`; `@disqus`), two companies that build comment management software for blogs. Through a debate in Twitter, they collaborated on some cross-functional features in their otherwise rival products to make both companies' customers happy and solve a problem.

Twitter can also help business networking in the employment sector — it's a fantastic way to meet and evaluate new employees, and also to find new work. This movement towards a "Hire 2.0" culture (applying so-called *Web 2.0* technologies to the job market), creates a more open and flexible hiring environment for all kinds of companies. You can observe potential employees while they talk about what they know, get referrals from people who know them, and introduce yourself — all in real time. Twitter also efficiently harnesses networks of loose ties — the friends of friends who are more likely to know about job opportunities and job candidates.

Freelancers who network and collaborate on projects can use Twitter to find former colleagues from past companies with whom they lost touch, and to get to know their existing employees and customers. We really can't overstate how versatile a networking tool Twitter can be. In so many ways, Twitter acts as a portable business networking event that you can pop into when the time and availability suit you. Bonus: You don't have to talk to anyone whom you don't want to.

Offering Promotions and Products

If you represent a company that has something to sell, you can find a unique home on Twitter. You may need to adjust your messages a bit so that you can shift from a hard-sell philosophy to an attitude of interaction and engagement that doesn't necessarily follow a direct path to a sale. But after you find and flip that switch from "talking at" to "talking with" potential customers, people on Twitter can interact with and respond to your company's information ideas and products in ways that often lead to benefits for both sides.

You can sell-without-selling just about anything on Twitter. Whether you want to sell something large (such as used cars) or something small (such as shoes), you can probably find people on Twitter who need and want them. These potential customers have questions for you about your item, your company, your staff, and *you* — and you can let them talk to you on Twitter about their concerns. You're in business because you solve problems and fulfill needs for people. Spend your time on Twitter being useful and informative about the types of problems you solve, and the rest really does follow.

One of the most popular examples of products and how Twitter can help sell them is @Zappos. Zappos has been a pioneer in business microblogging because a large number of its employees all use Twitter and all, in their own way, promote the brand and its products. Having more than 400 employees active on Twitter has improved communication and connection between Zappos' employees, increased its visibility and reach, banked large amounts of *social capital* (potentially valuable connections with people who know you and care about your work), and led to extensive press coverage and speaking opportunities.

Zappos is fronted by CEO Tony Hsieh, who tweets about his life, including his schedule, his company, and his personal thoughts — he even operates a separate Twitter account for his cat. The Twitter community embraced Tony and Zappos early on, and in return, Zappos periodically offers Twitter-only bonuses to its followers, such as free shoe giveaways.

But Zappos isn't the only company finding sales success on Twitter. @DellOutlet is another Twitter success story. We talk about Dell as a company that used Twitter to start reversing its reputation as a struggling brand with a poor customer image in the section "Customer service," earlier in this chapter. But Dell, like Zappos, has also started offering Twitter-only promotions, tweeting links to deep discounts that have generated over $1 million in revenues. Most notably, you can attribute more than $500,000 in revenues to less than 1,000 followers — demonstrating that the coupons not only got passed along on Twitter, but that they probably also got passed along via e-mail to people not even on Twitter. The airline JetBlue (@jetblue) has also had great success advertising deals on Twitter: A special $14 cross-country flight offer was snapped up by Twitter users almost instantly, and retweets helped spread the word. This past winter, it was estimated that more than 1,500 coupons and offers appear on Twitter every day. Dozens of coupon-aggregating accounts (like @dealtaker) and even Web sites (http://www.coupontweet.com and http://www.cheaptweet.com) are emerging to organize these coupons and find the best ones.

Two women making exceptional use of Twitter for discovering gift-givers in need are Melanie Notkin (@SavvyAuntie) and GiftGirl (@GiftGirl). Those who sell any kind of gift resource can use Twitter to reach their audiences and magnify their impact. Notkin and GiftGirl have found unshakable niches with their custom gift-finding service. How to find the right gift for loved ones for birthdays, weddings, and anniversaries is actually a pretty commonly tweeted question. The advice these women provide on their Twitter accounts and the commerce they offer through their Web sites (http://savvyauntie.com and www.giftgirl.com), place them squarely in Twitter's elite when it comes to product sales and knowledge contribution.

You can replicate their success be keeping these tips in mind:

✔ Be interesting.

✔ Be accessible.

✔ Be genuine (mean what you say).

✔ Be yourself.

✔ Don't hard sell.

✔ Don't link spam.

✔ Follow the 90/10 advice — 90 percent unselfish tweets to 10 percent promotional tweets.

Promoting Bands and Artists

If you're in any way in the business of creating, whether it's art, music, film, photography, or what-have-you, Twitter can become a home away from home. Twitter users are incredibly receptive to creative people who tweet — just ask MC Hammer (@MCHammer). The former rapper turned preacher turned producer had a terrible image: bankruptcy, bad decisions, and excess. But he joined Twitter around the same time that he co-founded a new Web startup, DanceJam (http://dancejam.com), and conversing with followers on Twitter let the world see another side of him.

MC Hammer is a pretty cool example of how you can use Twitter for rebranding, marketing, and self-promotion as an artist, but Twitter can also help relatively unknown people make it to the top for the first time.

Twitter also helps artists such as Natasha Wescoat (@natashawescoat) increase their prominence in the art world. Westcoat's work is finding a home in art galleries, movies, and more, and she can attribute some of that increasing reach to contacts that she made on Twitter.

So, how can you (as an aspiring musician, artist, photographer, or other person who makes a living in the creative industries) find success on Twitter if you aren't already on the level of Dave Matthews (@DaveJMatthews), MC Hammer, Ryan Adams (@ryanada_ms), John Mayer (@johncmayer), Ashton Kutcher (@aplusk), or Oprah Winfrey (@Oprah)? Here are some simple tips that you can follow:

- ✔ **Surround yourself with successful people.** We don't mean just others in your profession or field who are more successful than you! We also mean people in other fields or areas of creativity that inspire you. You can start to find them by finding out which of your real-world contacts in the industry are on Twitter or by doing a few Twitter searches to find like-minded people while you build your network.

- ✔ **Take it offline.** Take the connections that you make on Twitter and organize events and get-togethers that bring the experience offline. You can also find out about other members' tweetups that are relevant to your business. In creative industries, the talent is what counts, and so real-world connections can really lead to new opportunities, fan segments, and opportunities to build your loyal fan base.

- ✔ **Share your content.** You don't have to give away all your hard work, but put your music, art, videos, or other work out there for people to sample and play with. Start a Blip.fm (http://blip.fm) channel, upload a short video to YouTube, offer free mp3s on your Web site, or set up a page that features a few Creative Commons–licensed photos. Whatever you do, give people a way to take a look or have a listen so that they can get to know you and what you make.

  Creative Commons (http://creativecommons.org) is an organization that makes it easy for people to license their work so that they retain their copyright but allow it to be shared. For more information on how Creative Commons works, go to http://creativecommons.org/about.

- ✔ **Tweet on the go.** Give your fans and potential fans a look backstage, in the van, behind the canvas, on tour, or behind the lens. Take them with you by tweeting while you travel with your music, art, film, or other creative medium. Also, let them know where you are! Many fellow Twitter users would love to hang out with you if you happen to be in town.

- ✔ **Engage your fan base.** Don't just post static links to content or schedule changes! Talk to your fans and respond to them through Twitter. They probably want to ask you about the thoughts behind your work, your experiences, and you. Let them. Answer them. Engage them in good conversation, and watch as they spread the word about your work to their friends and followers.

> ✔ **Be yourself.** Put a good face forward, yes, but don't try too hard to project a persona that really isn't authentically you. Twitter is a medium that rewards authenticity, candor, and transparency. Try too hard to put your best face forward, and you may lose yourself and stop being genuine. Twitter people notice if you aren't being real. Don't worry about impressing people — just do what you do and be yourself, and the fans will follow.

For the most up-to-date examples of how musicians (`http://wefollow.com/tag/music`), TV personalities (`http://wefollow.com/tag/tv`), actors (`http://wefollow.com/tag/actor`), comedians (`http://wefollow.com/tag/comedy`), and other celebrities (`http://wefollow.com/tag/celebrity`) are using Twitter, check out some of the top most-followed individuals in each category on user-generated Twitter directory We Follow. For more in-depth reading on how musicians can use Twitter, see (`http://pistachioconsulting.com/musicians-guide-to-rocking-twitter`).

Sharing Company Updates

If you have a new or growing company that you want to introduce to the world through Twitter, start a separate account for the company, just as Laura did with @oneforty. You may find balancing traditional corporate professionalism with the level of transparency that Twitter users have come to expect to be a little tricky sometimes, so keep these guidelines in mind when you start your new account:

> ✔ **Provide value to the Twitter community.** Your company account can become a source of news, solutions, ideas, entertainment, or information that's more than just a series of links to products and services. Educate your Twitter followers. Reach out to people whom you can genuinely and unselfishly help. You can even offer sales incentives for products, in the way that @DellOutlet does, as long as what you offer has genuine value. Establish your company's leadership in providing ideas, solutions, and innovation.

> ✔ **Attach a real-world face to the account.** If you need to use a company logo as the avatar because of internal regulations or because multiple people are maintaining the account, make sure to list the names of the actual people who are tweeting in the Bio section of your business's Twitter profile, and consider signing each tweet with the author's initials. This approach lets your followers become familiar with who's behind the company voice and it makes them feel more engaged. People like to talk to other people, not brands.

✔ **Don't spam.** Don't flood the Twitter feed with self-promotional links or product information that don't deliver genuine value to readers. Whether self-promotional or not, you never want to clog up peoples' Twitter streams with irrelevant information. You might not talk about your cat or your marriage on a company account, but you can still make it personal. Profile an employee, talk about milestones for employees, or talk about what's going on in your office. You can even hold tweetups at your office and invite your followers to stop by, like Boston's NPR news station WBUR (@WBUR) does. This approach gives people a peek at what makes your company run.

Before tweeting in earnest for your company, it's a good idea to openly discuss your plans to demonstrate that you're taking a productive, innovative approach and to prevent any misguided fears that twittering means you will somehow suddenly start to leak sensitive company information or otherwise break reasonable corporate policies. As with any public communications platform, you do need to consider just how much you can say about what goes on inside your business. Transparency is key, but you don't want to disclose industry secrets in a public forum. Every company has a different style. It helps to have a good plan in place and make sure that the employees assigned to the company Twitter account are trustworthy and have solid judgment.

Building Community

Community-building sometimes suffers from a kum-ba-ya perception that devalues the importance of using tools such as Twitter to connect with people. But building a truly engaged community is extremely valuable.

Apple is an example of a company that benefits tremendously from its engaged community in terms of promotion, sales, and even customer support administered from one Apple fan directly to others. Apple built its community by building great products people get passionate about, not by worrying about any particular tools. So as you approach the Twitter opportunity, remember how powerful and engaged community can be and remember what people actually engage around — the things they really and truly care about.

At its best, the community concept of sharing and connecting can help you spread a positive image and good comments about your company; done wrong, it can veer into feel-good, self-help banter that's ultimately empty. Again, don't fuss too much about Twitter as a tool. Think more strategically about the community and what they care about and engage them with substance and real contributions.

Building a community is not necessarily the same as building a network:

- ✔ **Network:** Your network is there for you and your business, a kind of foundation for concrete professional growth.
- ✔ **Community:** Building a community means inspiring the people who follow you on Twitter to embrace your brand and create a feeling of solidarity around your business, service, staff, or product.

With a community, you can build a loyal corps of evangelists: people who are passionate about your brand, even though they have no professional or financial stake in the company. If you can engender the community feeling through your use of Twitter and how you interact with your customers, your customers begin to feel emotionally invested in your success online.

You can see this community feeling with Zappos. The Twitter users who follow the shoe retailer are so dedicated that they act like they're legitimately invested in the brand's success. Zappos fosters this effect by staying on top of what people on Twitter are saying about them, or about shoes in general, through the use of monitoring tools. Then they jump in with help, as needed. If you tweet about having trouble finding any kind of shoe, for example, you can expect a Zappos employee to send you a direct message (DM) or @reply in less than a day that includes links to the proper pages on the Zappos site. Plus, Zappos has spent so much time building a strong community that Twitter members who don't even work for Zappos will routinely pass along information they see or hear and will even reach out on behalf of the company and connect potential customers with Zappos.com.

You can also see the community around less popular products, such as Comcast's cable offerings. Even while people express frustration about their cable service, members of their Twitter network still point them to @Comcastcares to find help.

Community is also a huge aspect of many musicians' and artists' Twitter experiences, such as Imogen Heap (@ImogenHeap) and John Mayer (@johncmayer). Heap uses Twitter to interact more directly with her fan base, which increases the loyalty of her listeners, who have come to see a more human side of her and feel like they've even come to know her. If someone tweets something about Heap that her Twitter followers don't like, you can watch the community leap to her defense. At the same time, tweets from her Twitter community usually reflect the tone of her own calm tweets, remaining mellow and not shrill.

Musicians, actors and other celebrities are really personality-based businesses, and bringing forth those personalities on Twitter by asking questions and sharing parts of their lives cements a valuable engagement between the artist and fans.

You can build community through

- Genuine interaction
- Asking questions
- Honesty
- Transparency
- Following people back who follow you
- Not over-automating
- Being more than a link list
- Providing value

Conducting Research

Twitter is an excellent tool for crowd-sourcing and focus-group research. You can easily get the answers you seek after you establish a relationship with your followers that encourages participation, conversation, and sharing. The real challenge is finding reliable methods to extract and analyze the data: Twitter is still a very new medium, and analytics tools associated with it aren't yet that advanced. Larger corporations are diving in to conduct their own research and build their own tools that can make sense of the tremendous amount of data being generated on Twitter all the time.

If you're willing to experiment with different ways to watch the Twitter stream, you can collect *passive data* (what people happen to be mentioning), do *active research* (asking questions and conduction polls), and even engage actual focus groups and ad-hoc communities in live events.

As you build your network and start gaining more followers on Twitter, it becomes a very useful tool for informal conversational research. If you ask a really good question and send it into the world with a #hashtag to make the answers easier to find, you can even do research with a very small following, because the tag attracts curious bystanders who may later become new followers. As you ask questions, you can use any number of polling tools or even a simple manually generated tracking system (such as a Microsoft Excel spreadsheet) to collect the answers and data that you receive.

Twitter can be thought of as a global, human-powered, mobile phone-enabled sensing and signaling network. What Twitter knows about the world is pretty incredible, and once businesses understand how to work with that information, it can contribute toward closing some pretty important gaps in our economy between supply and demand.

Growing your numbers naturally

Although effective questions and good tagging can help your research spread beyond your direct network, in order to do most kinds of research on Twitter, you need a healthy following first. This network will have much more value in the long run if you grow your numbers through natural conversational methods and organic back-and-forth follows. (*Tip:* Don't advertise "please follow this account" the way that Ashton Kutcher did when he was trying to race CNN to a million Twitter followers.) When you know that you have a diverse crowd of intelligent people following you on Twitter, including those who are both fans and critics of your brand, then you can feel relatively comfortable starting to ask them for feedback and insight.

Take it slow and wait for a solid, engaged, relevant network to build up instead. But your business and you can begin to thrive on the real-time feedback about your products, services, and staff. Twitter can, among other things, help you find out before it's too late that a new flagship product is flawed, spread the word about your excellent customer service directly from the customers that were involved, and invite interested customers to come to real-life tweetups to find out more about your brand. Any forward-thinking business that has transparency on the mind or wants to remain on top of brand perception at all times has started to use Twitter.

Going Transparent

Transparency is a crucial marketing buzzword for some businesses and a scary reality for others. Lest you think we're asking you to live out that unpleasant dream where you forget to wear your pants to school, relax. Transparency doesn't require exposing company data to corporate spies or baring your soul for the Internet. More than anything else, it simply means being honest, disclosing your biases, admitting to mistakes, and not trying to force your message and spin on everyone all the time.

Although many Twitter users find themselves becoming more casual in their use of the service over time, you need to find your own personal comfort level between acting like a real person and over-sharing. After you find that line for yourself, your business, and your employees, being genuine and transparent on Twitter becomes second nature. Transparency fosters trust and relationships. It's no secret — people like to work with people they like.

Here's how to achieve transparency:

 ✔ **Release control.** Stop worrying about what might happen to your brand. Instead, listen to what your customers are trying to tell you and respond to that feedback. The truth is, you haven't been able to control your message for a while now: You might just not have known it. For example, look at the hashtags #motrinmoms and #amazonfail. In the former example, painkiller brand Motrin put out an online ad campaign that targeted mothers; it failed spectacularly when real moms took offense at its content. They used Twitter to express their anger and ultimately get the campaign suspended. The Amazon Fail incident happened when books pertaining to gay and lesbian themes were suddenly pulled from the online retailer's bestseller lists. Again, Twitter users smelled something fishy and instantly started spreading the word. Both companies learned from going through this process that a better Twitter listening practice would have helped them address concerns early and prevent a conflagration.

✔ **Admit to problems.** When you acknowledge that your business and you occasionally have rough patches, you can form stronger, more genuine connections with your community. That kind of open disclosure has limits when it comes to some professions. Obviously, people in the legal and medical professions, as well as government agencies, have to restrict and curtail their Twitter use because of privacy issues. But for most businesses, honesty is the best policy.

✔ **Reach out continually.** Don't stop seeking out the customers who are talking about you (you can find them by conducting regular Twitter searches; see Chapter 9) and reaching out to them. That personal touch goes very far in establishing and maintaining a positive perception of your business or brand.

✔ **Be proactive.** If you're engaged with the community in a genuine way, people forgive most mistakes. Twitter's community is pretty cooperative, and if you embrace it, you can be rewarded with unexpected benefits like loyalty, advocacy, and even organic, voluntary promotion of you and your work.

But, What If My Employees . . .

Like with any new tool, business owners often feel some uncertainty and concern about how to manage employees so that they don't waste time or make costly mistakes when using Twitter. Remember to apply common sense and manage based on behavior and results, not just specific tools. Your existing guidelines about e-mail, blogs, commenting on Web message boards and forums, and even conversations with outside individuals cover any concerns that you have about your employees' use of Twitter.

That said, it is important to take heed that information spreads fast on Twitter, and that Twitter is a very open and searchable public forum. Errors can — and will — go farther, faster, so the exercise of common sense is in order.

Before you start using Twitter for your business, provide staff with guidance on how to use it and what to be cautious about. Twitter is extremely new to many people, and they may not yet be familiar with just how public and open it is. Definitely set a few ground rules to help avoid common mistakes. You can simply write up a one-or two-page set of reminders or direct employees' attention to the parts of your existing HR policy that cover public communications.

Make the guidelines basic, clear, and easy to follow. Here are some thoughts to get you started:

✓ Remember that if you wouldn't say it in front of your parents, kids, or boss, perhaps you shouldn't say it on Twitter.

✓ If you do something confidential at a company, keep private information under wraps. Respect clients' privacy, as well as your company's.

✓ Respect the company brand when you're out at *tweetups* (Twitter-based meet-ups) and events. Anyone can get quoted at any time.

✓ Perception is reality. Even if the complaint you tweet right after a client phone call wasn't about the client, it can be misconstrued that way.

✓ Manage your time on Twitter well so that it doesn't interfere with your workload.

Unless your business has other issues that come into play (for example, if you work for a law firm or government agency), these basic rules should be enough to keep people from abusing their time on Twitter. Customize them however you want.

Twitter can be an extremely valuable tool when it comes to building your professional team and bringing them together. You can set up meetings, tweet notes, meet customers, and more — and your staff can connect more easily by using Twitter, as well. The more of a team you can build, the better you can weather any economic buffering.

Sharing Knowledge

You can also use Twitter to share knowledge, collaborate both inside the company and out, and gather business information and research. After you start to build a healthy network, you need to send out only a few tweets about your project, problem, or issue before people come out of the woodwork to try to help your business and you. If you haven't been building your Twitter network, you may have to wait a while for this aspect of Twitter to become useful for you.

Say that you come up with a major presentation about what your company does or sells, but you need something to complete it, such as a chart or a link to a relevant study. Twitter can probably help you find that missing piece. People on Twitter usually offer a helping hand when it comes to knowledge sharing, collaboration, and information gathering, especially if you spend time interacting on Twitter and building your network. Avid Twitter users are all aware of the same thing: By helping out others, they can get a hand when they need it.

The very existence of this book is an example of Twitter bringing people together for knowledge sharing and collaboration. Laura got to know two Wiley employees on Twitter and in person at conferences, which led to a conversation about Laura writing *Twitter For Dummies*. Laura in turn had met Michael and Leslie via Twitter-related conversations and events, and they had all come to trust one another over time. We also reached out via our personal Twitter accounts and @dummies on Twitter to ask the broader Twitter community what they thought belonged in a book about Twitter. Moving forward, we'll continue to listen and interact via the @dummies account, our Web site, and, of course, via the community at Laura's Twitter-powered community startup www.oneforty.com.

Chapter 12

The Social Side of Twitter

*J*ust as businesses can benefit from using Twitter to build goodwill, communicate with stakeholders, and establish personal relationships with customers (which we talk about in Chapter 11), the service can likewise be used by individuals to build strong social connections. Through these connections, one can tap a wealth of resources that were heretofore unavailable due to limitations of time or distance.

As we show in this chapter, your Twitter network can help in a myriad of ways that range from the prosaic (such as recommending a favorite pizza place in an unfamiliar town) to life-saving (coordinating disaster relief efforts in real time). We also go into detail about the social benefits of strong Twitter connections and provide tips for building and participating in a supportive Twitter community.

Using Twitter as a Support System

Most people don't realize this, but Twitter is a support system for your support system. Twitter keeps you connected in real time with the people in your life, providing support to your support system itself.

Many users instinctively turn to their Twitter network when they need to commiserate over a loss for their favorite sports team, when they get a promotion or a new job, when they lose a loved one, or when anything else happens that they want to share with a supportive network of people.

Twitterers have used the service to help displaced families, victims of natural disasters, abuse victims, job-seekers, animals in need, and even researchers who need people to take part in focus groups. Twitter has also proved useful for couch-surfers, who have come to know interesting and accommodating people in different fields of expertise.

Because Twitter helps people get to know each other on a more personal level, new friends can successfully meet and interact with each other offline.

As always, exercise caution when meeting people for the first time. Meet them in a public place, like a cafe or restaurant, and if you can, bring another friend with you, so you're not alone. Pay attention to your instincts — if something doesn't feel safe, it probably isn't.

For many, Twitter has replaced search-based electronic resources (such as Yahoo!, Live Search, or Google) and become their go-to place for help and support. Depending on the nature and the strength of your network, asking your friends on Twitter (both the ones you now have and the ones you're making) for guidance or opinions can yield more detailed and varied advice and help than you might receive if you had turned to only your offline network.

Of course, Twitter isn't meant to replace your offline network of lifelong friends and family — it's a technology designed to enrich that network. While connecting with your friends on Twitter, you may meet new friends and start to get a better feel for the people (both new and old) whom you can trust.

Although Twitter is useful for supporting global causes and events, the most poignant uses of Twitter can just as easily be found in the simple ways that users help each other, one at a time, all day, every day.

Twitterers reach out to one other through the trials and annoyances of every-day life (such as not having enough quarters at a laundromat) to crises of every size and measure. Twitterers have been support networks when loved ones are in hospital, when couples divorce, when relationships break up, and more. When you use Twitter, your expressions of frustration and loss are often met with an immediate response. Twitter empowers humanity to act humanely.

Connecting with People

Because all Twitterers use the same toolset and (as far as Twitter is concerned) play on the same level, it is remarkably easy to connect with people on the service. The more people you connect with, the more your follower/following numbers go up, thereby increasing the breadth of your network to a sometimes embarrassingly large number of people.

Gaming for followers

Twitter networks are based on trust and reputation, and one of the first metrics that people tend to use when deciding whether to follow someone is how many followers that user already has, and the ratio of following to followers.

Consequently, some Twitter users try to improve their follower/following reputation by collecting as many followers as possible. These individuals aggressively follow hundreds of people with the hope that the followed users follow them back (and many do). These people then unfollow the users who don't follow them back within a couple of days. The more aggressive "follow spammers" unfollow everyone in order to keep adding more and more and more. In fact, a couple of tools (which we won't name, and some of which Twitter has already suspended) automate this process. Does gaming followers give you a really high number on your follower count? Yes. But this behavior is seen as obnoxious, unethical, and strongly against the overall Twitter community spirit. It's also pretty questionable how engaged those tens of thousands of "followers" actually are.

Twitter, in an effort to curb these users, has limited the number of people that users can follow to 2,000 until the user is followed back, in turn, by a similar number of accounts. This is why the more ruthless gamers follow and then unfollow everyone that they target, to avoid hitting the "follow ceiling." If for some reason you hit that ceiling, you don't have to do anything but wait for your ratio to balance out, and then you will automatically be permitted to follow more new people.

You personally can help curb these gamers by not following back anyone you suspect is doing this, or even by clicking the block button on their Profile page. When a Twitter account is blocked by a large number of users, Twitter's spam team investigates the account and suspends any that are violating the terms of service.

Do yourself a favor and do not be tempted to play any of these games. It is *not* a good way to quickly build a Twitter following. The network generated is random and low-value, and you run the risk of losing your account entirely if other users block you or report you for abusing the system.

Some Twitter users (and we won't name names) are addicted to increasing their follower count and will use many tricks to artificially increase their number of followers. For more information, check out the sidebar "Gaming for followers," in this chapter.

Anxious to have lots and lots of followers? First, it doesn't matter as much as you might think. Second, be patient and build a network of actual connections, not collections of usernames and large follower numbers. It takes time for people to notice you; you'll need to have posted a few updates or tweets first. But if you share posts that others find valuable (in other words, you write tweets that people find interesting or informative), your follower count will grow organically. Getting more followers may take a while, especially if you have esoteric interests, but having a following of attentive and interested listeners trumps having a large number of followers any day.

Adopting the Fail Whale

Twitter is still a young service, and although it has grown exponentially, it has had some growing pains. Most frequently, its growing pains revolve around service outages, which typically occur when the servers become overloaded.

Twitter has a variety of kitschy graphics that appear when the service has problems. Best known is the Fail Whale, who comes out to play, towed by seven Twitter-logo-like birds (four of them are flying backwards), each time the service goes over capacity. The Fail Whale started life as a birthday card design called "Lifting the Dreamer," designed by Yiying Lu. There are other "failure" graphics — kittycats with screwdrivers (no longer used), the unscheduled maintenance caterpillar, the "just chill" ice cream cone, and owl and a Fail robot, but none has engendered the love and following of our dear Fail Whale.

Instead of becoming upset that their darling service was down, Twitterers reacted differently to the Fail Whale. The shared experience of losing access to the service fostered a sense of community so quickly among its users that they ended up adopting the Fail Whale as their mascot for banding together in tough times. They made t-shirts. They created a contest for designing a label for the Fail Whale Pale Ale, a mythical brew (see `http://tweetcrunch.com/2008/08/17/the-twitter-fail-whale-pale-ale-contest`). You can find Fail Whale plushies, mugs, t-shirts, and more. Few companies are able to transform a potential disaster into a point of culture for its users, but Twitter pulled it off.

What makes that plot twist interesting is how emblematic it is of how users feel the service as a whole. That sense of family and community transcends obstacles and gets things done. The adoption of the Fail Whale by the twitterverse was a sign that Ev, Biz, and Jack, the Twitter founders, had indeed hit a home run.

The first time you make a real, organic connection with a stranger on Twitter, it might feel a little weird, but it's also a bit thrilling. Whether you do something as simple as get (or give) a much-needed answer to a question, connect for business, or bond over something fun (such as music or sports), you've just made your first Twitter-friend.

Twitter is based around people and their networks. These interpersonal networks are the most important aspect of this simple and (we admit) quirky service. Real connections power Twitter — those connections are the heartbeat of your Twitter community.

In its early stages, Twitter went through some serious technological growing pains while it got more popular, leading to significant site downtime and unacceptable levels of quality of service. But the power of the connections and the format of the service kept it going. Without that network of connectivity, no one who uses Twitter would have had the patience to not only stick around while the people behind the service worked out the kinks, but also to embrace the problems and create solutions.

One of the most common issues with Twitter during its early days was down-time — the server frequently became overloaded with too many users writing too many updates. Although users couldn't access their Twitter accounts, the development team was nice enough to let you know what was going on: In place of whatever screen you expected to see, Twitter returned with a graphic of birds holding a whale out of the water. The picture and euphe-mism for Twitter down time was born: the Fail Whale, pictured in Figure 12-1.

So, what does all this connectedness have to do with you? If you listen to longtime Twitter users talk about it, you may start to feel like there are a whole lot of shared memories and assumptions that you're not a part of. Don't worry: New people are joining Twitter all the time. From the period of November 2008 until the final touches were put on this book, Twitter dou-bled at least three times. That means pretty much everyone is new, and you shouldn't feel shy about what came before. We're just filling you in on it so that you have some idea how these past feel-good moments apply to you.

For one thing, Twitter's past has established the underlying tone, lexicon, and conventions on Twitter. Also, the camaraderie among Twitter users is based on trust, and if you want people to trust you on Twitter (just like if you want people to trust you in any other circumstance), you really ought to give as much (or more) than you get back. To be effective, you really need to add value to the Twitter streams of others and act in a way that inspires trust. You will be rewarded with interesting new connections, ideas, and even life-long (virtual and real life) friends.

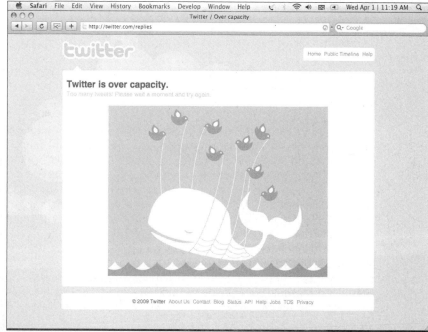

Figure 12-1:
The Fail Whale appears when Twitter's traffic exceeds their server capacity.

Making New Friends

In life, the word *friend* can have a number of different meanings. But on Twitter (and on most of the Internet), a friend is someone with whom you share a connection. Many Twitter users naturally follow people they know and trust; over time, however, many people start interacting with strangers. It's therefore not unusual to hear about the friends and real-life connections that people make on Twitter.

At first, you might have trouble believing it. Most people start out feeling like the stranger at a cocktail party, and existing Twitter users might not start a meaningful interaction with you right away. But most people will say hello and expect you to respond to them and tell them a bit about you — just as they would in a real conversation. Well, it *is* a real conversation.

Making friends on Twitter is much like making friends in the real world: If two people have things in common (for example, coming from the same home town), share a common interest (such as politics), or simply find each other fascinating, they may become friends. In fact, Twitter's interface makes it pretty easy to figure out if someone is worth following — just look at the person's Twitter Profile page, read her bio, check out her timeline, and follow her if she seems interesting.

Twitter users tend to share something unique or telling about themselves in their Twitter Profile page, either inside their biographies or URLs — or both. So, if you receive a flurry of tweets welcoming you to the service, take a look through those people's Profile pages and URLs to get a better feel for who they are, and whether you'd want to strike up a conversation with them . . . and then do so, if you want!

If you express interest in other people and what they say or do, they tend to reciprocate. In general, people love to know that you're interested in what they have to say, in real life and on Twitter.

You can find people with whom you want to start conversations through the public timeline, but if you want to look for individuals who share your interests, you can quickly and easily find those people by using Twitter Search (see Chapter 9) to see who's already talking about your interests. Laura frequently challenges new users to search for the most obscure keywords around their work or their favorite hobbies, to find people they have something special in common with.

You may find sending that first tweet to a potential Twitter connection a bit daunting. After all, what do you say to a total stranger? How do you say it? As a general rule, think of Twitter as a giant cocktail party. (In a perfect world, this party has cupcakes.) If you're the type of person who carefully chooses her conversations, Twitter gives you a lot of ammunition: Take a look at people's bios, their Web sites, and the things that they've tweeted so you can pick your conversations carefully. If you tend to be the life of the party, have at it! Go ahead and start @replying to people and stir up a conversation. You decide what approach you want to take, as there's no single right way to tweet. You'll ultimately find that your own personal style for meeting people in real life translates pretty similarly to Twitter.

Searching for topics of interest

Conversations crop up all the time on Twitter, so if you want to see what people are saying about something you're interested in, search for it.

Say that you're a huge cupcake fan and want to connect with other pastry buffs, so you want to see what people are saying. You can do this simply by running a Twitter Search for *cupcakes*. (We cover Twitter Search in detail in Chapter 9.)

Figure 12-2 shows a sample search for cupcakes. A recent search result, "about to bake cupcakes!<3<3" depicts a woman who seems excited at the prospect of making her cupcakes (those <3 characters are meant to be little sideways hearts showing how she loves cupcakes). By way of starting a conversation, you @reply to her, "I'm about to make cupcakes as well! What's your favorite recipe?" The two of you can go from there and may happen to start a relationship about your mutual love for baking cupcakes. The fancy name for this is *social object theory* — the idea that two people who discover a common interest are more likely to form some kind of direct connection to one another because of their connection to (and feelings for) the shared interest. Put differently, a whole lot of what goes on on Twitter is about "What do we have in common?" more than it is about "What are you doing?"

Or maybe you find the prospect of maple cupcakes intriguing. That user seems like a great person to ask for a recipe if you want to make them, too!

While you're going through the public timeline or the search results to find people who have information you want or people with whom you want to interact, you might feel tempted to try to direct message them. However, direct messaging works only if the person is following you. And because, in all likelihood, you haven't talked to them yet, they're probably not following you. Start a conversation by replying to them directly, for example: "@AliciaSue8 hey! Hey you! Maple cupcakes sound fantastic! Where'd you find that recipe?"

On Twitter, you'll find yourself getting to know people a lot better than you expected. Because Twitter profiles link to other resources and relevant information on their profile owners, you can get a pretty good sense of who people are. So, Twitter-based relationships often transition into relationships in real life. (Or, as some techies abbreviate it, IRL.)

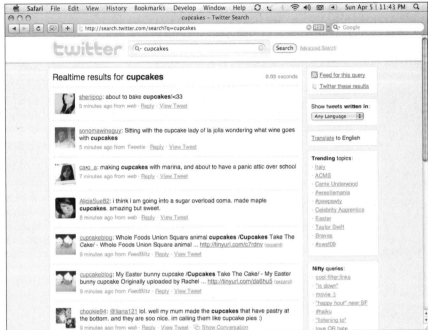

Figure 12-2:
Searching
for
cupcakes.

Twitter-based events

Through conversations on Twitter, many smaller communities have cropped up. The Twitter-based community occasionally organizes meet-ups in real life — the common thread being that they're all part of a community from Twitter. As with nearly every term relating to Twitter, it should come as no surprise that these meet-ups are sometimes referred to as *tweetups*.

Because Twitter is just another medium by which people connect, and because the medium allows you to easily build relationships, you may not see meeting offline as such a stretch. In our experience, because Twitter connections are based on trust within a community (which you can measure by seeing who people talk to, what they say, and what they're like), meeting people offline doesn't feel as taboo as it used to.

In fact, because Twitter makes reaching out to new people so easy, some people have had great success in meeting people in the most random of places — for example, in between flights during a layover.

Say that you're traveling from New Jersey to Colorado with a layover in Texas. You might send an update to Twitter: "Flying EWR to DIA, via IAH. Anyone care for a game of Scrabble during my 2-hour layover?" A fellow traveler might be, out of curiosity or boredom, searching Twitter for new people to meet and might take you up on your offer.

The real Shaq story

At first, Jesse Bearden didn't believe that his friend Sean was getting regular updates from the real Shaquille O'Neal on Twitter. After all, anyone could be masquerading as the much-loved star of 1996's smash-hit genie coming-of-age comedy, *Kazaam*.

So, when @THE_REAL_SHAQ updated his status to tell his followers that he was having a meal at the nearby 5 & Diner, Sean and Jesse decided to stop by and settle the identity question once and for all.

Sure enough, Shaq's truck was in the parking lot, and the man himself was tucked in a corner booth. While the two friends worked up the courage to say hello, Shaq tweeted again: "I feel twitterers around me, r there any twitterers in 5 n diner wit me, say somethin"

Within moments, they were being invited to share Shaq's booth, trade notes on Shaq's Android Googlephone versus Jesse's Window's Mobile device, and take pictures. In Shaq's words:

"To all twitterers, if u c me n public come say hi, we r not the same we r from twitteronia, we connect"

Celebrities and brands who use Twitter to build audiences become approachable on their own terms — even in real life!

You can find more information about the story at http://sesquipedalis.blogspot.com/2009/02/finally-use-for-twitter.html.

So, if you happen to be in a new town on business, or visiting friends or relatives (and need to get away), you might be able to find people in that city to meet for coffee or drinks. Twitter is another avenue by which you can find people; and, having the ability to figure out who they are before agreeing to meet them certainly benefits you. Not only can you look for common interests to talk about before meeting people (which certainly jumpstarts the awkward early phases of any conversation), you can also make such meetings safer by screening people before meeting up with them. Your mom was partially right about not talking to strangers, of course, but by meeting in public and by finding people you actually know in common, you can be a bit safer in making the jump to an offline connection.

In addition to impromptu tweetups, the digital-media folk on Twitter (the *Twitterati*) have organized and promoted a number of charity events through Twitter; two popular charity events, as of this writing, are @SM4SC (Social Media for Social Change; www.sm4sc.com), shown in Figure 12-3, and @Twestival (www.twestival.com). In just a few short weeks, @Twestival jumped to international consciousness — and headlines the world over — by drawing out 10,000 Twitterers to 200+ events in cities around the world. When all was said and done, a massive series of tweetups on February 12, 2009 raised $250,000 for charity: water (www.charitywater.org) to build safe, clean drinking water wells in developing nations. In April 2009 the main @twestival organizer Amanda Rose (@amanda) traveled to Ethiopia with charity: water founder Scott Harrison (@scottharrison), Twitter investor Chris Sacca (@sacca) and others to film and dedicate the first @twestival well drilled.

Figure 12-3:
On the
Social
Media
for Social
Change Web
site, you can
see what
events are
coming up.

By being active on Twitter — practicing the philosophy of transparency and having genuine interactions — you can increase your circle of friends and connections both on- and offline. You can also merge your offline circle of friends with your online circle of friends in ways you never could before, increasing your social reach exponentially. We talk more about being genuine in Chapter 10.

As it turns out, the more solid connections you have with your Twitter following, the more your network works for you. Although you may find meeting people in airports for board games an advantage to having some Twitter credibility, you can use your online network as quite a resource beyond the fuzzy stuff (which we discuss in the section "Using Twitter as a Support System," earlier in this chapter). If you have a valuable network, you can get your followers to answer questions you can't find answers to anywhere else!

To Follow or Not to Follow?

Everyone has their own methodology for whom they follow and how they follow people on Twitter. Some people tend to follow everyone they interact with, but others judiciously control their following counts. Some people diligently review who they follow and trim out users who are no longer relevant to their lives, and others never look through their Following list.

There is no single "right" way to go about deciding who to follow; other twitterers may use the Following tool differently than you — just because they don't immediately follow you back doesn't mean they're not going to in the future. Our rule is simple: Follow someone if you have a reason to follow him, not just because he's following you. (If you're on Twitter for business purposes, we have different advice for you in Chapter 11.)

To prevent spam, the Twitter team has limited the number of twitterers that users can follow to 2,000 until they have roughly that number of followers themselves. Once a limited account reaches close to or over 2,000 followers, Twitter once again allows it to go out and follow more accounts.

Every user has a different ritual when she gets a new follower: Some people @reply their new followers to acknowledge the follow; some direct-message their new followers to say hello; and others do nothing at all. Twitter doesn't have an official protocol about what you're supposed to do, and you naturally gravitate towards a routine that works for you.

Some people and businesses choose to make first contact with their new followers by sending a direct message. You can write a very personalized direct message to say hello, thank the recipient for the follow, and mention why he might want to keep in touch. Some users enjoy receiving such direct-message greetings, but others might view a direct message as intrusive or antisocial. There's no hard and fast rule, and it's not always possible to tell which approach your new follower prefers, so play things by ear and develop your own personal style of what you are comfortable with.

Some Twitterers go so far as to use third-party services to automatically send a thank-you direct message to people who follow them.

If you decide to use that kind of technology, be forewarned that many users hate these automatic DMs. That sort of outreach can be antisocial and irritating; and, if the person doesn't like receiving direct messages from new people that she follows, sending her a DM can be insulting. So, use these technologies with caution.

As a side note, some Twitter users have rallied around the hashtag #endautodm in solidarity against auto-direct messages. Search for the endautodm hashtag on Twitter Search to get a sense of how unpopular auto-direct messages can be. (We cover hashtags and Twitter Search in Chapter 9.)

If you're on the fence about what to do to acknowledge someone who follows you, make first contact openly to keep with the transparent and welcoming nature of Twitter. Direct messages are meant for private conversations, which usually happen only after you spend time to get to know someone, both in person and on Twitter.

Getting Quick Answers

Have you ever had a seemingly simple question that has bothered you for days and days? Well, why not ask Twitter?

If you have a solid network of Twitter friends, someone can likely answer your question. People tend to know a variety of things, or have unknown talents and knowledge bases, so go ahead and ask! You might be surprised by the answers you get.

In fact, someone probably knows what you're looking for or is having a similar conversation somewhere, whether locally or on the other side of the world. For example, if you're awake at 5 a.m. in California trying (vainly) to remember the name of the fifth Beatle so that you can stop obsessing and go back to sleep already, someone who knows the answer is probably awake on the East Coast or not yet asleep in Europe. Hop on Twitter and ask!

(The Fifth Beatle's name is Stuart Sutcliffe, according to some; you can read more about it here: `http://en.wikipedia.org/wiki/Fifth_Beatle`. So, go to bed already!)

Some people consider tweeting a question whose answer you can easily search on your favorite Internet search resource impolite. Try hunting down the answer first by yourself before asking your Twitter network. Some users consider it rude and inconsiderate to waste their time with silly questions, and they may unfollow you. So, perhaps asking the fifth Beatle's name is poor form. You might ask your followers if they have any movie recommendations, though.

In addition, some brands and companies are beginning to use Twitter as a customer-service tool, and are willing and ready to answer customer queries. For example, JetBlue, shown in Figure 12-4, uses Twitter to send customers information on flight delays. (In Chapter 11, we explain how businesses can use Twitter to their advantage to help, educate, and communicate with customers.)

Accessing the experts

By using Twitter, you can find quick, knowledgeable answers to more serious questions, not just to simple ones. If you're doing some research for work and want to find the most useful sources, ask Twitter. Of course, you still have to do additional normal research and fact-checking, but you can definitely get pointers in the right direction much faster than you can on your own.

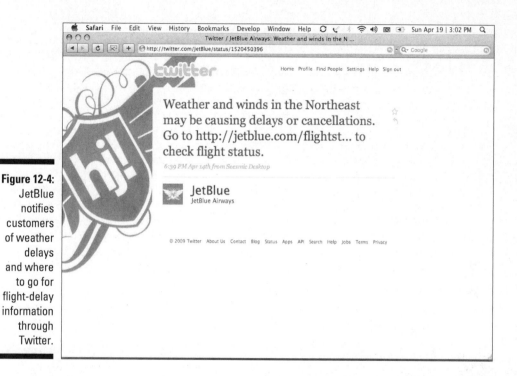

Figure 12-4:
JetBlue
notifies
customers
of weather
delays
and where
to go for
flight-delay
information
through
Twitter.

While Twitter grows in popularity, more professionals, celebrities, and point people at companies are actively using the service to further their own publicity, knowledge, and outreach. For example, if you want to get a better sense of what it's like to be an Australian actor working in America, ask Hugh Jackman (@RealHughJackman). Want to know what Yoko Ono thought about when she was writing one of her pieces? Go ahead and ask her! (@yokoono). Despite their celebrity, they have the exact same tools that you do and are as accessible as they want to be on Twitter. If they have the time and see your question, you just might get an answer. But again, respect their time by asking something relevant and interesting to them, not just something selfish or easily looked up elsewhere.

As you can probably imagine, many celebrities and industry mavens have many, many followers — and those popular folks are often inundated with questions and @replies. If you ask something of them and don't get a response, your question may have just gotten lost in the noise. Feel free to try to talk to them in the future, but if you're sending them public messages in your timeline, remember that everyone else reading your updates gets all those messages, too. In short, don't be a rabid fan.

You'll also find many industry analysts, number crunchers, stats hounds, and fact checkers on Twitter who aren't famous but are eager to help you. So, with your Twitter account comes an army of experts and pundits who have research-heavy charts, graphs, and reports on a wide array of topics. People on Twitter can be very generous with their time, knowledge, and information. After all, many of the relationships you have on Twitter are with people whom you trust and who trust you.

Twitter is a trust-based network. In the process of building connections, interacting with the community, and sharing your ideas and knowledge, you earn trust. That trust-building goes both ways. Your growing network of contacts on Twitter also earns your trust. So, if someone in your trusted network sends you a link, you can probably trust that the link will take you to a page that's helpful to you. Always check your facts, but you can get valuable, reliable, and accessible information through Twitter.

Information about breaking news

The real-time nature of tweets makes Twitter an ideal resource for breaking news. If anything newsworthy happens on the local level, someone on the scene probably has Twitter and is telling his network about it as it happens. If the twitterer uses any of the services that can post to Twitter accounts (such as Utterli, TwitPic, or Brightkite), his network is also getting real-time pictures, audio, geo-location, and sometimes video information, as well.

Follow @breakingnewson for the latest in breaking news, a favorite amongst many Twitter users.

Although Twitter has proven itself to be a great tool for getting live updates and eyewitness reports, traditional journalism and fact-checking still has a place. Sometimes, in the heat of an event or moment, rumors can spread as easily as fact across Twitter, so take each piece of information with a grain of salt. Depending on how much you trust the person who's providing the updates, you know how much legwork you have to do (if any) to validate her claim. By the same token, perpetually spreading false rumors reduces your reliability as a source to your followers.

Getting recommendations

Twitter's a great resource for getting recommendations from your friends and contacts. Say that you're an employer looking for a reliable office manager. A great way to start is by asking your Twitter network for help in staffing that position. In fact, your next office manager may come from your Twitter following.

Or perhaps you're looking for the best Chicago-style pizza in New York City. Ask your Twitter network for suggestions on where to go. If you have contacts in both Chicago and New York, you might have a bit of fun reading their tweets while they argue the finer points of crust thickness, cheese selection, and topping distribution. In the end, you'll likely have a few pizzerias and restaurants to try out (and more information about your contacts' food preferences than you bargained for).

Sharing Information

One of the things that new users notice quickly on Twitter is the abundance of shared information. You'll find that people share everything — from recipes to complex PowerPoint presentation files or *slide decks* — seemingly without a second thought.

Sometimes, people question the motives of those sharing or worry that the people who see and use the information might somehow steal it. Addressing that concern requires a fundamental psychological shift in thinking: Part of the success of Twitter is the concept of giving up some control over the information you release to your network. To quote an old adage, "Sharing means caring." Sharing with your network increases the value that you have to that network and allows your network to grow. It also shows that you care enough about the people in your network to share what you know, what you're doing, or what you're thinking about.

Giving up control might sound a little scary, but it doesn't have to be. You've built (or are building) a network of Twitter users whom you can trust. You can control who you interact with on Twitter and what kind of network you find value in cultivating. Whom you share with can be just as important as what you're sharing.

Like with any online service (or any gathering of human beings for that matter), nefarious characters do crop up on Twitter. They might try to socially engineer networks, artificially build reputation, or poach information for not-so-up-and-up purposes. The nice thing about Twitter is that it's pretty self-policing: If you're concerned about a user, either block or simply ignore him. If you're concerned about your information becoming public, protect your updates (you can find instructions on how to protect your updates in Chapter 3) and allow only people you trust to receive your tweets.

Another way many Twitter users share information is by linking to other Web sites, blogs, and Internet resources. We cover linking in Chapter 9, including how to go about linking to other sites, ways you can reduce your character count so that you can maximize the information and commentary you can include, and linking etiquette.

Chapter 13

Changing the World, One Tweet at a Time

*T*witter is a great communications tool for businesses and persons alike, and it has the potential to connect people and create relationships over a variety of discussions, interests, and geographies. When people use Twitter to grow their communities and share observations and insights on issues and situations that matter to them, interesting things start to happen. Twitter becomes a touch-point by which users try to improve their worlds.

In this chapter, we share true stories of global and social-change initiatives that either started or were facilitated by the use of Twitter, as well as world and local events aided by Twitter. We close the chapter with a few examples that illustrate Twitter's ability to spread messages of goodwill and world improvement through its user base.

Twittering the Globe for Change

Twitter offers a platform for immediate news delivery and instant communication with millions of twitterers around the world. So, despite the seemingly confining 140-character limit, Twitter has become accepted by many as an extremely effective tool for social change on both a local and global level.

Twestival

Twestival, a worldwide event with more than 200 participating cities, was held on February 12, 2009, to benefit a nonprofit called charity: water (`www.charitywater.org` and `@charitywater`). This night of music and friends got its start in the U.K. from a single Twitter user who had fewer than 2,000 followers. But the idea caught on when some of those followers decided to make it a worldwide effort.

Ultimately, volunteers raised more than $275,000 around the world for charity: water, which uses donations to build wells in developing countries, where access to clean water is scarce. Generating the interest took a matter of days, and most Twestivals were put together in only a few weeks, thanks to Twitter's ability to rapidly disseminate ideas and information. In April 2009, Amanda traveled to Ethiopia to witness and share the drilling of the first Twestival well and to raise awareness of charity: water's work and provide a behind-the-scenes look at clean drinking water issues.

Quite a few individuals and organizations have begun to use Twitter for outreach, sharing news, publicizing activities and events, raising funds, mobilizing grassroots efforts, and a number of other ways for effecting positive change. Users who know how to tap Twitter's potential for swiftly spreading their ideas are able to get rapid and powerful results.

One can call attention to issues or events by consistently tweeting relevant information in digestible snippets, as well as occasionally sending links to valuable and verifiable information. You also increase your reputation as an authority on a given topic if you write credible posts and articles and share these with your followers.

But, on the simplest and most mundane level, tens of thousands of users have made strong personal connections on Twitter: new friendships and relationships, as well as new and fruitful professional connections. These connections spring up on Twitter all the time, and even new twitterers are likely to encounter someone who can share one of these only-on-Twitter stories. Heck, you may become a Twitter story yourself — you just have to reach out.

Charity events

Twitterer Amanda Rose (`@amanda`) is widely acknowledged as the driving force behind Twestival (`www.twestival.com` or `@twestival`), shown in Figure 13-1, a series of events that raised awareness and funding for a non-profit organization called charity: water (`www.charitywater.org`).

charity: water (founded by Scott Harrison, @scottharrison) is one of the best-known charities with a presence on Twitter, largely because of a note Twitter founder Biz Stone (@biz) included in an August 2008 e-mailed newsletter. Internet luminaries such as Mashable.com founder Pete Cashmore and Facebook developer Dave Morin have hosted Twitter campaigns for donations. Just as Twestival planning was kicking off, Laura's own Christmas-and-birthday wish effort @wellwishes raised $25,000 and placed charity: water and the concept of microgiving (donations were $2 each and made directly through Twitter) onto TechCrunch, The Huffington Post, Mashable, Howard Lindzon's blog (@howardlindzon), and dozens of other old and new media outlets.

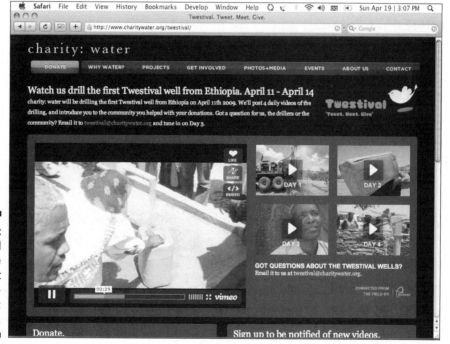

Figure 13-1: Twestival supports the nonprofit organization charity: water.

charity: water is not the only nonprofit to have benefited from Twitter's broad reach and influence. Social Media for Nonprofits guru Beth Kanter (@kanter) conducted the first Twitter-based charity fund drive we know of when she decided to send a young Cambodian woman to college with a little help from her friends. Beth's ongoing work usually benefits Cambodian orphans via The Sharing Foundation. Other Twitterers donated money and gathered at a fundraising social event in Boston to help victims of domestic violence through Gradon Tripp's (@gradontripp) Social Media for Social Change (@SM4SC), shown in Figure 13-2).

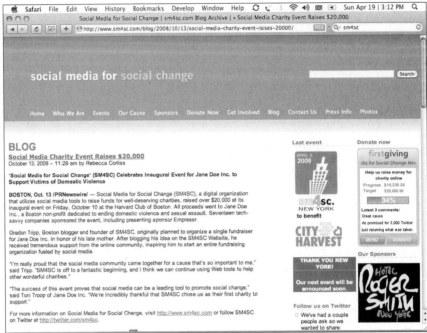

Politics

You can gauge the impact of an issue around the world by checking Twitter. During the 2008 United States elections, news junkies used Twitter to follow not just the issues, but also the sentiments of people from around the world: disillusionment with the administration of George W. Bush, the shortcomings of U.S. foreign policy, the rapidly deteriorating economic situation, and the rise of Barack Obama (@barackobama). In the weeks leading up to the election, Twitter even launched a page specifically for campaign-related tweets and worked closely with Al Gore's (@algore) company Current.TV on a video-text integration of tweets into their election-related broadcasts.

Twitter users began to follow and monitor politics in real time, bonding over some candidates, making fun of political gaffes and snafus, and overall creating a real-time political metric that instantly became a media favorite. Twitter users live-tweeted debates and stump speeches, and even less-active twitterers turned to the service to keep tabs on what was going on in the world of politics as it happened.

Staffers caught on to the fact that politicians can use Twitter to measure the buzz about them in real time. During the election, Barack Obama's team was in on the ground floor when it came to the use of Twitter as a publicity and organization tool, choosing the platform as an important way to interact with prospective voters.

The night of the U.S. presidential election, Twitter was nearly brought to its knees by millions and millions of shared concerns, excitement, questions, voting reports, and a massive buzz of connection around the events that were unfolding. Twitter's technological system took on massive traffic from all over the globe and managed not to crash, although there were time delays, especially in the SMS-to-Twitter message flow. It was amazing to share it all virtually with friends and loved ones from around the globe in real time on our phones and computers.

The reactions were varied, but no matter which side of the fence you were on, you were a part of the first, truly real-time, global reaction to a national election. Barack Obama's election victory was historic for twitterers, in more ways than one.

Twitter also helped people around the world aggregate their reactions from other social-media services. TwitPics, YouTube videos, Qik channels, Utterli and TalkShoe voice posts, and plenty of other services all fed into Twitter in a massive data stream that pretty much anyone around the world could access.

Natural disasters

Twitter has also caught on as an extremely important medium for natural-disaster reporting, such as hurricanes Gustav and Ike, wildfires and earthquakes in California, and the massive and tragic 2008 earthquake in China, as well as countless smaller hurricanes, earthquakes, volcanoes, and tornados. These days, with so many people using the service, news of major weather events often break on Twitter long before the mainstream media reports it.

You can use Twitter as a sort of tracking service for weather events and other surprises across the globe. Follow weather in real time while it moves from place to place, just by watching the tweets of people you follow.

Government agencies (see Figure 13-3) can find tremendous value by tapping into Twitter as a real-time system for sensing and signaling events around the globe. Because of Twitter's open application program interface (API), programs that use Twitter's search and trends data to help people survive and thrive in future disasters are only a matter of time.

Twitter has value to individuals beyond news reporting and storm tracking, too. Twitter users can also connect with far-off family, friends, and colleagues to check on their status after a major weather incident in their area. You can use Twitter as an immediate channel to get information about what's happening and, more importantly, do something about it.

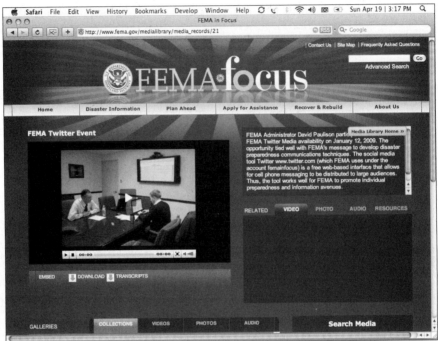

Figure 13-3:
FEMA
embraces
Twitter.

Helping others

Using Twitter for social change goes beyond fundraising, though. People also use Twitter for some very unique problem-solving: Among the more unusual projects is fronted by user @maratriangle, who has been on Twitter since its early days and uses the service to track and catch poachers in Africa (see Figure 13-4). With a standout avatar in a green beret, he has developed a network of Twitter users all over the globe who make sure no reports of poaching go unnoticed.

Twitter can effect real global change by facilitating data-sharing for professionals across borders. One teaching hospital tweeted during a live surgery to educate students who couldn't actually be at the surgery. Other people have suggested using Twitter to share medical and prescription data anonymously from doctors to pharmaceutical companies so that pharmaceutical firms can see in real time which prescriptions are being prescribed where. The ability to collect this type of data also has implications for disease tracking and outbreak control, though anyone trying this must tackle the obvious privacy issues before such a use could be considered.

Twitter certainly has lofty potential for global connections on a large scale. So, how can you use it yourself? Be patient. After you build a following on Twitter and become a respected member of a strong network, you can help rally others to a cause, or even get a hand when you need some help. Your Twitter network can help you relocate across town or across the globe, find a new job, reconnect with lost family members, and even research your history and genealogy.

In one dramatic example, the use of Twitter helped someone escape potentially dire circumstances. When James Karl Buck was arrested in Egypt, he immediately tweeted a single word: "Arrested". Instantly, his followers and colleagues were alerted to his situation and mobilized the help needed to secure his release. Read the story at `www.cnn.com/2008/tech/04/25/twitter.buck`.

Figure 13-4:
`@mara triangle` makes sure that poachers don't go unnoticed.

Organizing People Online and in Real Life

Twitter makes organizing group activities both online and in real life easy. People have used Twitter to solicit volunteers for events, rally a group around a cause, push get-out-the-vote efforts, find speakers for conferences, scout locations for get-togethers, or just have impromptu *tweetups* (a term twitterers use to refer to spontaneous real-life meet-and-greets).

TIP

Twitter helps people take online interactions into the real world. As Twitter becomes more popular and enters the mainstream, however, Twitter users may want to exercise some basic common sense when meeting people offline for the first time. Make sure to meet in groups and in public places, and tell someone where you're going and with whom. While the vast majority of the people we've met on Twitter are trustworthy, we advise you not to make rash decisions about your safety.

You can use Twitter in such a wide variety of ways because of — you guessed it — how open-ended it is. Because Twitter doesn't have any forced rules of use, beyond common courtesy and a few guidelines about balance in followers (see `http://twitter.com/faq`), Twitter users can craft their own strategies for how to use it. You can read more about Twitter etiquette in Chapter 7 and security and safety in Chapter 10.

Perhaps the best example of Twitter's organizational power is Barack Obama's 2008 presidential campaign. The Obama campaign used Twitter in conjunction with other social-media tools to rally grassroots support. Representatives from Obama's team used the Twitter account @barackobama to post updates on the candidate's whereabouts, announce rallies and donation drives, and answer questions from ordinary twitterers. By using Twitter, the campaign helped to foster an idea of transparency and togetherness.

Even more interesting than Obama's use of Twitter was how his supporters used it. When Obama supporters on Twitter began to use their avatars and background images to display their support for him, the idea caught on and spread rapidly across Twitter. Twitter avatars changed to Obama-themed icons in solidarity to the cause; twitterers updated bios and tag lines; and people pointed their personal profile Web links to Obama's campaign site. For a service as simple and stripped-down as Twitter, Obama supporters certainly found creative ways to use it to show their affinity.

Now that Obama has been in office for some time, you can see an alternative organizational effort underway among conservatives on Twitter. Feeling underrepresented on Twitter, pugilistic, and calling themselves the Top Conservatives on Twitter, these individuals use the #tcot hashtag to represent themselves, and to stir support for their after-election goals and events (see Figure 13-5).

Organizing on Twitter does come with some risks. Because of the crowd mentality, Twitter opinion can turn on a dime. Everything discussed on Twitter is so real-time and in the moment that something can be trendy one moment and passé the next. Take the time to set up some foundation work first — a Web site that has accurate information, a universal hashtag, and keyword tracking. Your potential attendees and volunteers will know that you mean business if you use such tools. As we go to press, infighting amongst the

`#tcot` community has disabled some of the Web sites built to support and display their efforts, but you really can't own or stop a hashtag. It belongs to those who use it most.

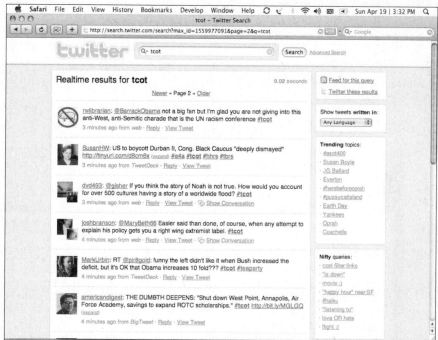

Figure 13-5:
A #tcot search, showing politically conservative tweets.

Organizing on a small scale

You can use Twitter to rally people around a cause at any level. We mention some bigger examples in the preceding section, such as Beth Kanter (see Figure 13-6), who once raised $9,000 for The Sharing Foundation orphans in 90 minutes onstage and via Twitter during the Gnomedex technology conference, and Twestival nonprofit raising $275,000 for charity: water. But what can you do in your own communities?

Even if your big idea is a local one, you can take advantage of Twitter to make it happen. Twitter empowers the user to locate and organize like-minded people online around a common goal or idea. If you need volunteers to fundraise for your child's class trip or school supplies, you can probably find them through your Twitter network. If you want to start a book club, try using Twitter to find members.

Taste Live

Wine and spirits enthusiasts have caught on to using Twitter as a community platform, especially the international community of wine lovers that organizes virtual tastings and real-world events. If you turn to Twitter on most Saturday nights, you can catch a glimpse of the Twitter Taste Live phenomenon (hashtag #ttl), shown in the figure.

This online event was started by Massachusetts wine shop Bin Ends Wines, and it has taken off as a concept all over the U.S. and abroad. The store didn't just stop with Twitter Taste Live online events, though: They tapped the power of their Twitter network to take it offline, as well as onto other social-media channels, such as Ustream.

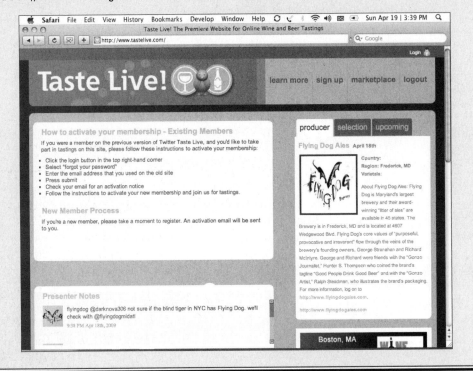

Organizing on Twitter does help serious causes, but it doesn't have to be all work and no play. You can use Twitter as a tool to organize whatever kind of group you want, including those on the lighter side of life. Food and spirits enthusiasts have been taking advantage of Twitter lately: A thriving foodie community, for example, socializes online and plans dinner parties, restaurant weeks, and other offline excursions to celebrate their passion for food. This community is both international and local, at the same time. They trade recipes and ingredients, solve cooking problems, and spread the word about new restaurants together (see Figure 13-7).

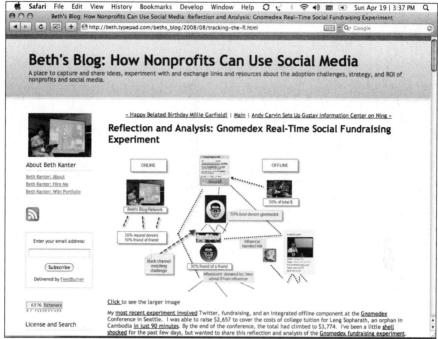

Figure 13-6:
Beth's
Blog is a
resource for
how non-
profits can
use social
media,
including
Twitter.

Figure 13-7:
Planning
to eat food.
Mmm!

Banding together for creative purposes

If you want to drum up user-generated content for your company or clients, or use that content on a Web site or blog, then you can often find enthusiastic participants by reaching out via Twitter. Twitter users have banded together on creative projects of all sizes, some of which were started by corporate marketers. Tyson Foods uses Twitter and its blog to generate blog comments that trigger in-kind donations to food pantries. Marketer HubSpot often gathers people in the Boston area — both company employees and outsiders — to "star" in musical videos about inbound marketing on YouTube, and they do it by rallying the troops on Twitter.

Creative content from Twitter is definitely not limited to commercial purposes. Twitter users have planned, written, and cast whole online *Webisodics* (television-style video series based online only) via the service. When they need to change a plot or scout a location, Twitter can come to the rescue, letting interested participants help the project in real time.

Do you need to organize an audio or music challenge, such as the RPM Challenge (`www.rpmchallenge.com`), shown in Figure 13-8? Twitter can help you do that, by allowing people to participate or express interest in your idea. Twitter is also a fantastic tool for collaborating on projects. You can find co-authors, lyricists, people who play various instruments, and more, just by shooting out a few strings of 140 characters into the Twitter universe.

Figure 13-8:
The RPM
Challenge
Web site.

Planning an event

If you plan events — whether they're small, impromptu meet-ups or large weekend workshops or seminars — Twitter can help. You can use Twitter to find speakers, scout locations, score discounts, locate equipment, and drive attendance.

Here's how you can make the most of Twitter for your event:

1. **Create a landing page.**

   Even though you're doing most of your organizing on Twitter, Twitter itself isn't feature-heavy enough to provide all information to your potential event-goers and volunteers. Make the landing page an off-site location for signing up, recording offers of help, and generating interest. Your landing page can be a blog, a Web site, or an event page on a site such as EventBrite, Amiando, or Upcoming. TwtVite is a relatively new event-planning site purpose built for Twitter that incorporates the Twitter avatars and profiles of those who sign up.

2. **Choose a hashtag (keyword) for your event.**

   Take a minute to check Hashtags.org (`www.hashtags.org`) or Twitter Search (`http://search.twitter.com`) to make sure that no one else is using that hashtag. A unique hashtag will eliminate confusion.

3. **When your event landing page is ready, set up basic alert tracking for your event.**

   Several free services such as Google Alerts or BlvdStatus conversions (see Chapter 9) will meet your basic requirements.

   You can also use a paid media monitoring service such as those offered by Radian6 (see Chapter 9) to track your event. When you need to decide what to track as your keyword, your hashtag is a great place to start. You can also track the venue, the theme, and other related keywords.

4. **Now that you have laid the foundation for tracking interest and attendance to your event, start spreading the word!**

   Don't let talk of the event completely dominate your Twitter stream — you can lose followers that way — but make sure to highlight your event adequately. You can generate interest and allow the tweet to get legs and be retweeted (RTed).

 If you're planning something larger than a simple two-hour tweetup, make sure to keep up with who has volunteered assistance, who signs up for the event, and venues that have offered help (see Figure 13-9).

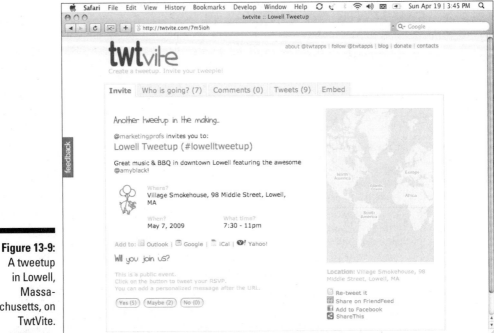

Figure 13-9:
A tweetup
in Lowell,
Massa-
chusetts, on
TwtVite.

Can you plan a full-blown conference by using Twitter as your main tool? Yes, you can! Planning a conference takes a little more finesse than a short tweetup or business function, but it's very doable.

If you do plan to go big by organizing a large event on Twitter, keep thorough records to help you manage all the tweets related to it. You can even use a free tool such as WebNotes (`www.webnotes.net`) or EverNote (`http://evernote.com`) to track what people have offered to do, who's coming, and other logistical issues. Coupled with your tracking methods, you may find planning a big event the 140-character way relatively painless.

Engaging in Citizen Journalism

You may have first been turned onto Twitter by hearing about it in the main-stream media. News outlets such as CNN (`@cnn`, `@cnnbrk`) and popular shows such as *The Ellen Show, The View,* and *The Oprah Winfrey Show* have all begun to incorporate Twitter and the global, real-time conversations it fosters into their on-screen time.

Twitter is cropping up in print media, too. Celebrities are adopting it as a way to beat the paparazzi at their own game and give their fans a more direct voice to listen to (see Figure 13-10). Musicians are tweeting to bypass regular radio and sell more music, as well as interact with more fans. Twitter is even making it into nontechnical print publications such as the *New York Times.*

Even before its exposure on mainstream media, Twitter had already become a natural outlet for the phenomenon known as *citizen journalism.* Thanks to services technologies like mobile phones and portable video cameras, real people can report on real events as they're unfolding.

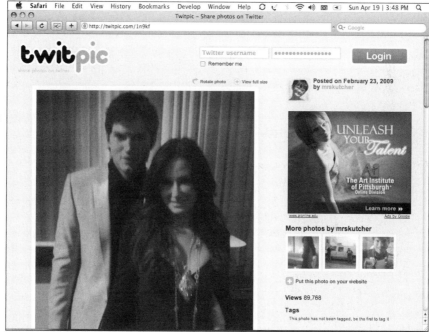

Figure 13-10: Ashton Kutcher (@aplusk) and his wife Demi Moore (@mrs kutcher) dive into Twitter, full force, by using TwitPic.

Citizen journalism hits the mainstream

Mainstream media outlets have been turned on to the social-media craze, and CNN has been at the forefront with its *iReport initiative* (see Figure 13-11), which allows anyone to upload photos, videos, or stories to CNN's Web site; CNN then features some of those iReports on TV. Twitter is a big part of this phenomenon. We don't know whether CNN was the first national news outlet to embrace citizen journalism, but they were the first to embrace it so openly via Twitter. Now, thanks to Twitter; the CNN iReporter interface; and other technology, such as Pure Digital's popular Flip video camera, and better phones with Twitter-friendly services (such as Qik); man-on-the-street report-ing has become a reality — and an important part of 21st-century journalism.

That man on the street can be any person who has access to computers, phones, cameras, video cameras, or audio recorders. Now, anyone can be the journalist, and Twitter brings that roving band of citizen reporters into sharp focus.

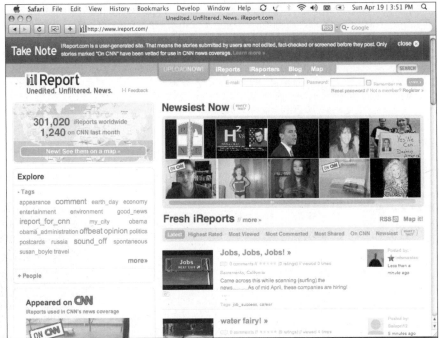

Figure 13-11: iReport and citizen journalism.

How does Twitter fit in? Twitter is the darling of the instant-gratification crowd, and it allows you to report events right away with no fact-checking at all, so do take everything you read with a grain of salt. If it's a story that's not being reported on by the major, respected media outlets, do a little fact-checking before you take it as the gospel truth.

Being a Twitter journalist

Twitter, like user-created encyclopedia Wikipedia, seems to be very good at self-policing. When a fraud starts making the rounds on Twitter, sharp-eyed users are quick to catch onto it and are just as quick in telling their friends and colleagues what's going on. Twitter users offer a kind of natural checks-and-balances system for the twitterverse.

A January 2009 news event that highlighted Twitter's potential for citizens to act as journalists was the emergency landing of a plane in the Hudson River in New York City after a run-in with migrating birds led to the loss of both engines. Twitter users were arguably the first people to hear about it because eyewitnesses posted instant reactions.

Janis Krums, @jkrums, a Twitter user on board a ferry that raced in to rescue passengers, took an incredible iPhone picture of the floating plane and the passengers being evacuated. He instantly posted it to Twitter (http://twitter.com/jkrums/status/1121915133) using a third-party service, which hosts photos and tweets a link to them on the user's Twitter account. The astonishing photo was retweeted and passed around Twitter so quickly that it hit international media outlets within minutes (see Figure 13-12). The Web traffic going to the photo was so overwhelming that TwitPic's servers temporarily went offline.

Figure 13-12: Pictures of the plane that landed in the Hudson River first ended up on Flickr, Tumblr, and TwitPic, directed by the Twitter users who took them.

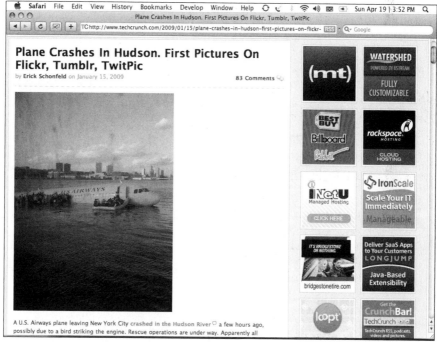

Citizen journalists can do more than just observe — Twitter's immediacy and portability (because of its availability on mobile devices) makes it possible for people to report during the moment, not just afterwards. During the November 2008 terrorist attacks in Mumbai, Twitter was used to pass word of a blood drive to help victims.

As a part of the citizen-journalism movement, Twitter is helping make the world safer for children. Recently, the number of Twitter-generated #AmberAlerts has risen, and several children have been reunited with their families because of the observations of regular people who cared and paid attention (see Figure 13-13).

Help Find My Child and other similar organizations have also been working on finding lost children through Twitter. Unlike the unofficial #AmberAlerts, which don't come from a centralized source, @helpfindmychild is an organized international effort coordinated through one office to use Twitter to find missing children.

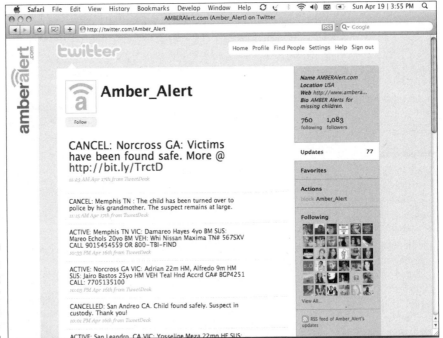

Figure 13-13: Amber Alert on Twitter for missing children.

Twitter and other forms of citizen journalism are changing the world for the better, but users need to fact-check, credit the proper sources, and flag those twitterers who are inaccurate or worse, deliberately misleading. While Twitter and the rise of the citizen journalist both augment and replace mainstream news, you must be vigilant and ensure that the news you're spreading is true.

Tweeting accurate info

How do you credit a source on Twitter or assure people that the news you tweet is accurate? As much as possible, offer proof that your news is valid. Here's how:

- ✔ **Include a link.** The most basic thing you can do is link to a reliable source or, if you can't verify, post the item as a question, asking others to share verification. The BBC learned this lesson the hard way when they posted an unverified rumor during the November 2008 Mumbai attacks. Their page said Twitter was the source but did not link to a tweet that would support or deny its validity. Once BBC had reported the rumor, subsequent tweets linked to the BBC page, and the rumor persisted, where most Twitter rumors tend to die out.

- ✔ **Create a companion blog.** In this blog, you have more space to credit the sources of your news. Link to that blog in your tweets. Make sure to go into your blog after you send your tweets and credit each story wherever possible.

- ✔ **Build a network based on trust and continued reliable information.** Not only should you make sure that the people you follow and associate with are trustworthy, but you should also be certain that the people in your network feel the same about you.

- ✔ **Don't underestimate the power of the retweet.** The retweet (where one your followers repeats your tweet for the benefit of her own followers) is critical to networking and viral spread. Retweets of your posts give them a level of validity because retweets prove what you say is worth repeating. Most third-party Twitter clients have built-in buttons next to each tweet in your stream that let you easily set them up for a retweet, and we suspect Twitter will add this feature soon.

- ✔ **If you retweet, try to credit the original poster.** Sometimes when retweeting, the 140-character limit means that you have to take out names or letters to make the message fit. Always make sure that you leave the name of the twitterer you are retweeting to acknowledge your source.

Gathering your journalistic tools

You can use these tools to prepare for your Twitter-inspired citizen-journalist moment:

- ✔ **A mobile phone that has a camera and/or video camera:** Most cellphones have at least the former these days. And make sure that you have a cellular data plan so you can send your photos.

✔ **Qik:** A free Web application (www.qik.com) that lets you record short, live videos and broadcast them for free online. It posts a link to Twitter so that your followers can view the stream live, and even chat, and the video posts to YouTube, as well as to the Qik site. Two different videos of pro-Tibet protests made it to the world from the 2008 China Olympics because of Qik, even though both videographers were detained.

✔ **Utterli:** A free program (www.utterli.com) that lets you record short, live audio and video files and then posts them to the Web, similar to a live audio podcast. It posts to Twitter, as well, and you can attach still photos and other articles to each audio or video file.

✔ **A Flip video camera:** A nice, affordable way to grab live video of an event while it happens, then post it to the Web. Pure Digital Technologies manufactures this video camera, but several other electronics companies (such as Kodak) make similar, pocket-sized video cameras.

✔ **An account on a free photo-sharing service:** These services include TwitPic and Flickr, which accept mobile uploads for sharing your still photos.

If you ever take live video or pictures of people, it should be common sense to get their permission or, if circumstances don't require permission, to at least warn them that you plan to broadcast the images or post them online. Depending on where you are, it may be illegal to post those images without the subjects' permission. If you intend to capture video or pictures for distribution online with regularity, consult a legal professional.

Part V
The Part of Tens

The 5th Wave   By Rich Tennant

"This is getting downright annoying. He tweets me every time he's about to go down a chimney."

In This Part . . .

Like every *For Dummies* book, we include the Part of Tens in *Twitter For Dummies*. In this part, we highlight neat tools, services, and uses for Twitter that you may want to check out while you're tweeting away.

Chapter 14

Ten Twitter Tools

In This Chapter

▶ Organizing your Twitter world with the right applications

▶ Getting down to business with the help of Twitter tools

▶ Connecting your Twitter account to your other online accounts

*Y*ou need the right tools to get the most out of Twitter. New tools, services, Web sites, and applications are created for Twitter users every
day, so the list of tools that you can choose from is always growing. To help
get you started, we want to tell you about a few of our favorite examples,
which give you a fun sampling that will give you some sense of different ways
you can use Twitter.

Each time we tried to come up with a list of the top ten tools, we realized it's
just not possible — too many great innovations are being built on Twitter's
"platform." What is the best tool for you really depends on your needs, and,
of course, popular new tools emerge all the time. Literally, because of this
problem, Laura is working on a startup, www.oneforty.com, that will make
it easy for anyone to find, use, and share the best Twitter-related applications
and services. Stay tuned to that site for help making the most of your Twitter
experience.

TweetDeck: Connecting with Many

www.tweetdeck.com

Type: Desktop client

TweetDeck is an Adobe Air application that gives you the tools you need to
keep track of large numbers of people in your Twitter stream. (For more on
Adobe Air, see Chapter 9.) It allows you to put people in groups, keep permanent search windows open, view your Facebook account (and post to it selec-
tively, as well), keep track of who's talking to you or about you, and much
more. It does all this in a customizable interface.

Six essential types of tools

The Twitter ecosystem is really complex. It can be overwhelming. A shortcut to make sense of it is to think about six essential types of tools that most any twitterer should try. We also include some of the best examples for each:

✔ **Networking (Twellow, FriendorFollow):** Your network is *the* most important thing about Twitter, but tools to find, follow, and keep track of your connections aren't that great yet. For now, we have directories.

✔ **Desktop client (TweetDeck & Seesmic Desktop):** Dedicated software on your computer that makes interacting with Twitter easier.

✔ **Smartphone client (Tweetie/iPhone, TwitterBerry/BlackBerry, PocketTwit/**Windows Mobile):** Dedicated software on your phone that makes interacting with Twitter easier.

✔ **Search and listening (Twitter Search):** Search tweets in real time, monitor keywords and hashtags, and subscribe to search results.

✔ **URL shortener (bit.ly):** Make links fit into 140 characters, keep track of what you've linked to, and preferably, keep some kind of records of how many people clicked, repeated, or also shortened the link.

✔ **Multimedia sharing (TwitPic, Qik, Last.fm, Utterli):** Embed and share links to photos, video, or audio, to make your Twitter stream a whole lot more than a bunch of text.

TIP

Recent contender to the throne is Tweetie for Mac OS X (`www.atebits.com/tweetie-mac`) and iPhone (`www.atebits.com/tweetie-iphone`), mainly because of the one-two punch of mobile plus desktop, combined with some favorite TweetDeck style features.

Seesmic Desktop/Twhirl: Managing Multiple Accounts

`www.twhirl.org`

Type: Desktop client

Twhirl is owned by Seesmic, a video messaging company that has fully integrated its video service into the new desktop application for Twhirl. Twhirl is missing a few key features for managing (and listening to) many followers, but it makes up for its shortcoming in the ability to have multiple accounts open at the same time. As this book went to press, Seesmic was publicly beta testing its Twhirl replacement Seesmic Desktop, which offers a great deal of new functionality.

Twhirl offers ways to interact with some of your other favorite social services, such as identi.ca (`http://identi.ca`) or 12Seconds (`http://12seconds.tv`), Facebook (`www.facebook.com`), and FriendFeed (`http://friendfeed.com`), for example.

CoTweet: Corporate Tweeting

`https://cotweet.com`

Type: Business dashboard

If you want a corporate solution that lets multiple users monitor and update a single account and displays all of your Twitter accounts in a single interface, you should look at CoTweet. Like the social media listening tool Radian6, CoTweet lets companies assign individual tweets to employees for follow-up. Still in *beta* (meaning that new features and functions are being added all the time), this service is hit or miss on features, but the planned feature set should take care of most of your company or organization's Twitter needs, from keeping organized and letting more than one person maintain an account to scheduling tweets ahead of time.

Make sure that you have full disclosure in your profile somewhere if you have multiple people tweeting for your company or you have a ghost tweeter tweeting for you. For shared accounts, authors usually sign the end of their tweets with an ^ and their initials.

Speaking of disclosure, Laura advises both CoTweet and a service named TipJoy that appears in Chapter 15. She played no part in selecting which companies to profile in these chapters and, in fact, only found out which ones Leslie and Michael chose just before the book went to press. Both CoTweet and TipJoy are unique innovators in their areas and got into the book on their own merits.

Smartphone Clients Tweetie, PocketTwit, and TwitterBerry

`http://www.atebits.com/tweetie-iphone`
`http://code.google.com/p/pocketwit`
`http://www.orangatame.com/products/twitterberry`

Type: Smartphone clients

If you have a mobile phone, you may have trouble finding the perfect Twitter client. Even more frustrating, all carriers use different browsers and standards, making it impossible to find one client to fit all phones. Here are some of our favorites for each platform:

- ✔ **Tweetie:** If you have an iPhone, Tweetie is the way to go. It's like having TweetDeck on your phone, in a slick iPhone interface. It also has a companion desktop client — an added bonus. (We talk about TweetDeck in the section "TweetDeck: Connecting with Many," earlier in this chapter.)

- ✔ **PocketTwit:** For Windows Mobile phones that have touch screens, PocketTwit is made by Google Labs and offers several nice features, multiple-account management, and a nifty, avatar-included interface.

- ✔ **TwitterBerry:** The current most popular solution for BlackBerry devices, TwitterBerry works with BlackBerry's proprietary interface, so you can easily tweet on the go. Laura whinges about how many basic Twitter features TwitterBerry lacks, but nothing great for the BlackBerry has taken its place. Yet.

Check your carrier's data and text charges before using these services. Twitter may be free, but some of the attached services may come with hidden costs for use if your phone is not already on unlimited data.

Twellow: Finding People to Follow

www.twellow.com

Type: Networking

Many directory sites have come and gone, but Twellow was the first. It doesn't have the sexiest interface, but it has a fantastic database of easily searchable, accurate information about people, companies, and categories.

Use more than one solution to find followers if you want to get a more interesting and beneficial demographic.

FriendorFollow: Managing Followers and Followings

http://friendorfollow.com

Type: Networking

This Web site lets you see whom you're following, who's following you, and which follows are mutual — all in a nicely tabbed, avatar-based grid. And you can fix any follower/following discrepancies right from the site interface.

Don't unfollow people just because they don't follow you back. Twitter doesn't require you to follow someone back, and you never know whether that user might have just missed you. Try saying hi with an @reply to see whether you can get to know that person better.

TwtVite: Event Planning

> `http://twtvite.com`

Type: Miscellaneous

This quick and easy Web site lets people tweet out their RSVP to your event. It then keeps track of who has RSVPed for you. This service offers the added bonus of marketing before the event while people tweet about their attendance.

Also make an EventBrite (`www.eventbrite.com`) or Facebook Event (`www.facebook.com/apps/application.php?id=2344061033`) page to make sure that you're giving people a way to connect if they don't use Twitter yet.

It's worth mentioning that TwtVite parent `www.TwtApps.com` also offers eight more helpful and nicely integrated Twitter tools covering polls, jobs, greetings, travel, business, and even virtual pets.

Twitterfeed: Getting Your Blog Posts to Twitter

> `http://twitterfeed.com`

Type: Publishing

This handy service lets you schedule periodic scrapes of your blog for new posts, and then link these blog bits up on Twitter. Twitterfeed gives you a simple and easy way to drive traffic to your site or alert friends to a new post without having to remember to do it separately.

Set Twitterfeed to check your blog only every few hours to prevent your Twitter stream from seeming spammy.

TwitPic

`www.twitpic.com`

Type: Multimedia sharing

TwitPic is a popular image-sharing service for Twitter. Users can upload photos via camera or mobile phone and then share those photos on Twitter. You can also add comments on the pictures themselves.

Xpenser: Keeping Track of Your Expenses

`http://xpenser.com`

Type: Financial

Xpenser is a neat tool that integrates with sites such as FreshBooks (`www.freshbooks.com`) and applications such as Quicken to help you keep track of your business and personal expenses on the go. After configuring your account, simply send a direct (private) message to xpn to keep track of your spending. Now, reporting your business lunch or tracking your gas mileage is only a tweet away.

You can use Xpenser to get yourself in the habit of recording your expenses. Because the updates are made via direct message, you don't have to worry about your followers seeing the information.

Chapter 15

Ten Useful Twitter-Based Services

*W*ith events like the Hudson River plane crash, Demi Moore, Ashton Kutcher and Oprah coming to Twitter, buzz about the service is making Twitter go mainstream fast. Because of that, many businesses, causes, and people are creating Twitter-based presences, and hundreds of innovative Twitter-based services are emerging to support that. Some have separate Web sites, and some you just use directly through Twitter. In no particular order, here are ten that stand out because of their usefulness and overall appeal to Twitter audiences.

BreakingNews

`@BreakingNews http://www.bnonews.com`

Type: News. This simple feed gives you ongoing breaking news from around the world. Actual humans maintain and update it, not an automatic RSS feed. It has a good track record of beating many of the major news outlets for breaking news — and it has a good track record for accuracy, as well.

StockTwits

`@StockTwits http://www.stocktwits.com`

Type: Financial. Cofounded by Howard Lindzon, best known for mashing up Wall Street with video podcasting to create the highly successful WallStrip, StockTwits plays off the fact that investors who tweet like to tweet about stocks. StockTwits is essentially a community and social exchange of snippets of conversation about stocks, using Twitter as the conversation medium at its core. You can use StockTwits at its Web site, by following @stocktwits, or by using the TweetDeck plug-in.

Tweecious: Use Delicious to Organize the Links You Tweet

> http://friedcell.net/tweecious/get

Type: Publishing. If you post links to Delicious (http://delicious.com; a social bookmarking service that allows you to share links with your friends), this little tool makes it easy for you. Now, your posts to Twitter that include links can also automagically go to Delicious. Tweecious even looks at the rest of the tweet and automatically tags the link with relevant categories or keywords. Once you have a Delicious account, Tweecious takes only a moment to set up, and it even reads shortened URLs and extracts the original link.

People who like to keep track of a variety of Web pages and tend to lose them on Twitter may find this tool very handy.

TipJoy

> @Tipjoy or www.tipjoy.com

Type: Financial. This payments service offers you a way to pay the person, business, Web site, or charity of your choice. Originally developed to let you tip bloggers — or any Web site — you can make payments with TipJoy right on Twitter incredibly easily. Follow @tipjoy on Twitter or go to its Web site to create an account. After you fund that account (you have to go to the Web site to do so), you can pay any amount to anyone on Twitter by simply tweeting **p $amount @username**.

Many people like to include a note or link about what the payment is for right in the tweet, which can help spread the word about an interesting cause, project, or product.

TipJoy was founded by husband and wife team Abby and Ivan Kirigin and launched in a startup incubation program known as Y Combinator. After working together to raise $25,000 for Laura's @wellwishes holiday and birthday charity campaign for charity: water, TipJoy invited her to become an advisor. We can personally vouch for their legitimacy and reputation.

ExecTweets

www.exectweet.com

Type: Networking. Like millions of other people, Laura pretty much laughed at Twitter when she first heard about it. Turns out that's pretty normal. But what made the difference for her was noticing that she could use it to surround herself with successful, interesting people who would motivate her as a homebound working mom.

Nowadays, we have ExecTweets to let you easily follow the tweets of some of the world's smartest, most successful executives. Richard Branson? Check. Jack Welch? Check. Dive in and find inspiration, leadership, ideas, and resources from some of the brightest business minds in the world.

EpicTweet

www.epictweet.com

Type: Entertainment. EpicTweet is a service that delivers only the tweets that Twitter users have determined to be the funniest, most retweeted, most important, or smartest. Twitter users vote on which tweets get included. An example:

> **"BarackObama**: We just made history. All of this happened because you gave your time, talent and passion. All of this happened because of you. Thanks" 2:34 PM November 5, 2008 (http://twitter.com/BarackObama/status/992176676)

Link Bunch

http://linkbun.ch

Type: URL shortener. In Chapter 7, we discuss that you can use Twitter to link to one URL, but Link Bunch offers a URL shortener for bundles of links. It takes several links and shortens them into one minimal URL that people can click to access the links. When the user clicks the Link Bunch link, he's taken to a page where he sees all the links you bunched together and click on whichever ones he's interested in.

Tweetree

```
www.tweetree.com
```

Type: Reading. This little service threads your tweets into a tree, which includes inline links, videos, and other files. If you think the Adobe Air application that you use to view Twitter leaves your stream looking cluttered, or if you have a hard time following conversational "threads" back and forth, Tweetree might be your answer to making your Twitter conversations easier to read.

TwitterGrader

```
http://twitter.grader.com
```

Type: Directory. This Twitter-based service ranks you using a secret formula developed by its creators at HubSpot. The system takes into account not only how many followers you have, but how you converse and engage, who follows, talks to and retweets you, who you follow and more. Your TwitterGrade of ## is a percentile, claiming that you are more, well, gradeable, than ##% of other Twitterers. The service helps you see how you measure up to other tweeters around the Web and specifically in your area and helps you find people whom you may want to follow because they mesh well with your ranking, interests, and location. Ultimately the grade doesn't mean a whole lot, but it will definitely show you who is active in your area.

Blip.fm

```
http://blip.fm
```

Type: Multimedia sharing. You can use this Twitter-based music service to DJ songs onto Twitter. It has an outstanding database of songs, and the service allows you to make mixes for your Twitter following.

Chapter 16

Ten Cool Ways to Use Twitter

*Y*ou can use Twitter for much more than keeping up with your friends and family. Track your expenses, get your latest homework assignment, get restaurant reviews or recommended wines. . . . The possibilities are endless and expanding every day. In this chapter, we introduce you to ten cool ways you can use Twitter.

Plain Old Networking

Twitter is an extremely powerful networking tool for several reasons. As contrived as it is when you think about it, in practice, Twitter actually mimics the natural process of how humans get to know one another. People don't like demanding, confrontational, face-to-face interaction; they prefer side-by-side, random interaction around gradually discovering the things they have in common. Routine, random, low-level interactions weave the fabric of community that builds trust and holds us all together. Twitter also creates an environment of random interactions that's really conducive to discovering new people with shared interests and for getting to know a more total picture of who someone is and what interests them.

On a strictly utilitarian basis, just being able to forge an electronic connection using something as short and simple as a Twitter handle is incredibly powerful, especially since you can make that connection via mobile phone right when you first meet. Since October 2007, Laura has barely used business cards at all. It's so much simpler for her to connect to the person she's just met on Twitter by sending **f username** as a text message to 40404. It leaves an easy breadcrumb trail back to someone she's chatted with and sets the stage for gradually getting to know more about them — or not — over time.

Breaking News

Twitter continues to grow as a resource for breaking news. Events like the recent earthquake in China, terrorist attacks in Mumbai, or the Hudson River emergency landing in January 2009 all broke first on Twitter and were then picked up by the mainstream broadcast media. Journalists and media organizations, along with consumers, now look to Twitter as a legitimate source for news.

Sourcing standards for journalism still apply, of course, and you can easily lose what really has happened until a definitive account is posted on a major news site, such as *The New York Times* or CNN.

CNN, in fact, is now one of the top Twitter accounts, at least by following. Anchors have integrated Twitter into their on-air shows, and @CNNBrk competed with Ashton Kutcher (@APlusK) to be the first on Twitter to get a million followers. (Ashton won, by the way, and donated 20,000 malaria nets to charity.)

Travel

Airlines, trains, car companies, and more all use Twitter to keep their corporate finger on the pulse of a lot more than just brand perception. Some airlines, like Southwest (@SouthwestAir), have taken it one step further and use Twitter to track flow at various airports, monitor problems in real time, report delays, and so on.

You can connect with many travel-focused companies using Twitter. If you lose a bag or are experiencing flight delays, some airlines, like JetBlue (@JetBlue), are trying to reach out and help customers through Twitter. You can even find cab companies on Twitter that offer more innovative ways to find a ride once you're on the ground, especially if you have an iPhone.

Finance

As new Web applications like StockTwits, Xpenser, and more crop up to help you manage your money, Twitter has become a more viable method to track spending. Add in helpful financial advice from your fellow Twitter users, and you can see how Twitter might become a genuine force in the financial world.

Food, Wine, and Spirits

Yelp, Chowhound, food blogs, and endless Web sites that aggregate reviews or impressions of the restaurant industry are on Twitter. They're looking to consumers, many of whom are sharing thoughts on where and what they're eating in real time, right from the mobile phone.

If you're wondering about a specific restaurant, increasingly you'll be able to search for the name and see what people are saying about it.

Wine lovers have found a whole new world for their passion for the grape on Twitter. Whether it's Twitter Taste Live (#TTL) by Bin Ends Wine (@binendswine), live streaming of tastings from personalities like Gary Vaynerchuck (@GaryVee), or just on-the-fly commentary about what and where people are drinking, Twitter is bridging serious gaps in the wine industry. More people are discovering wine or spirits that they might not have encountered before, thanks to the real-time recommendations of Twitter friends.

Books

Authors and readers alike have discovered new books to read and recommended books to others on Twitter. Famous writers, such as Neil Gaiman (@NeilHimself) or Paolo Coelho (@PaoloCoelho), actively engage fans around the world. Some authors have been able to land publishing deals through Twitter. Others release serials, one chapter at a time on Twitter. One service, 140Story, actually uses tweets to write stories.

However you look at it, Twitter is full of readers. When you start listening, you'll find book clubs, writing groups, and more. And when you begin contributing, you'll often discover a phenomenal amount of instant connection and support available on both sides of the pen through Twitter.

Music

Musicians, both signed and unsigned, are finding Twitter an effective tool to build a fan base, connect more deeply to fans, and get the word out about their music. John Mayer (@JohnCMayer), Dave Matthews (@DaveJMatthews), Britney Spears (@BritneySpears), and P. Diddy (@iamdiddy) are among the most famous musicians twittering, but thousands of recording artists at all levels are making innovative use of it, including Twitter veterans Matthew Ebel (@MatthewEbel) and Samantha Murphy (@thehighwaygirl).

Fans find Twitter a great place to discover new music, as well — especially with tools such as Blip.fm around. (Blip.fm allows you to share your favorite songs with your followers on Twitter.)

Education

Teachers are starting to tweet their lessons. Students are tweeting questions about their homework. Schools are using Twitter to communicate with their communities, quickly getting out information and cutting down on the cost of mailings. Conference attendees share insights and links from the conference, creating a virtual community for remote colleagues. Classes with a Twitter-fueled *back channel* (ideas, observations, questions, and comments coming from the audience) have been taught at colleges and universities around the world, including the esteemed Harvard Business and Law Schools.

Charities and Causes

Charities and causes find Twitter an easy way to get word out about their passions. You can even use Twitter to give microdonations to your favorite charity. The charity Social Media for Social Change (@SM4SC) exists only because of people who came together on Twitter. People use Twitter to raise awareness and money for a wide variety of international causes and charities. The ease of use makes it appealing to many agencies and groups.

Event Planning

The immediacy and reach Twitter allows can really help you get your next conference, party, or social-networking event off the ground. You can find everything you need, right in your Twitter stream. You can manage events on Facebook using a custom application within the platform, pulling tweets right into the launch page. You can even update both at once with TweetDeck or Seesmic Desktop. Twitter is also integrated with other event planning Web sites, such as EventBrite, allowing attendees to find and follow each other before and after the event itself.

Glossary

. . . .

AFAIK: Abbreviation of As Far as I Know.

bot: An account run by an automated program. You can find good bots, such as the ones that pull in all breaking news headlines from a media outlet. But you also can find bad bots, which put out only generic tweets, usually filled with links to Internet marketing sites or porn. You can often spot these bots by a generic "hot chick" avatar or their uneven follower/following ratio (meaning that they're following hundreds or thousands of people but have only a few following them back).

DIAF: Abbreviation of Die in a Fire; expresses extreme anger with a person or about an idea.

direct messages: Private messages sent to specific Twitter users in your network (abbreviated DMs).

dweet: A tweet sent while under the influence. Drunken tweeting can be amusing for your Twitter stream, but it can have lasting consequences for you because Google indexes all tweets. Be careful with dweeting!

early adopter: The enthusiastic people, often closely tied to the Silicon Valley digital-media community, who tend to be the first to use a new gadget or technology. Twitter's early adopters, for example, are the ones who joined before or during the SXSW (South by Southwest) conference in March 2007, when Twitter made its first big splash.

FailWhale: The image of a cartoon whale that appears when you try to load a page on the Twitter.com domain when the domain's servers are overloaded. In Twitter's early days, the tiny startup was known for unreliability because its rapid growth had outpaced its server power. Back then, the FailWhale made an appearance as often as several times a day, and many Twitter users casually use the expression FailWhale to show disapproval of anything on or off Twitter that isn't working properly. But don't get too worried: The days of the FailWhale's rampant appearances on Twitter have been over for months.

FTL: Abbreviation of For the Loss. The opposite of FTW, FTL is a quick way to show disappointment or dissatisfaction.

FTW: Abbreviation of For the Win; a quick way to show appreciation or enthusiasm. The term comes from gamer and hacker speak. Many of the shorthand abbreviations on Twitter have their roots in the vernacular that arose in video games, hacker forums, or instant-message programs as far back as the 1980s.

FWIW: Abbreviation of For What It's Worth.

hashtag: Words preceded by the # symbol. Basically, hashtags flag something as a keyword for searches. They're surprisingly powerful, as real-time (but virtual) events, and even communities can (and do) form around them. At the time of writing, #journchat is a community of PR pros and journalists who discuss their trade every Monday evening.

IMO or IMHO: Abbreviations for In My Opinion or In My Humble Opinion.

metrics: A way to measure what the service means for business and individuals as it relates to return on the time invested. Because Twitter has so many analytical applications built on its API, you can find tons of Twitter metrics out there.

After using Twitter for a little while, check out your Twitter grade at TwitterGrader.com (http://twitter.grader.com).

microfunding or microgiving: A means of using microblogging to raise charity donations. Several Twitter apps, such as TipJoy (www.tipjoy.com), specialize in microfunding, and nonprofits, such as charity: water (www.charitywater.org), have made Twitter microfunding a priority.

microsharing or microblogging: The niche of social media that encompasses Twitter. Other services — such as Jaiku, Pownce, and Plurk — have also specialized in microblogging, but none of them has achieved anywhere close to the following that Twitter has. Several microsharing services have already been shut down by their creators.

mistweet: A tweet that you send in error, either because you send it to the wrong person or you accidentally send a public tweet that you intended as a DM. Either way, it's a tweet you regret sending.

noise river: While you add more and more people to your Twitter stream, or if you turn on Show All @Replies (in your Twitter settings), you're going to see more and more tweets. You may have to put forth more effort to sift through to the good stuff. Twitter users who start to encounter this problem sometimes start to refer to their Twitter stream as the noise river.

OH: An abbreviation for overheard. Used to anonymously quote something funny that you heard, usually in real life. OHs look like this: "OH: 'Did somebody smell bacon? Because I sure did.'"

To see all tweets that are prefaced with OH, follow @overheard on Twitter.

@replies: Public tweets directed at specific people — anyone can see them and jump into the conversation.

RT or R/T: Stands for retweet, Twitter's equivalent of quoting. If you come across a tweet that you want to quote, giving credit to the original user, type **RT** at the start of a new tweet, put the Twitterer's username in an @reply format, and copy the contents of the tweet. A retweet looks like this: "RT @pistachio Boston - outdoor skating party this weekend, Sunday at 1pm. DM me if interested?" By putting RT at the front of the retweet, your also make sure that everyone can see your tweet because some members choose to turn off @replies that are not directed at them.

Keep in mind, however, that retweeting adds characters to a tweet and may force it over the 140-character limit. If that's the case, you might just want to link to it directly, instead. When prolific Twitter users put out a tweet that they want people in their network to retweet (for example, when they announce an event or charitable cause), many of them consciously keep it short to prevent that problem.

spammers: Spammers clutter up your Twitter stream (if you choose to follow them) and, just like with e-mail and other Internet tools, they send you useless content, usually trying to sell you something. Luckily, spamming on Twitter is hard because you don't have to follow anyone, and because Twitter works hard to remove accounts that are trying to take advantage of others and violating their terms of service (TOS).

tweeple or tweeps: Some Twitter users say tweeps to refer to the Twitter community overall, whereas others use it to refer only to those in their networks.

tweet: Either a noun or a verb. Your 140-character updates on Twitter are called tweets, and you can also say, "I tweeted."

tweetaholic or twitterholic: Someone who's addicted to Twitter. Many avid users toss this term about in a self-deprecating way if they find themselves using Twitter more often than seems normal. Also, the term *twitterholic* can refer to Twitterholic.com (http://twitterholic.com), a Twitter metrics application that measures the relative popularity of Twitter users.

tweetup: A pun on meet-up, tweetup refers to a gathering of Twitter users organized through Twitter. Tweetups can take many forms: a get-together for Twitter users who happen to be in the same town for a concert or festival, locals who want to try out a new restaurant or bar, or even a late-night meeting of karaoke enthusiasts.

twinfluence: Short for twitter influence. Can be based on criteria such as number of followers, how often they're retweeted, how many people @reply to them, or any other variety of metrics. An actual site at `www.twinfluence.com` that social network analysis to approximate the influence of different Twitter accounts.

TwitPic: One of the most popular third-party applications built on Twitter's API. TwitPic lets you upload a photo, often from the camera on your cellphone, to TwitPic (`www.twitpic.com`), which automatically sends a tweet that links to the picture and provides the caption of your choice.

twittcrastination: Using Twitter to procrastinate on a project or an unpleasant task.

twitter: Can be used as a verb ("I twittered that") but not a noun. ***Note:*** Don't say "twit" ("send a twit" is never correct, for example) because of that word's negative connotations in some parts of the world.

Twitter squatter: Much like a domain squatter on the rest of the Web, someone who claims the Twitter username that corresponds to a popular brand name or the name of a famous person, often in hopes of some kind of personal gain or monetary profit. Luckily, the guys behind Twitter deal with these people quickly if the person or brand in question wants that name back (William Shatner, Steve Wozniak, and others have been victims of squatters). You're also not allowed to *squat* on any account name without using it as an active account. New users can request (and frequently receive) usernames abandoned for more than six to nine months.

Twitter stream: The constantly updating and flowing timeline of everyone that you choose to follow on Twitter; also called a feed.

Twitterati: A pun on *literati* and *glitterati,* these are Twitter's perceived A-listers whom users want to follow or be followed by. It's a lot beside the point of Twitter, which is to connect to the people that interest *you* the most, not just the most popular. Fortunately, bona-fide celebrities are starting to tweet, and with time, this word won't mean very much.

twitterverse: The universe of people, tools, applications, and services on Twitter, meaning the entire Twitter community and ecosystem of other related things.

Index

BUSINESS, CAREERS & PERSONAL FINANCE

Accounting For Dummies, 4th Edition*
978-0-470-24600-9

Bookkeeping Workbook For Dummies†
978-0-470-16983-4

Commodities For Dummies
978-0-470-04928-0

Doing Business in China For Dummies
978-0-470-04929-7

E-Mail Marketing For Dummies
978-0-470-19087-6

Job Interviews For Dummies, 3rd Edition*†
978-0-470-17748-8

Personal Finance Workbook For Dummies*†
978-0-470-09933-9

Real Estate License Exams For Dummies
978-0-7645-7623-2

Six Sigma For Dummies
978-0-7645-6798-8

Small Business Kit For Dummies, 2nd Edition*†
978-0-7645-5984-6

Telephone Sales For Dummies
978-0-470-16836-3

BUSINESS PRODUCTIVITY & MICROSOFT OFFICE

Access 2007 For Dummies
978-0-470-03649-5

Excel 2007 For Dummies
978-0-470-03737-9

Office 2007 For Dummies
978-0-470-00923-9

Outlook 2007 For Dummies
978-0-470-03830-7

PowerPoint 2007 For Dummies
978-0-470-04059-1

Project 2007 For Dummies
978-0-470-03651-8

QuickBooks 2008 For Dummies
978-0-470-18470-7

Quicken 2008 For Dummies
978-0-470-17473-9

Salesforce.com For Dummies, 2nd Edition
978-0-470-04893-1

Word 2007 For Dummies
978-0-470-03658-7

EDUCATION, HISTORY, REFERENCE & TEST PREPARATION

African American History For Dummies
978-0-7645-5469-8

Algebra For Dummies
978-0-7645-5325-7

Algebra Workbook For Dummies
978-0-7645-8467-1

Art History For Dummies
978-0-470-09910-0

ASVAB For Dummies, 2nd Edition
978-0-470-10671-6

British Military History For Dummies
978-0-470-03213-8

Calculus For Dummies
978-0-7645-2498-1

Canadian History For Dummies, 2nd Edition
978-0-470-83656-9

Geometry Workbook For Dummies
978-0-471-79940-5

The SAT I For Dummies, 6th Edition
978-0-7645-7193-0

Series 7 Exam For Dummies
978-0-470-09932-2

World History For Dummies
978-0-7645-5242-7

FOOD, GARDEN, HOBBIES & HOME

Bridge For Dummies, 2nd Edition
978-0-471-92426-5

Coin Collecting For Dummies, 2nd Edition
978-0-470-22275-1

Cooking Basics For Dummies, 3rd Edition
978-0-7645-7206-7

Drawing For Dummies
978-0-7645-5476-6

Etiquette For Dummies, 2nd Edition
978-0-470-10672-3

Gardening Basics For Dummies*†
978-0-470-03749-2

Knitting Patterns For Dummies
978-0-470-04556-5

Living Gluten-Free For Dummies†
978-0-471-77383-2

Painting Do-It-Yourself For Dummies
978-0-470-17533-0

HEALTH, SELF HELP, PARENTING & PETS

Anger Management For Dummies
978-0-470-03715-7

Anxiety & Depression Workbook For Dummies
978-0-7645-9793-0

Dieting For Dummies, 2nd Edition
978-0-7645-4149-0

Dog Training For Dummies, 2nd Edition
978-0-7645-8418-3

Horseback Riding For Dummies
978-0-470-09719-9

Infertility For Dummies†
978-0-470-11518-3

Meditation For Dummies with CD-ROM, 2nd Edition
978-0-471-77774-8

Post-Traumatic Stress Disorder For Dummies
978-0-470-04922-8

Puppies For Dummies, 2nd Edition
978-0-470-03717-1

Thyroid For Dummies, 2nd Edition†
978-0-471-78755-6

Type 1 Diabetes For Dummies*†
978-0-470-17811-9

---

* Separate Canadian edition also available
˄ Separate U.K. edition also available

Available wherever books are sold. For more information or to order direct: U.S. customers visit www.dummies.com or call 1-877-762-2974.  WILEY

INTERNET & DIGITAL MEDIA

AdWords For Dummies
978-0-470-15252-2

Blogging For Dummies, 2nd Edition
978-0-470-23017-6

Digital Photography All-in-One Desk Reference For Dummies, 3rd Edition
978-0-470-03743-0

Digital Photography For Dummies, 5th Edition
978-0-7645-9802-9

Digital SLR Cameras & Photography For Dummies, 2nd Edition
978-0-470-14927-0

eBay Business All-in-One Desk Reference For Dummies
978-0-7645-8438-1

eBay For Dummies, 5th Edition*
978-0-470-04529-9

eBay Listings That Sell For Dummies
978-0-471-78912-3

Facebook For Dummies
978-0-470-26273-3

The Internet For Dummies, 11th Edition
978-0-470-12174-0

Investing Online For Dummies, 5th Edition
978-0-7645-8456-5

iPod & iTunes For Dummies, 5th Edition
978-0-470-17474-6

MySpace For Dummies
978-0-470-09529-4

Podcasting For Dummies
978-0-471-74898-4

Search Engine Optimization For Dummies, 2nd Edition
978-0-471-97998-2

Second Life For Dummies
978-0-470-18025-9

Starting an eBay Business For Dummies, 3rd Edition†
978-0-470-14924-9

GRAPHICS, DESIGN & WEB DEVELOPMENT

Adobe Creative Suite 3 Design Premium All-in-One Desk Reference For Dummies
978-0-470-11724-8

Adobe Web Suite CS3 All-in-One Desk Reference For Dummies
978-0-470-12099-6

AutoCAD 2008 For Dummies
978-0-470-11650-0

Building a Web Site For Dummies, 3rd Edition
978-0-470-14928-7

Creating Web Pages All-in-One Desk Reference For Dummies, 3rd Edition
978-0-470-09629-1

Creating Web Pages For Dummies, 8th Edition
978-0-470-08030-6

Dreamweaver CS3 For Dummies
978-0-470-11490-2

Flash CS3 For Dummies
978-0-470-12100-9

Google SketchUp For Dummies
978-0-470-13744-4

InDesign CS3 For Dummies
978-0-470-11865-8

Photoshop CS3 All-in-One Desk Reference For Dummies
978-0-470-11195-6

Photoshop CS3 For Dummies
978-0-470-11193-2

Photoshop Elements 5 For Dummies
978-0-470-09810-3

SolidWorks For Dummies
978-0-7645-9555-4

Visio 2007 For Dummies
978-0-470-08983-5

Web Design For Dummies, 2nd Edition
978-0-471-78117-2

Web Sites Do-It-Yourself For Dummies
978-0-470-16903-2

Web Stores Do-It-Yourself For Dummies
978-0-470-17443-2

LANGUAGES, RELIGION & SPIRITUALITY

Arabic For Dummies
978-0-471-77270-5

Chinese For Dummies, Audio Set
978-0-470-12766-7

French For Dummies
978-0-7645-5193-2

German For Dummies
978-0-7645-5195-6

Hebrew For Dummies
978-0-7645-5489-6

Ingles Para Dummies
978-0-7645-5427-8

Italian For Dummies, Audio Set
978-0-470-09586-7

Italian Verbs For Dummies
978-0-471-77389-4

Japanese For Dummies
978-0-7645-5429-2

Latin For Dummies
978-0-7645-5431-5

Portuguese For Dummies
978-0-471-78738-9

Russian For Dummies
978-0-471-78001-4

Spanish Phrases For Dummies
978-0-7645-7204-3

Spanish For Dummies
978-0-7645-5194-9

Spanish For Dummies, Audio Set
978-0-470-09585-0

The Bible For Dummies
978-0-7645-5296-0

Catholicism For Dummies
978-0-7645-5391-2

The Historical Jesus For Dummies
978-0-470-16785-4

Islam For Dummies
978-0-7645-5503-9

Spirituality For Dummies, 2nd Edition
978-0-470-19142-2

NETWORKING AND PROGRAMMING

ASP.NET 3.5 For Dummies
978-0-470-19592-5

C# 2008 For Dummies
978-0-470-19109-5

Hacking For Dummies, 2nd Edition
978-0-470-05235-8

Home Networking For Dummies, 4th Edition

Java For Dummies, 4th Edition
978-0-470-08716-9

Microsoft® SQL Server™ 2008 All-in-One Desk Reference For Dummies
978-0-470-17954-3

Networking All-in-One Desk Reference For Dummies, 2nd Edition
978-0-7645-9939-2

Networking For Dummies, 8th Edition
978-0-470-05620-2

SharePoint 2007 For Dummies
978-0-470-09941-4

Wireless Home Networking For Dummies, 2nd Edition
978-0-471-74940-0

OPERATING SYSTEMS & COMPUTER BASICS

Mac For Dummies, 5th Edition
978-0-7645-8458-9

Laptops For Dummies, 2nd Edition
978-0-470-05432-1

Linux For Dummies, 8th Edition
978-0-470-11649-4

MacBook For Dummies
978-0-470-04859-7

Mac OS X Leopard All-in-One Desk Reference For Dummies
978-0-470-05434-5

Mac OS X Leopard For Dummies
978-0-470-05433-8

Macs For Dummies, 9th Edition
978-0-470-04849-8

PCs For Dummies, 11th Edition
978-0-470-13728-4

Windows® Home Server For Dummies
978-0-470-18592-6

Windows Server 2008 For Dummies
978-0-470-18043-3

Windows Vista All-in-One Desk Reference For Dummies
978-0-471-74941-7

Windows Vista For Dummies
978-0-471-75421-3

Windows Vista Security For Dummies
978-0-470-11805-4

SPORTS, FITNESS & MUSIC

Coaching Hockey For Dummies
978-0-470-83685-9

Coaching Soccer For Dummies
978-0-471-77381-8

Fitness For Dummies, 3rd Edition
978-0-7645-7851-9

Football For Dummies, 3rd Edition
978-0-470-12536-6

GarageBand For Dummies
978-0-7645-7323-1

Golf For Dummies, 3rd Edition
978-0-471-76871-5

Guitar For Dummies, 2nd Edition
978-0-7645-9904-0

Home Recording For Musicians For Dummies, 2nd Edition
978-0-7645-8884-6

iPod & iTunes For Dummies, 5th Edition
978-0-470-17474-6

Music Theory For Dummies
978-0-7645-7838-0

Stretching For Dummies
978-0-470-06741-3

Get smart @ dummies.com®

- **Find a full list of Dummies titles**
- **Look into loads of FREE on-site articles**
- **Sign up for FREE eTips e-mailed to you weekly**
- **See what other products carry the Dummies name**
- **Shop directly from the Dummies bookstore**
- **Enter to win new prizes every month!**